W9-CNG-603

Understanding Children

Understanding Children

Richard A. Gardner, M.D.

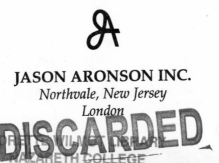

JASON ARONSON INC.
Northvale, New Jersey
London

THE MASTER WORK SERIES

1997 softcover edition

ISBN: 0-87668-726-5 (hardcover)
       1-56821-225-9 (softcover)

Library of Congress Catalog Card Number: 84-45133

Manufactured in the United States of America. Jason Aronson Inc. offers books and cassettes. For information and catalog write to Jason Aronson Inc., 230 Livingston Street, Northvale, New Jersey 07647.

About the Author

Richard A. Gardner, M.D., a practicing child psychiatrist and adult psychoanalyst, is Clinical Professor of Child Psychiatry at the College of Physicians and Surgeons, Columbia University. Among child therapists he is recognized as one of the leading innovators in the field. His books, articles, and audio tapes (numbering over 250) on various aspects of child psychotherapeutic technique are considered to be among the most useful and creative in the literature. Dr. Gardner is a Fellow of the American Psychiatric Association, the American Academy of Child and Adolescent Psychiatry, and the American Academy of Psychoanalysis. He has lectured extensively throughout the U.S. and abroad on issues relevant to child psychiatry.

To children:

>whose infectious *joie de vivre*
elates us,

>whose ingenuousness
refreshes us,

>whose guilelessness
embarrasses and teaches us,

>whose undiscriminating love
flatters us,

>whose optimism
gives us hope,

>and who, as our progeny,
provide us with our most meaningful
link to immortality.

CONTENTS

The love of the child for the parent · The love of the parent for the child

"We have the greatest respect for our child's natural impulses." · "I can't stand to let him cry." · "I would never let my child use a pacifier." · "I would never go to work and leave my children. What kind of a mother do you think I am?" · "I can't stand for him to be angry at me." · "He's everything I have in the world." · "But you promised." · "You can never repay us for all the sacrifices we have made for you." · "I want to give them everything I didn't have when I was a child." · "My son the doctor" · "My son the doctor is drowning!" · "Comes the Revolution, you'll like wine." · "The rich man's son syndrome" · "He catches cold very easily." · "My Joey would never do such a thing." · "He's a genius." · "We're like pals." · "All I want is respect." · "You're not old enough to understand things like that." · "Mother knows best." · "I don't know what I would

do without her." · "Where did we go wrong, doctor?" · "When I studied psychology in college..."

and then she called him a son of a bitch." · *"My father gave my mother a black eye after she threw a dish at him."*

Parental Anger toward the Child 142
"Anyone who hates children and dogs can't be all bad." · *"My daughter is turning into a tramp."* · *"Just because you go to college, you think you're smarter than your parents."* · *"He takes after his father—the same stubborn streak, the same laziness."* · *"A zadeh you call a 'shithead'? Fuck you!"* · *"The first thing you have to do is attract his attention."*

The Child's Anger toward the Parent 145
"He has the worst temper tantrums. They can drive you crazy." · *"I can't stand to see him so angry at me."* · *"I'll never get used to his long hair. From the back he looks just like a girl."* · *"Who do you think you're talking to? Your mother?"* · *"To a zadeh you say, 'Fuck you'?"*

Anger within the Child and Anger between Children 150
"You must have been very angry when the coach had you sit out the whole game on the bench." · *"How did you feel when Gail broke your doll?"* · *"Hardly a week goes by when he doesn't have a terrible fight on the way home from school."* · *"Nice boys don't fight."* · *"My father can beat up your father."*

Anger between Siblings 154
"They never seem to stop fighting, doctor." · *"Don't touch that." "Stay away from that," etc.* · *"A fight a day keeps the psychiatrist away."* · *"You always give him the biggest piece of cake."* · *"The oldest was always a hellion."* · *"We restrain our praises of Bob because it makes Jane feel so bad."* · *"In our home, everything is shared. No one owns anything."* · *"Billy says I'm a sneak (baby, tattletale, etc.)."* · *"Their fighting is a constant drain on us."* · *"Who started it?"* · *"I can see how that makes you angry, but you still can't flush her fish down the toilet."* · *"Thank God we only have one child."*

win?" · *"Timmy's such a sore loser."* · *"How about a game of checkers?"*

PREFACE TO THE 1983 EDITION

It is now eleven years since this book was first published. One could certainly have predicted eleven years ago that the world would be different over a decade after the book's publication. I believe, however, that all our changes notwithstanding, the differences are small compared to the similarities when we are concerning ourselves with the child-rearing process. Accordingly, I consider this book still applicable and relevant.

Of course, there certainly have been some changes. Adolescent boys no longer use long hair as a statement of rebellion. They still, however, need to rebel. The need remains to scorn parents and view them as anachronisms from the Middle Ages—in part to overcome their fears of leaving home. If they were to view their parents as all loving and accepting, it would be difficult for them to break their dependent ties and face a less benevolent world. And adolescent rebellion serves parents in that it makes it easier to tolerate the separation from their children. As they did a decade ago, parents continue to say: "Although on the one hand it's painful to see them grow up and leave, on the other hand (between you and me) it's also a relief. There's just so much of their antics one can take."

Elementary schools maintain the principle that it is psychologically devastating to a child to be criticized. Accordingly, an elaborate system of euphemisms designed to protect children from criticisms (no matter how benevolently provided) is utilized. However, there appears to be increasing appreciation that the "respect" of children that justified overindulgence ten years ago may not have been in their best interests. Schools are beginning to recognize that true respect of children involves teaching them that real life inevitably requires tolerance for discomfort if one is going to achieve one's goals. The school is one of the best places to start teaching children this important reality. This does not mean that education cannot also be fun, but only that drill and self-abnegation are also important parts of the educational process. We are seeing some appreciation of this principle in the "back to basics" movement that is presently coming into vogue.

We are observing, at the present time, what may be the beginning of an educational revolution that will change our traditional education system. I am referring to computer-assisted instruction (CAI) and what can best be described as an epidemic of the utilization of computers in education, often introduced on the nursery school level. There is good reason to believe that computers enhance children's motivation to learn, and that they have far more patience than even the most dedicated and involved teacher. A computer never gets tired or irritable, never screams at a child, and can tolerate repeated student mistakes without a scintilla of exasperation. It is too early, however, to know how effective this new teaching tool will prove to be. We don't know its long-range effects on student curiosity, motivation, and dedication to the educational process. The early evidence indicates that the effects in these areas are promising. However, the labor and expense of creating computer programs for complete courses at the high school and college level makes these courses impractical at this time. In addition, computer teaching seems to be more applicable to the sciences than to subjects like English and social studies. The word processor, however, appears to increase children's motivation to do their written assignments, since it is so easy to change mistakes and avoid the laboriousness of written assignments.

Television is still very much with us, and the controversy over the detrimental effects of television is still raging. Over a decade later, I hold to the views stated in the original printing. I do not believe that television viewing plays a significant role in street violence, mugging, raping, and other kinds of severe antisocial behavior. People who engage in such activities do so because of serious problems in their home and family life. At worst, television may provide the criminal with some ideas and techniques for criminal activities, but it does not produce the basic rage that generates and promulgates antisocial behavior.

My views on childhood sexuality are still applicable. My criticisms of the Oedipus complex are receiving more support as mental health professionals become increasingly aware of many of the absurdities of classical psychoanalytic theory. Freud was a great pioneer, yet some of his ideas have not held up over time. The psychoanalytic movement is in far less prestigious a position today than it was over a decade ago. Of particular relevance to Freud's theory of the Oedipus complex is our recent awareness that sexual abuse of children appears to be far more common than previously believed. It is probable that Freud's first idea, that his patients were indeed being sexually abused, was probably closer to the truth than his revised theory that such sexual experiences were products of his patients' fantasies. Child sexual abuse appears to be a widespread problem and is receiving far more attention than ever before. This attention can result in better ways to deal with the problem as well as greater understanding of the role of childhood sexual experiences in the development of psychopathological states both in childhood and in adult life.

There remain the kinds of eating problems described in the initial printing. However, emphasis on anorexia and bulimia are in vogue. If one were to read present newspaper and magazine articles, these disorders are epidemic. Physicians are stating that these disorders are more widespread than we have previously realized and, with presumably increased diagnostic acumen, are more frequently diagnosing these illnesses. At the same time more youngsters are developing the symptomatology of anorexia and bulimia as part of the process of keeping up with peers. Being anorexic or bulimic is almost the "in" thing to do, and everybody knows someone who is suffering with an eating disorder. Although increased attention may lead to greater knowledge about the etiology and treatment of these disorders, there is no question that overdiagnosis produces overtreatment, and many will be thereby involving themselves in therapeutic programs that are not truly applicable to their difficulties.

An unfortunate trend in the first printing sadly continues. I refer to the increasing psychopathy of our society. Whereas Freud's primary goal with his early patients was to help diminish their guilt, many psychiatrists today find themselves trying to *increase* their patients' guilt. Society still appears to be moving in the direction of increased egocentrism and decreased consideration for the feelings of others. Thinking of "Number 1" is the prevalent guideline by which growing numbers of people operate, producing a progressively more exploitative and insensitive world. Although some may view this to be an overly pessimistic view of our society, I hold it to be accurate. I believe that the best antidote for psychopathy is a stable home life in which children are not only taught values that will reduce their propensity for psychopathic behavior, but have parents who serve as models for healthy and humane behavior. In the service of these goals, this book is still very much applicable.

Richard A. Gardner, M.D.

ACKNOWLEDGMENTS

I am deeply grateful to my child patients and their parents, who have taught me most of what I have put down here. This book is an accumulation of the answers to their questions—answers that have been derived from my observations of and experiences with them.

More than anyone else, I am indebted to Dr. Jason Aronson, my publisher. It was he who first suggested that I write this book, and it was he who provided me with his encouragement and advice. As both psychiatrist and publisher he was in a unique position to contribute. As well, I am grateful for the dedication of Miss Jennifer Mellen at Jason Aronson, Inc. and Miss Gail M. Griffin in editing the manuscript. I am deeply appreciative, also, of the extensive help given me by Mrs. Frances Dubner in editing the original manuscript and providing valuable suggestions.

Mrs. Linda Gould, my secretary, indefatigably typed the manuscripts in their various renditions and offered helpful editorial advice as well.

I appreciate the permission granted to me by the editors to quote from the following previously published works of mine :

Sexual Fantasies in Childhood. *Medical Aspects of Human Sexuality*, 3(10):121-134, 1969.

Therapeutic Communication with Children: The Mutual Storytelling Technique, New York : Science House, Inc., 1971.

On Using Anger. *Harper's Bazaar,* July, 1971.

"They Never Stop Fighting. . . ." *The New York Times Magazine,* November 28, 1971.

Lastly, I am deeply grateful to my wife, Lee, who as dedicated mother of our children (Andrew, Nancy, and Julie) and as a child psychiatrist has taught me much (by both example and instruction) that is contained herein.

Understanding Children

Introduction

The history of the world is replete with examples of man's brutality to his fellow human beings. As far back as we can go, we learn of crime, wars, and bloodshed. Although the advancement of our knowledge has certainly been used for the distinct benefit of mankind, it has simultaneously served in the creation of ever more ingenious devices for inflicting pain and suffering on our fellow humans. We cannot pick up a newspaper today without reading about wanton murder, cruel prejudice, massive pollution, senseless wars, rampant muggings, extortion, rape, political corruption, bribery, poverty, and a host of other acts of cruelty and injustice to one another. Yes, there is love, benevolence, concern, and philanthropy; but these pale in comparison to the scourges of our world.

The causes of each of these manifestations of man's enormous hostility are multiple and complex. And there is certainly much we have yet to learn about them. The whole range of biological, familial, social, cultural, and historical contributing factors must be considered in trying to understand them. And these cannot be studied in isolation from one another, but rather as parts of a complex interrelated pattern of causative factors. As time goes on, it becomes ever more urgent for us to come to grips with this grave problem of our inhumanity to one another. In fact, the very survival of mankind depends upon our doing so. We are on the verge of polluting ourselves out of existence, and there are a few individuals in this world who have it within their power to bring about the destruction of us all within a few hours or days.

Of the many approaches to this ever-pressing problem of man's hostility, the one that, in my opinion, offers us the greatest hope is the study of human psychology, both normal and abnormal. After all, it is man who is the perpetrator of these iniquities. His thoughts, feelings, and actions are the central factors that bring about the horrors that we all fear and deplore but, to a greater or lesser degree, continue to perpetuate. If we could do something to improve the behavior of man, to lessen his proclivity for violence and brutality, then there is still hope for his survival. As a psychiatrist, I believe that the sick forms of thinking and acting that cause an individual to wreak sorrow on those about him have their roots in his childhood. Although hereditary factors may certainly play a role, I believe environmental ones to be far more instrumental in bringing about the kinds of cruel behavior I am discussing here. And of the various environmental influences, I believe the family to be the most crucial. The more we understand about the early life of the individual and the more we can utilize such understanding to prevent the development of psychological disturbance, the fewer deranged people there will be and the better our world will become. It is my hope that this book will serve some role, no matter how small, toward this goal.

Writing a book such as this is an awesome task. The question of how we want our children to be is not far removed from the question of how we want our world to be. The more we think about such questions, the more confused we become and the more we realize that few, if any, definite statements can be made. There are few generalizations that will hold for all children in all families. Even if we try to confine ourselves to principles that will hold in western society in the 1970's (as I do here), the variations within children and families are so great that all suggestions must be tentatively made. Yet, we have to act; we have to make decisions; we have to follow some guidelines. The newborn child cannot wait for us to learn all we need to know (if we ever can) about how to bring him up.

I am reminded at this point of an experience I had almost thirteen years ago, when I brought my first child home from the hospital. He was then four days old and, as I brought him over to lay him down in his crib, I was suddenly faced with a conflict : should I put him on his abdomen or on his back? I anxiously pondered the question. What I did at that moment, I thought in my anxiety as a new father, might determine his sleeping posture for his whole lifetime. What an awesome responsibility I had. I decided in favor of the abdominal position, as that was closest to the way *I* was most comfortable sleeping. I anxiously placed him on his belly, hoping that I was doing right, and I continued to place him in this position whenever I put him in bed. However, as soon as he was able to turn himself over, he elected to lie on his back and has slept that way ever since.

We have to act; we have to guess; we have to make decisions for our children. Sometimes we will be right and sometimes wrong. Sometimes we will be able to rely on some forces within our children to rectify or alter (as in my experience with my boy) our mistakes. Other times they will suffer from them. No one is so omniscient that he will not make mistakes. No one is so free from the blindness of his own problems that he will not in some way have a deleterious effect on his children. Regardless of how hard we try, our children will exhibit traits that may not be in accordance with those we wished for them and may even be in the category of psychological disturbance. There are children who grow up in homes that are quite disturbed, yet they appear to overcome the handicaps of their childhood and grow up into stable and productive adults. On the other hand, there are children whose parents do not appear to have exposed them to significant deleterious influences, yet they suffer with psychiatric disorder. There is still much we have to learn, and the parent who assumes that he was the sole or primary cause of his child's disorder may be taking on an unnecessary and inappropriate burden of guilt. None of us is completely free from psychologically inappropriate and unhealthy traits, and it is unrealistic to expect that we can raise our children to be totally free from them either. It is my hope, however, that this book will serve to lessen the extent and intensity of such disorder. The insights I will describe and the suggestions I will propose are not presented as irrefutable rules. Rather they are recommendations that I have derived from my clinical experience and have found applicable to most children at this time. As we learn more and as the world changes, my suggestions may become progressively outdated; but these guidelines are, I believe, relevant to the children of today. It is grandiose of anyone to claim to be able to provide more.

This book does not provide simple explanations or easy approaches. Human behavior is complex, and there is still much we do not understand. Simple formulas are always more attractive, and there is no dearth of those who propose them. But if the reader is to genuinely profit from this book, he must be willing to consider the child's behavior in its complexity. If he is willing to expend the effort to read it and to attempt to apply the multiple and, sometimes complicated, suggestions it offers, the child with whom he is involved should benefit. Although this book may not have the appeal of those that offer simple solutions, it will not cause the disappointment and disillusionment that inevitably follows the failure of the easier approaches. Like so many other ventures in life, child rearing is a slow and difficult process. Patient consideration and thoughtful deliberation are far more likely to make the venture success-ful than are quickie solutions. There is no such thing as magic and magic solutions to life's problems, and those who believe in them invariably end up disillusioned and frustrated. It is hoped that the reader of this book will be helped to avoid such disappointments.

It is not the purpose of this book to help parents and others involved with children to rear children who will be happy most of the time and who will become adults who are most often happy. No one is happy most of the time. Life is a mixture of both happiness and sadness, of both contentment and misery. Everyone has his share of suffering. Life is such that there are predictable frustrations and deprivations. It is the book's purpose to help children become *relatively* happier, to suffer fewer periods of unhappiness than they might otherwise have had, and to grow up with the appreciation that periods of unhappiness are part of man's lot. It is my hope that thereby they will suffer fewer disillusionments about life—disillusionments and unrealistic expectations that can significantly impair their relationships with all those whom they may encounter.

There are those who believe that if a child is given genuine love he will not suffer significant psychological disturbance. Although I am in agreement that parental love is essential to the development of psycho-logical health, I am also in agreement with the well-known psychologist Bruno Bettelheim that "love is not enough." Love, as necessary as it is for the child's healthy growth and development, is not all that he needs. There must also be knowledge. There must be understanding of what is going on in the child, of what he needs and what he doesn't need, of what is in his best interests and what isn't. Love is not the general preventive of all psychological disturbance; nor is it its panacea. In addi-tion, the kind of knowledge one needs for child rearing is not only the "common sense" type. This is *not* a common sense book about children. I do not have an abiding respect for the common sense of men—whether it be mothers' or fathers' or others'. I do not believe that we all have within us some innate pool of knowledge of those things that are best for our children. What is rational to one may be irrational to another. Some of the most detrimental things done to children have been considered to be common sense. Much that I say here is "uncommon sense." This book is a mixture of common sense approaches as well as those that are not. My hope is that I will convince the reader that those approaches that may not initially appear to be reasonable come to be so and that he will appreciate that some uncommon sense suggestions may be in the child's best interests.

Some of the ideas presented in this book are entirely conventional. They have been selected because I consider them important and worthy of emphasis. Others are less well known but have not been given the attention they deserve. Some of the conventional ideas are modified in accordance with experiences that have indicated to me that some alteration of traditional views is in order. And there are other proposals that are quite unconventional but that I believe are worthy of the reader's serious consideration. In addition, I will attempt to rectify what I consider to be misconceptions about childhood—some of which, unfortunately, have been originated or perpetuated by colleagues in the fields of psychology and psychiatry.

This book is an outgrowth of my work as a practicing child psychiatrist. The greater part of my working day is spent trying to understand what goes on in the minds of children. I attempt to use this knowledge to help children work out their psychiatric problems and to advise parents on how to handle their children. This book is a compendium of those issues and problems most frequently brought up in therapy. It covers, I believe, the broad range of common difficulties that confront *all* children—not only those who seek help from a therapist. Time and other limitations prevent the therapist from helping but an infinitesimal fraction of all those who could profit from his assistance. A book such as this enables me to overcome some of that frustration. It provides me with the hope that many more will profit from what I have learned and found to be useful. It is my hope that those who read it will enhance their understanding of and sensitivity to children and that such knowledge, when applied, will play a role in their bringing about a future in which there will be children who are less wracked with emotional disorder and freer to enjoy the richness of life. In such a world, there should be far less of the misery we suffer today because of those with psychologically deranged minds; and there should be more opportunity for the rich gratifications that mankind, even now, has the potential to enjoy.

1

Parent-Child Love

Love is probably one of the vaguest and most misused words in the English language. It is often used to mask feelings that have little to do with love: to alleviate guilt, to seduce, and to describe intentions quite removed from benevolence and affection. Even in the love between a parent and a child these confusions and misrepresentations often occur, though frequently unintentionally. To describe what I mean by the word *love,* I will divide my discussion into two categories: the love of the child for the parent and the love of the parent for the child. It must be remembered, however, that the two contribute to and enhance each other, for love, whatever the kind, if it is to be worthy of the name, cannot exist without some reciprocity.

The love of the child for the parent. If there is any single word that describes the nature of the love of the child for the parent it is *dependency.* The child's love is primarily based on the gratification of those needs that he depends on his parents to supply. The more consistently the parents provide these satisfactions, the more gratifying the child will find his relationship with them and the more affection he will feel and display. Although this is self-evident at the survival or subsistence level, the basic needs that the child looks to his parents to satisfy go beyond food, clothing, and shelter. As an infant, he also requires sensory stimulation and protection from danger; and as he grows older, he relies on his parents to provide him with the wherewithal to function in a social setting: to teach him the *do's* and the *don't's*, the *right's* and the *wrong's*, so that he may more adequately cope with adult reality.

In addition, there are yet more subtle needs to be satisfied if loving feelings are to be engendered in the child. He must feel that he is wanted and needed by his parents, that he is important to them; but even more vital and more difficult to describe is his experiencing a kind of "warm inner glow" (for lack of a better term) that results only in response to a similar warmth produced in his parents by his presence. This phenomenon, this mutual resonance similar to that which one vibrating tuning fork will set up in another having the same fundamental frequency of vibration, is central to the young child's loving response to a parent. The need for love is so vital that the child who receives food, clothing, and shelter but is deprived significantly of these other elements may lose his appetite, become unresponsive to his environment, and may actually waste away and die. Others similarly deprived may survive infancy but may develop such severe withdrawal from others that they become effectively nonfunctioning individuals, living in their own mental worlds and gaining whatever little gratification they can from their fantasies. The deprivation need not be overt (such as physical abandonment) but can result from psychological rejection in the form of parental withdrawal, hostility, coldness, or other kinds of negative interaction with the child.

The love of the parent for the child. Despite my belief in strong, instinctive urges for procreation within each of the sexes, I believe that the mother's tie to the newborn infant is probably stronger than that of the father's. It is she who carries the developing fetus within her, and it is she who is physiologically capable of providing the newborn with food from her own breasts. These capacities make it *likely* that she will develop a stronger psychological tie to the infant than the father; but although the father's psychological bond to the child may not be as intense as the mother's during this period, it is still quite strong as long as cultural or personality factors do not suppress it.

The genuinely loving father and the mother frequently experience a warm inner glow when they are involved with the child. I say "frequently," because there are inevitably times when the parent will have hostile feelings toward the child. He enjoys giving the child pleasure, and the child's delighted response produces in the parent even greater joy. And the cycle spirals upwards. The loving parent is interested in the child's welfare and becomes upset when the child's health or well-being is endangered. He has found a healthy balance between what the child wants and what he thinks is in the child's best interests. He respects the child's requests but complies with them only insofar as it benefits the child that he do so. He does not consider the child to be indebted to him for the sacrifices and deprivations he may suffer in the child's upbringing, but considers the gratifications he derives from the *process* of child rearing to be his primary rewards.

The loving parent recognizes as well that his feelings toward the child are not pure affection, and he is comfortable with this ambivalence. He can accept the periods of hostility that the inevitable frustrations and resentments of child rearing often evoke, and he accepts too the fact that he may not be equally responsive to the child at different stages in their relationship. (Some parents do better with dependent infants, others with the school-aged, and others with the adolescent.) Yet in spite of these variations in the intensity of this involvement, the loving parent still derives deep gratifications from the various stages of the child's growth. He has pride in his youngster's accomplishments both because he has contributed to the child's ability to achieve them and because he is happy for the child's own gratifications regarding them.

An important manifestation of a parent's love is that he enjoys spending time with his child. In fact, daily periods of "time alone together" can ward off potential future psychic disturbance in the child, as well as serve as a powerful therapeutic measure in the treatment of such disturbance. I usually recommend to all parents, regardless of whether their child is in therapy, that they set aside a time every day when they can be alone with the child without distraction or interruption. Each sibling should have his own time, from which the others are firmly excluded; and this time alone together should be cancelled only under unusual circumstances.

These periods are most effective when both parent and child are genuinely enjoying themselves. If the parent only *pretends* enjoyment in a game or activity, the child will sense the inevitable resentment of the parent's reluctant involvement, and the time spent together will thereby become a deleterious experience for the child. This time can also be profitably used for talking about one's feelings and for sharing the day's experiences—for finding solace, commiseration, and understanding and for relating anecdotes, achievements, and disappointments. It is during these moments of shared feeling and empathy that loving feelings flourish, and both the child and the parent become enriched by them.

As mentioned earlier, a human relationship cannot appropriately be called loving if it is one-sided. Claiming to love someone who provides no significant affection in response may be called many things—for example, self-delusion and masochism—but it cannot be called love. The child will not develop loving reactions unless he receives loving attention and affection. The parents, in turn, cannot be expected to love for long a child who does not respond to their ministrations. The affection of each is enhanced or diminished in accordance with the response of the other, for love is based on interaction and cannot exist unilaterally, in isolation.

PSEUDO-LOVE

The pseudo-loving parent exhibits behavioral patterns that only ostensibly manifest affection but that basically do not. The deficient parent uses pseudo-loving mechanisms to conceal from himself and others his inability to provide his child with meaningful affection. There is no parent who does not exhibit, at times, one or more of these forms of interaction with his child. If, however, many of these patterns are present or if they are exhibited frequently, then there will probably be significant difficulty in the relationship between the parent and the child.

The manifestations of parental pseudo-love described here do not exist in pure form; there is often significant overlap. In addition, a parent rarely exhibits only one of these mechanisms in isolation; rather one usually sees several in combination. Although a particular pattern usually originates with the parent, the child's behavior soon plays a significant role in determining both its perpetuation and the form that it may take. In addition, constitutional factors may be operative. For example, an innately passive child is more likely to comply with a parental pseudo-loving maneuver than the child who is innately more aggressive. As the child grows older, the pattern becomes one in which both parties contribute equally to its perpetuation—complaints to the contrary notwithstanding.

"We have the greatest respect for our child's natural impulses." There are parents who believe that the primary, if not exclusive, criterion for deciding what is good for a child is the child's own impulses. They believe that the instincts should reign supreme if the child is to grow up healthy and that the restrictions of society are repressive, and cause abnormal behavior.

Parents who are exaggeratedly committed to the philosophy of "respect" for the child's instincts may be doing him a great disservice.

Such children may be permitted to eat on demand, to go to sleep whenever they choose, to destroy household articles in the name of "exploration," and in extreme cases, even to defecate wherever and whenever they wish. Temper tantrums often produce whatever they want. I do not believe that such children are truly respected. They are not being helped to adapt to the world, which will not so indulge them. They cannot but be anxious because they are deprived of the protection and guidance that every child needs for his healthy growth and development. They often grow up "spoiled," dependent, and distrustful of the world; and although some may become quite self-assertive and independent, their basic trust and faith in others is usually markedly impaired.

In his early work, Freud concluded that neurosis was the result of society's repression of instinctual impulses and that their free expression would cure the neurosis. He later came to appreciate that things were not so simple and that only a few psychiatric disorders would respond to such an approach. Today, however, there are many, both within and out of the field of psychology, who hold Freud's earlier view and advocate allowing the child, whether or not he is in therapy, the greatest degree of free expression. Although proponents of this view differ in the degree to which they will place limits on the child, there is general agreement that the fewer such restrictions the greater the likelihood that the child will be psychologically healthy.

Favoring Freud's later position on this question, I do not have as much respect for the inner wisdom of the child as many of my colleagues. I believe that there are both instincts (for food, warmth, physical contact, etc.) and characterological differences (such as passivity, assertiveness, and activity level), which probably exist on an hereditary basis. However, external factors can significantly influence the way hereditary patterns will manifest themselves, and cultures vary in their means of modifying instinctual urges. Although I would not propose that the child be brought up to submit to every social restriction, I do believe that environmental modification is important, *along with* a respect for the child's innate impulses.

I wish to emphasize that I do not use *adjustment* or *adaptation* to mean total compliance to society. The healthy person reaches a compromise. He learns to question things around him and to evaluate them. He *tries* to alter what he does not believe to be valid and in man's best interests (Revolution may even be necessary to effect such changes), and to accept and comply with what he considers sound and reasonable. The healthy person recognizes that he cannot possibly change all the things he would like to and that frustrations and resignations are inevitable, and he accepts the fact that he can devote himself only to a small fraction of all the things in the world that need changing. This is what I mean when I use the term *adjustment* or *adaptation*.

Ideally, the parents should take into consideration the child's desires, respect his instinctual cravings, and gratify them or not (either fully or partially) in accordance with what the parents consider to be to the child's benefit. The parents must maintain the balance between the child's desires and what is in his best interests, both immediately and ultimately. This is true respect for the child.

"I can't stand to let him cry." There are parents who try to compensate for their feelings of insecurity and inadequacy by trying to rear what in their scheme of things is a "perfect" child. When such parents decide that the perfect child is one who is completely happy and never frustrated, the child's cry then takes on special meaning to them. It becomes a danger signal, implying both that some need of the child is not being satisfied and that their efficacy as parents, and consequently their own self-worth, is being questioned. The cries must be stopped if they are to have any respect for themselves and not feel that they are failures as parents, and they may devote themselves to anticipating the child's needs in order to avoid the psychological pain they feel when he cries. (And this pattern may continue as long as the child remains in the home.)

Such parents, like those who profess deep respect for the child's innate impulses, deprive their child of the important experience of learning "frustration tolerance." The world will never be as indulgent as parents; and if the child is to successfully function in it, he must learn to wait for his gratifications. In addition, the child feels unprotected by parents who submit to his every whim and, rightfully, comes to look upon them as weak. They thereby become poor models for the child to identify with and make it likely that the child will grow into a similarly weak adult. It should not be surprising that such children become quite anxious without the feelings of protection and security that parental limits provide.

"I would never let my child use a pacifier." My focus in this section is not on the pros and cons of pacifiers but rather on the use of a controversial issue for unhealthy motives. Comments like "I would never let my child use a pacifier" are often made to enhance one's self-esteem by putting other people down, and there are parents who latch onto a particular child rearing practice for its one-upmanship value rather than for any of its intrinsic merits. There is practically no advice to parents for which a good refutation does not exist, and there are differing "schools of thought" on just about every childrearing practice. It is, therefore, easy to find something one is doing that one's neighbors aren't that can be used to lord over them. The person who is taken in by such patronizing and who feels loathsome for having so neglected his child, merely provides such flaunters with the sick kind of gratification they seek and so perpetuates their neurosis. He would do better to appreciate that such condescension compensates for feelings of inadequacy and that the truly secure person expresses his differences of opinion without the need to downgrade those whose opinions differ from his own.

"I would never go to work and leave my children. What kind of a mother do you think I am?" There is no question that the younger a child is, the more intensive the care he requires—especially from his mother. However, there is also no question that affectionate care given by a mother surrogate can, to varying degrees, be an effective substitute for the mother's own care. Since there is also no question that child rearing, under the best of circumstances, is often boring and wearying work, all mothers, in my opinion, do well for both themselves and their children to have frequent "breathers"—periods when they can be away from their children. It matters not whether they are working, going to school, relaxing, or involving themselves in recreation as long as they have the opportunity for a change of scenery and new stimulations. Thus refreshed, they can return to their child with renewed vigor.

The mother who does not have the opportunity for such variation (or who does not avail herself of it when she does) generally becomes increasingly unhappy with the child's upbringing. Her growing resentment cannot but deprive the child of the kind of relaxed and satisfied mother so important to his healthy development. In addition, as the child grows older he must gradually experience and accept separations from his mother if he is ultimately to become an independent adult. And this process can begin in the first days of life without having a deleterious influence on the child.

"I can't stand for him to be angry at me." There are people who subscribe to the dictum : "If he's angry at me, I must be terrible. I must, therefore, avoid annoying anyone." Such people do not seem to be aware that, no matter how hard one tries, there will still be those who will dislike us ; and in their attempt to be loved by everyone, they avoid saying or doing anything that might alienate. These people live by the dictum : "If a situation is such that someone has to end up angry, I'd rather it be me than the other person." They go through life passive, friendly, and compliant but inwardly hating themselves. They are not concerned with the appropriateness of the other person's anger or with

the distortions that may have occasioned it, for anger is to be avoided if one is to preserve one's self-respect.

Some people in this category are even threatened by the anger of their children, because they fail to appreciate that much of the child's anger is inappropriate. They are so conditioned to preventing or avoiding anger at all costs that they automatically react to their child's anger by running away from it. Their children become "spoiled" and over-indulged, for they quickly learn the manipulative value of their temper tantrums: with a screaming outburst the child can get just about anything he wants. Such children, clearly, grow up ill-equipped to function in the adult world (unless they find someone who will similarly indulge them, and some do).

"He's everything I have in the world." Some parents' lives are so limited that their total feelings of usefulness are derived from their children, and they have no other involvements to provide them with meaningful gratifications. Such parents may be threatened by the child's growing-up because his ultimate independence would deprive them of their primary source of satisfaction in life. Such parents may utilize every excuse to retard the child in his emotional growth and development. Their children are not permitted to ride their bicycles away from the home, cross the street alone, or venture far from the home when others their age are doing so. Such parents see the neighborhood as far more dangerous than other parents do. Their children are not old enough for overnight visits, sleep-away camp, or staying at home alone, at the age when others are doing these things.

The healthy parent has other sources of gratification and, therefore, need not retard his or her children in their development in order to maintain a sense of usefulness. For example, many women in ghettoes, women without adequate education, and mothers without husbands, may have many more children than they can adequately provide for—both economically and psychologically. Yet they continue to have them, in part, because of their dread of the time when their youngest will be out of the house and they fear they will then be of no use to anyone. This is one of the reasons why such women may be particularly lax in effectively using contraceptive measures. But the syndrome is by no means confined to the socio-economically deprived. There are women from every stratum of life who find themselves significantly depressed when their youngest goes out on his own. Some of these women have had deficient relationships with their husbands and have used their children to make their lives more rewarding. The "involutional depression" (a deep depression generally occurring in the forties or fifties) has many contributing factors. One, is the feeling of uselessness that is experienced by people who have been so extensively devoted to their children that they have no other satisfactions to turn to when the youngsters grow up and become independent of them. Treatment of such persons is predictably futile if it does not help the patient provide himself with new and meaningful sources of gratification.

Parents' anxiety over their grown children's impending separation may be clearly seen in many maneuvers. They may find fault with every prospective marital partner. They may engender guilt in a child who is preparing to leave the home: "How can you leave your poor old mother?" "After all the sacrifices I've made for you, how can you do this to me?" Or, they may inculcate the notion that the ideal child is one who is continually concerned with his parents' welfare and that marrying is an abnegation of this obligation.

"But you promised." The parent who plays this game, although he may not consider promises made to his spouse, peers, friends, etc., inviolate (breaking such promises is usually preceded by the term "I'm sorry but," which is supposed to absolve guilt and gain absolution), somehow regards the promise made to a child to be something sacred. If a promise is broken, he reasons, the child will lose respect for or trust in him—with psychologically devastating results. I believe that parental adherence to a promise for which he no longer has conviction does more to produce the child's distrust and disrespect than breaking it; whereas breaking a promise for appropriate reasons will enhance a child's admiration.

An example will illustrate this. A father promises to buy his daughter a certain kind of doll on a specific day. They set aside an hour for the purchasing trip. The first store is out of the doll and the second has already closed. Driven by the girl's relentless "But Daddy, you promised to get me the doll today" and fearful of the supposed deleterious effects of her disappointment, he doggedly searches for the doll (ignoring, all the while, the people who are awaiting his return). Although the girl may have been successful in getting her doll that day, she cannot have too much respect for a man who runs around like a frightened mouse, crazed with the importance of getting the doll that day. She cannot admire a man who has so little concern for those who are awaiting his return nor have much respect for a father she can manipulate so easily. She does not learn compassion for the father's position; she is not helped to learn that certain things in life are not controllable; and she cannot trust him to provide her with appropriate guidance and limits. The father, on the other hand, who says, "Look, we've tried two stores and haven't been able to get the doll. I know you had your heart set on getting it today, but we just can't. There are people waiting for me, and we have to go back home now. I'll call up some stores and do everything to get you your doll within the next few days," is strong, firm, and respectful of all parties concerned. He is not fearful, weak, or manipulated. He truly commands his child's respect and trust.

The wise parent communicates to the child what the word *promise* really means in the real world. It means that the promiser will go to reasonable efforts to keep his word. It means that if the situation so changes that the promise is no longer appropriate, both parties concerned will be agreeable to make alterations in the agreement. It does not mean that one will go to any length, no matter how absurd, to adhere to it. The parent who plays the "But, you promised" game is not fulfilling this obligation to his child. Lastly, the parent can share with the child the disappointment that both of them suffer when a promise, made in good faith, cannot be realized. This not only provides the child with a learning experience about the uncontrollable vicissitudes of reality but can provide mutual sharing of disappointment—a most salutary parent-child experience.

"You can never repay us for all the sacrifices we have made for you." The healthy parent does not look upon the inevitable frustrations of child rearing as sacrifices for which the child will someday repay him. This would be a one-sided bargain since the child did not ask to be born and did not agree to provide future services in return for those given to him by his parents when he was young. The healthy parent is compensated for the inconveniences and discomforts he suffers in the child's upbringing by the pleasures and gratifications he also experiences during the child's growth years. Hopefully these satisfactions will more than compensate for the deprivations.

It is reasonable to expect and hope that when our children are older they will want to maintain some relationship with us, have some interest in our welfare, and help us in time of crisis and incapacitation. But the healthy parent does everything to provide for these exigencies himself so that he will be less dependent on others, regardless of their relationship to him. The healthy parent is gratified when his child is leading his own life and enjoys the satisfaction of knowing that he has contributed to the growth and maturation of a self-sufficient adult who is now contributing to the betterment of the world.

The parent who does not derive real pleasure from the *process* of raising his child may try to compensate by priding himself on sacrifices he has made for the child's welfare. He may believe that the only way he can get love is to suffer, and he measures the depth of his love by the pain he is willing to bear on behalf of the loved one. The more he elaborates on the extent of his sacrifices, the more he may convince others and himself of his affection.

The martyr-parent may advertise his woes in order to elicit sympathetic admiration; or he may suffer in silence, praising himself for his courage and strength in not crying out, though he may still communicate his agony through sighs and pained facial expressions. The former technique gains the esteem of those who are impressed by such maneuvers, while the latter earns additional veneration from those who consider suffering in silence an added virtue.

The child who is used as a vehicle for the parent's self-aggrandizement through overt suffering cannot but feel guilt over the pain he is told he causes his parent. He is made to feel unworthy and unable to ever repay the debts he owes them for their sacrifices. Children are uniformly unappreciative of most of the day-to-day discomforts their parents experience on their behalf, but the child of the martyr is made to feel that there are *other* children who would be far more appreciative of their parents' efforts than he is. Under the guise of love, then, such parents are manifesting hate and self-aggrandizement. And the child cannot but recognize, at some level, this rejection.

"*I want to give them everything I didn't have when I was a child.*" Because life is such that we can, at best, gratify only an infinitesimal fraction of our wishes, it is natural to want to extend our limited realities by sharing vicariously in the experiences of others. By identifying ourselves with the figures we read about and see on the stage and in films, we achieve, in a compensatory way, some of their satisfactions. We cry and we laugh with them; their emotions become ours, and it is as if we ourselves were actually experiencing the same events.

Our children can provide similar extensions of our experience. We adults cannot allow ourselves the abandon, the silliness, and the free expression of joy that are so natural to the child. By identifying ourselves with our children, their revels can become ours; by observing their pleasures, we partially achieve similar gratifications. An uneducated parent may aspire for his child's college education, in part, for similar reasons. And the economically deprived parent can, through his child's success, partially compensate for his own privations. Such instances are ubiquitous and generally healthy. They are beneficial to both the child and the parent. Knowing that his parents derive so much pleasure from his accomplishments may serve as a strong impetus for the child, and the parents' frustrations can be lessened through such vicarious satisfactions.

This mechanism becomes abnormal, however, when it is used to excess.

"My son the doctor." When parents place excessive pressure on the child to pursue an area he may be basically unmotivated toward, the child soon senses that his parents are only partly interested in his welfare and that they also are using him for their own self-glorification. In such situations the child generally becomes confused. He doesn't know whether he really wants to be a doctor, priest, teacher, nurse, etc., or whether he is simply giving in to his parents' desires. Even when their pressures are not excessive there is often, in career choice, some measure of compliance with parental wishes. However, when the pressure is inordinate, the groundwork is laid for career problems.

Some children withstand the coercion and go on to truly "do their own thing." Yet even some of these are not truly independent, for "their own thing" is often—though not always—uncannily similar to that which thousands of their peers seem to have concluded is *their* own thing at that particular time. Although doing one's own thing can possibly be a manifestation of true independence, it may also be a reflection of passive compliance to the influence of non-parental figures, *i.e.*, peers. Some react with the "freedom" of doing just the opposite thing; but if one has to do the opposite thing *because* it is opposite, he is not really acting independently. Others pursue the parentally prescribed course, but do so ambivalently. They appear to be working toward a particular goal but never seem to get there. For example, the child may work hard on his report, under parental domination, and then lose it on the way to school. Or he may get sick on the day of tryouts for the football team— much to the chagrin of his highly sports-oriented father. Still others react with such hostility to their being used by their parents that they may bring about their own defeat as a side effect of thwarting their parents. Those who submit with less ambivalence, with less acting out may go on to enter the career of their parents' choice—and may live out their lives in dissatisfaction.

"My son the doctor is drowning!" The humor in this mother's plea for help relates to the hostility toward her son that it reveals. This mother's need for self-glorification is so great that she is willing to lose vital time getting help (by inserting the words "the doctor") in order to satisfy this exhibitionistic need.

Another element in the hostility relates to jealousy of the son. The greater the disparity between the parents' and the child's accomplishments, the greater the likelihood the parents will be jealous of their child. The fact that they are related to one another does not prevent the development of jealous feelings, which, in my opinion, are inevitable in such situations. Other common forms of this phenomenon are revealed by statements such as "You think you know everything, just because you went to college" and "Now that you've risen so high you'll probably be ashamed of your parents." These remarks not only reveal the parents' feelings of inferiority and jealousy but their hostility as well.

The child, of course, may actually be a snob and an ingrate, in which case such accusations may still reveal the parents' hostility, though they also happen to be true. The healthy child, even though he may be more successful than his parents, does not look upon them as inferior. Rather he realizes that they had fewer opportunities and recognizes that this does not make them less worthy as human beings, possibly only less lucky.

"Comes the Revolution, you'll like wine." The Russian revolutionary, firing up his audience to join the movement against the Czar, proclaims to the crowd, "Comes the Revolution, there'll be wine flowing in the streets." A voice from the rear meekly responds, "But, I don't like wine." The revolutionary replies "Comes the Revolution, you'll like wine!"

There are parents, like this revolutionary, who have decided what is good for their children and who will shove it down their throats whether the children like it or not. Once again, the benevolent act attempts to enhance the self-esteem of the giver. He *knows* he is doing something worthwhile. When the child refuses to accept these favors, thereby depriving the parent of the enhanced sense of self-worth, the parent may resort to coercion, thereby also releasing his hostility and gratifying his need for power. The situation may also be complicated by parents' deep-seated dependency needs, which he cannot allow himself to gratify openly but attempts to satisfy vicariously by mentally projecting himself onto the child. It is as if each time the child responds with pleasure to his giving, he himself is receiving the pleasure. If the child is unreceptive, the parent may resort to force to gratify his dependency needs.

"The rich man's son syndrome." In this disorder in parent-child relations the child is indulged as an extension of the parents' own self-indulgence or as a means of exhibiting the parents' wealth. This is well described in the anecdote about the rich lady and her son who pull up in their chauffeured limousine to the front entrance of an ultra-expensive hotel. As the doorman assists the chauffeur in putting the son in his wheelchair, he comments to the mother, "I'm sorry your son can't walk, Ma'am." To which she replies, "Of course, he can walk. But thank God he doesn't *have* to." The story beautifully demonstrates the principle of

the child's being indulged for the parent's own glorification. The effects of this kind of abuse can be devastating.

I recall an eleven-year-old boy who was brought to me because he lacked motivation in school. Although basically bright, he was doing very poorly. His father, in his mid-thirties, worked in the business of the paternal grandfather who was a multi-millionaire. The boy stated that he knew that it didn't make any difference whether or not he did well in school because, no matter what happened, he would ultimately go into the family business. The boy's father had been asked to leave a series of prep schools because of poor academic performance as well as refusal to comply with the school's routines and regulations. Although he had progressive difficulty gaining admission to others, his father's donations ultimately resulted in his acceptance. His experiences in college were similar. After graduation, he entered his father's business where he had little involvement. There, he was treated with the deference due the boss's son, but he was not basically respected. The patient's mother, a very good-looking woman, married her husband primarily for his money, and both seemed to be waiting for the paternal grandfather to die in order to inherit his fortune.

From early childhood on, the father had had a recurring dream in which he would be drowning. But just as he was about to suffocate, he would suddenly realize that he could breathe under water. The dream clearly reflected his life situation: no matter how overwhelmed he might become over the repercussions of his laxity and no matter how oppressive life became for him because of his failure to effectively fulfill his obligations, he would suffer no consequences. At the last moment some magic force (his father, of course) would enable him to survive.

The father had many problems. He drank in excess and would have violent outbursts when inebriated (during which he would beat his wife). He was chronically agitated and flittered from pleasure to pleasure in an attempt to gain some gratification from what was for him a very ungratifying life. The boy was already following in his father's pattern. He was deprived of nothing material and took at his whim. He had no motivation for change or treatment and my attempts to engage him met with failure.

To want one's child to have some of the things one was deprived of himself is fine, but to give the child the idea that the primary purpose of those around him is to satisfy his every whim ill-prepares him to function adequately in reality and deprives him of the ego-enhancing sense of mastery that can only come from doing things on one's own.

Many parents who grew up in the Great Depression have tried to compensate for their own childhood frustrations by giving their children "everything they didn't have." A sad mistake. They would have done far better had they *given* their children a little privation (still possible in the midst of affluence) and prevented their the-world-owes-me-a-living attitude that is one of the effects of this well-meaning, but misguided, indulgence.

The child who is overindulged with material things in order to make him happy brings to mind James Thurber's comment: "The world is so full of a number of things, I am sure we should all be happy as kings. And you know how happy kings are."[1]

"He catches cold very easily." There are two common myths that contribute to the concerns of parents and entrench this manifestation of overprotection. The first is that one can catch a cold by exposing oneself to cold air without the protection of warm clothing. There are, unfortunately, even physicians who subscribe to this theory. It is indeed unfortunate that the name of the disease "the common cold" (or simply "cold") is the same as the word to describe a state of relatively low temperature. The first is a disease caused by a virus and characterized by nasal congestion and sneezing; it is rarely accompanied by fever (although at times one may feel a little "chilly"). The second word is often used to refer to the temperature in a given place. Most important, it has never been demonstrated (to the best of my knowledge) that there is a cause and effect relationship between the two. In other words, one does not "catch a cold" from cold air. One gets a cold by being infected with a particular virus; and this can only occur if one ingests, inhales, or otherwise introduces into the body the particular virus (or, more accurately, one of the class of viruses known to cause the disorder) at a time when the body defenses cannot successfully fight it. (I will elaborate on this point in greater detail in my discussion of myth number two.) These viruses do not have wings and they do not fly around like bats in the night air. They are much more comfortable in the nasal passages of our friends and relatives, and one is much more likely to come in contact with them by someone's sneezing in his face. Exposure to the cold (whether indoors or outdoors) does not give us a cold—at worst it only may make us a little more uncomfortable and chilly if we already have a cold in the first place. Exposure to cold has no effect on the duration of the illness. There is an old medical adage that states this quite well: "A cold, if untreated, lasts a week; if treated, it lasts seven days."

---

[1] Thurber, James, *Fables From Our Times,* Garden City, New York: Blue Ribbon Books (Harper and Brothers Publishers), 1943.

What I have just said is well appreciated by most physicians and is standard medical knowledge. Yet it is very hard to convince even well-educated and otherwise intelligent parents of this simple truth. Extensive studies by the U.S. Army have demonstrated that the incidence of colds is no greater among men out on winter maneuvers (with all its cold, mud, rain, sleet, etc.) than among those who remain in the warm barracks. Quoting these studies has generally been a waste of words, so deeply ingrained is this myth. Parents who can rise above their ignorance in this matter and allow their children more freedom and flexibility of exposure will have children who are not only psychologically healthier than they were before but, for reasons that I will now present, physically healthier as well.

The second myth is that the most important factor in determining whether an individual will contract a disease is exposure to it. If this were the case, our hospital beds would be filled with doctors, and there would be no room for anyone else. Practically everyone has wondered, at some time or other, how it is that doctors don't get sick very often, that they seem to be less susceptible than others to catching diseases from their patients. The answers to this question are simple—and well known among most physicians. In the first place, physicians, as a group, are not the kinds of people who quickly take to bed when they get sick. If for no other reason, their livelihood depends on their being up and about. Not too many people are going to seek medical advice from a doctor who is sick in bed. In the second place, there are many mechanisms in the body (such as serum antibodies and white blood cells) that serve to fight off invading germs, and these defense mechanisms are strengthened by exposure to the organisms that produce disease. Each time we are exposed to disease-producing organisms, the body intensifies its production of antibodies and other disease-fighting agents. When we have successfully fought off the germ, these defense mechanisms remain for varying periods of time and serve to protect us from future infection. Sometimes we have contracted a disease and may not even be aware of it because the symptoms are so mild. Even when we have had such "sub-clinical" cases of the disorder, we have built up our protective mechanisms.

We do children a service then when we expose them to the variety of infections they may encounter. We thereby enable them to acquire many "sub-clinical" infections that serve to protect them from the numerous reexposures they will encounter. Parents who try to protect their children from exposure to germs (and this is difficult to do, so ubiquitous are the organisms) deprive their children of the opportunity to build up their immunity and thereby may cause them to be more sick than they would have been had they been allowed the usual exposures.

Although some children are constitutionally very susceptible to infection, most who are considered to be in this category do not differ from others in their germ-resisting mechanisms but in having parents with phobias and germ preoccupations. One way a parent can compensate for basic feelings of inadequacy about his parental abilities is to be excessively cautious about exposing his child to infection and other traumas of life. He can then look upon other parents as neglectful and feel superior. However, such overprotectiveness may bring about the very disorders such parents are ostensibly trying to avoid. Frequent references to sickness provide the child with preoccupations he might not have otherwise entertained and introduce modes of behavior that might not have entered so readily into the child's scheme of things. The sickness adaptation enters the child's repertoire and thereby increases the likelihood that he will feign or exaggerate illness (either consciously or unconsciously) to gain certain neurotic gratifications. Bombarding a child with the possibility that something terrible will happen is one of the most effective ways of bringing about the feared occurrence.

One father sought help with the following story : "When the doctor told me that my wife had given birth to a son, the first thought that came into my mind was, 'I hope he doesn't grow up to become a homosexual.' When he was five, in order to be sure that he wouldn't become one, I showed him pictures of the kinds of things homosexuals and heterosexuals do—so that he would learn right from wrong. As he was growing up, every once in a while, I would sit down with him and we'd have long talks in which I'd explain to him how terrible homosexuality is. When he was thirteen, I took him to a prostitute so he would learn early about how to have sex with a woman."

The man came for consultation because the previous day his son, then seventeen, was discovered in a homosexual act. This is no surprise. With such programming, with such inculcation of homosexual imagery, with so many warnings to stay away, the child could not but be tempted. This father, although he had never engaged in a homosexual act himself (in fact, he exhibited disgust and anger toward anyone who had), was a man who basically had strong homosexual inclinations that he could not admit to himself. His preoccupation with the fantasy that his son might become a homosexual was basically the wish that he do so—disguised as a fear. The image that appears in a person's mind is the most important manifestation of his genuine wish. The words that one conjures up in association with the image can serve to deny the wish's true intent. The thought "I hope he doesn't grow up to become a homosexual" reflected the father's basic wish that the boy do so (to satisfy vicariously, through his son, his own unconscious wish to become one). Putting the desire in the negative, or in the form of a fear, served to lessen guilt over an unconscious awareness of the basic wish. The boy was driven to comply with his father's wish, and allowing disclosure was most probably his way of communicating his compliance.

In a similar manner, the parent who frequently visualizes his child being ill—when there is no evidence for sickness or real danger of such—reveals his basic wish that the child be so. There are many reasons why a parent may want a child to be ill. The sick child can enable the parent to satisfy vicariously his own dependency needs, for each time the parent ministers to the sick child, he is ministering to his own projected self. In addition, taking care of the helpless child provides the parent with an enhanced sense of usefulness and may be an opportunity to prove his competence as a parent. And this is especially important for the parent with feelings of inadequacy.

Visualizing or anticipating a child's illness can also serve as well as an outlet for parental hostility. All relationships are ambivalent, and in even the most loving relationship there is some hostility. The loved one must, by the very nature of living, at times frustrate us; and our children may, in fact, cause us more frustration and inconvenience than many adult relationships. The infant gets up at all hours of the night, wets, soils, makes irrational demands, needs our constant surveillance, etc. He cannot but produce in us angry feelings at times, as well as the thought that we would have been better off without him. Some parents, however, feel very guilty about such thoughts and believe that some fine folks somewhere have no such ambivalence, but have only loving feelings toward their children. Since such hostility cannot be admitted to conscious awareness, it is repressed and may be released via a variety of disguised mechanisms, one of which is to imagine or wish that the child is physically ill. The guilt over this wish is alleviated by the associated fear that the illness will occur.

I am not saying that such parents *really* wish their children ill. Generally, their hostility is not that extreme, and the loving components are still the major ones. What I am saying is that the illness image is the symbolic expression of hostility toward the child and a reflection of the primitive way in which the human mind works. It is a pictorial and concrete way of expressing anger that, as an abstraction, cannot be visualized. The visual imagery of illness allows for some release, through fantasy, of the hostility. What these parents are doing, in a way characteristic of the mind, is releasing some of the pent-up hostilities that inevitably arise in the child rearing process.

The father of the boy who engaged in the homosexual act only partially wished his son to be a homosexual. He, like the parent who fears that his child will become ill, was ambivalent. There was another healthier part of him that wanted the boy to be heterosexual. He shared in common with the parents who protect the child against germs the ambivalence and the transformation of the wish into its opposite (the fear) in order to lessen guilt over the wish.

There is often a realistic element in this type of overprotection. Homosexuality is a possible mode of adaptation for any child; automobile accidents do occur, and children need to be watched; certain neighborhoods are dangerous, and it is neglected to deny this. However, the overprotective parent can be identified by the degree of precaution he exercises. His exaggerated concern and his precautions above and beyond what is reasonable distinguish him from other parents and are the criteria by which I judge such worries inappropriate and harmful to the child. The child may not only fulfill such parental wishes and become sick (thereby complying with their neurotic demands), but utilize the parents' fears to his own advantage. He may feign physical symptoms in order to avoid unpleasant tasks and obligations and the parents may comply because his being ill provides them with the aforementioned neurotic gratifications. And the stage is set for the development by the child of other neurotic reactions centering on bodily symptoms.

"My Joey would never do such a thing." A certain kind of parent considers any defect in his child a reflection of deficiency in himself and may deny his child's faults in order to protect his own self-esteem. Other parents who utilize this maneuver know quite well that their child has indeed performed an unacceptable act; but they believe that the good parent always sticks up for his child, no matter how obvious it may be that the child has misbehaved. They fear that admitting a child's transgressions to an outsider will cause the child to lose faith in them as parents and will undermine his relationship with them. Parents of both kinds are depriving their child of important knowledge about himself that is necessary if he is to function adequately in the world.

"He's a genius." A certain amount of parental overvaluation is normal and healthy. The parent who does not distort at least a little in the positive direction regarding his child's attributes is usually somewhat deficient in providing affection. The parent who harbors no delusions about his child, who sees his liabilities quite accurately, and who does not at all overestimate his child's assets is depriving the child of a vital

stimulus to growth and development. The child requires praise, reward, and other forms of positive reinforcement for his accomplishments if he is to be motivated to repeat them and pursue others. Such encouragement, by the very nature of the child's immaturity, requires a certain amount of exaggeration and overevaluation by the parents.

For example, a four-year-old comes home from nursery school with a Mother's Day card that, by most adult artistic standards, is certainly not extraordinary. However, the child's pride in presenting it, the feeling of mastery he enjoys over having made it, is clearly present. The healthy parent responds to these additional feelings on the child's part. He is filled with pleasure in response to the child's joy and responds with enthusiasm.

Emotions tend to get transmitted and picked up by others. If we enter a room where everyone is depressed, we may find ourselves getting depressed as well. Humorous films are generally less funny in an empty theater. When I was a teenager, there was a popular phonograph record that, from beginning to end, played nothing but people laughing. Within a few seconds after turning it on, everyone in the room began to laugh. We didn't know what in the world we were laughing at—which tended to make us laugh even more. And it was not uncommon, by the end of the recording, for all of us to be hysterically laughing with tears rolling down our cheeks and some people even rolling on the floor. And yet, no one had the faintest idea what he was laughing at. As already mentioned, emotions are like vibrating tuning forks. If two with the same intrinsic frequency of vibration are placed a few inches apart and one is struck, the second will vibrate as well.

These "vibrations," which are transmitted by the child as he proudly shows his parents his Mother's Day card, contribute to the parents' overvaluation and enthusiastic response, and they exclaim, "That's beautiful!" Intellectually, they know that the card is not beautiful. What is beautiful, is the total situation: the child's vibrations and the parents' responding resonations. These contribute to the parents' belief that the card is "beautiful." The parent who does not respond with such resonance is deficient in his ability to provide his child with meaningful affection, and this particular defect on his part may play a significant role in lessening the child's motivation for further creative endeavors.

There are parents, however, who go too far in this regard and whose delusions become too divorced from reality. They cannot permit themselves to see enough of their child's defects and exaggerate his assets to an inordinate degree. If our children are psychological extensions of ourselves, we can enhance our feelings of self-worth through their accomplishments. But, when the parent's need for this particular mode of enhancing his self-esteem is excessive, when he has too few other modes of gaining it, he may develop delusions about his child that go far beyond those of the normal parent. The child may then be seen as a genius or a prodigy, and others who do not show proper appreciation for the child's unusual abilities are seen as blind, jealous, etc. In such a setting, the child may not develop an accurate image of himself, may select unreasonably high goals for himself and may lead a life of considerable frustration. In addition, he learns to take a very jaundiced view of people around him and believes that they are ignorant, hostile, and unappreciative of his talents—not a situation conducive to the formation of meaningful friendships.

"We're like pals." There are parents who pride themselves on the equality of the relationship they have with their child. A certain amount of egalitarianism between a parent and a child is normal and can contribute to the child's healthy development. For example, in the earliest phases of life, involving one's self with a child at his level is pleasurable to the child and allows the adult to gratify his own regressive tendencies (which all of us have) in a socially acceptable manner. Life would be very dull if we were "mature" all the time. Periodic satisfactions at earlier levels of childhood functioning seem to be necessary for the psychological well-being of all adults. Joking, laughing, dancing, singing, and various forms of sex play are examples of this phenomenon in normal adult behavior. Playing with children can provide the adult with another such outlet. In the earliest phases of the child's life both the adult and child can gain pleasure from teasing, tickling, giggling, and playing games like peekaboo. In the late pre-school period, storytelling and reading can provide mutual enjoyment; and throughout later childhood, there are a host of childhood games and sports that adults can enjoy along with their children. Throughout the child's life, a certain amount of "palsmanship" is desirable. This helps the child in the identification process, enhances his self-esteem, and provides him with the pleasure of the adult's company. The older the child, the more areas of egalitarianism there are to serve as the basis for such "friendships."

So much for the normal situation. Problems arise if a parent has inordinate needs for egalitarian experiences with his children. A basically immature parent may function along with the child at his level as an excuse to gratify his own regressive tendencies. For example, a father may become excessively involved in his son's Little League experiences, thereby trying to relive his own boyhood or compensate for early deprivations in this area. He may spend many hours with the boy in practice and training and place great pressures on the child to win. It is not at all uncommon for the whole atmosphere of the Little League games to be contaminated by parents who are excessively involved in the competition. The children, of course, are being used as pawns in their parents' competition with one another.

Another example is the mother of a teenaged girl who goes far beyond the healthy confidante relationship. Under the guise of being intimate, the mother may try to extract information about her daughter's love life and may even subtly foster sexual involvements that the girl might not have otherwise engaged in, in order to vicariously gratify her own sexual desires. Such a mother may try further to relive her youth by dressing like her daughter, using teenage language, becoming a rock music enthusiast, etc. Such a mother's greatest compliment may come when she and the daughter are confused as sisters. Unfortunately, this phenomenon is being culturally reinforced. Youth's pattern of style and speech has become the model for many of their elders—without doubt a manifestation of the attempts by adults to recapture youth in a society that places a high premium on being young.

Although children enjoy and need a certain amount of parental camaraderie, too much can produce anxiety. Although he may at times deny it, every child wants a strong parent who has control over him and who can be relied upon to prevent him from getting into difficulties. Without such parental authority, the child feels unprotected. Having a parent who is more child than adult leaves the youngster devoid of the guidance he so deeply needs. Even the adolescent, who is constantly talking about independence, sorely needs his parents' guidance and may only be able to accept it when it is forced upon him, since then he does not have to admit overtly that he is dependent and still in need of supervision. Instead he can believe that he courageously submitted to overwhelming pressures. The "pal" parent, who preaches and practices "togetherness," deprives his child of these important benefits of the parent-child relationship.

"All I want is respect." It is important to differentiate between true respect of a parent, which is engendered in a child in response to genuinely admirable qualities that a parent exhibits, and specious respect, in which the child merely acts as if there were respect or refrains from verbalizing disrespectful thoughts. The parent who does not genuinely earn the first, may resort to trying to get the second—that being better than nothing. The parent who says, "All I want is respect" is, in the very process of making the statement, losing it. In order to compensate for the lack of real admiration they detect in their children, they pathetically try

to obtain respect by demanding it ("I want you to show respect around here."), or by evoking guilt ("What a terrible thing to say to a parent."). Such maneuvers can only cause the child to *lose* respect for his parent. How can he respect a parent who asks to be lied to—either through coercion or out of guilt?

In the healthy situation, the child truly admires many qualities in his parents and genuinely respects them in response to attributes that are exhibited by the parent and appreciated by the child, not to some nebulous inner quality. I am not an adherent of the philosophy that holds that true love ignores and transcends the loved one's deficiencies—no matter how alienating they may be. Rather, love is a response to readily observable attributes that far outweigh the loved one's deficiencies. When the latter outweigh the former, the terms *love* and *respect* have little applicability.

Parents who believe that they have to present a perfect image to their children try to hide their deficiencies with rationalization: "I wouldn't want him to lose respect for me." This is an excellent way to lose a child's respect since most children, as they grow older, inevitably discover their parents' deficiencies and since the parent's duplicity in hiding his faults lessens the child's respect of the parent.

The healthy parent recognizes that he has both assets and liabilities. Hopefully, the former will outweigh the latter so that the child will profit far more than suffer from his relationship with his parent. Such a parent can tolerate the revelation of his deficiencies because they are more than counterbalanced by his assets. Admitting one's defects (in situations where their revelation is reasonable and appropriate) truly gains the respect of the child. He respects the honesty and the strength of character intrinsic to such admission, and he acquires realistic ideas about what his parents are really like—that they are not perfect, but rather a composite of both admirable and alienating qualities.

Children who grow up with the notion that their parents are perfect will often have trouble in their future relationships with others, whom they may similarly expect to be perfect; and they will inevitably be disillusioned and frustrated as each human being they encounter proves to be fallible. They may spend their lives in the futile quest for the perfect mate or be unable to adjust to marriage, where the acceptance of deficiencies in the mate is vital to survival. In work situations, they may be deprived of satisfaction because they are unable to accept fallible superiors and colleagues, and their continual disappointment and dissatisfaction with other relationships as well may result in significant loneliness.

The younger the child, the more likely he is to be blind to his parents' defects. The very young child, in the early years of the identification process, tends to accept everything his parents do and say as Gospel. Their distortions about reality become his, and although some of them are often rectified as he gets older (for example, their prejudices and superstitions), others may not be (for example, "It's bad to be angry" and "Sex is evil"). Many things occur in psychotherapy. But one process that is central to the treatment of all patients, regardless of their age, is the correction of the distortions about life that they have gotten from their parents. In my work with children there invariably comes a point, usually quite early in treatment, when I will tell the parents, in the presence of the child, that their approach or ideas on a certain subject are, in my opinion, misguided, false, etc. Many parents become fearful that such confrontations will undermine their child's respect for them. This has not been my experience. Rather, the child generally welcomes these conversations and the accompanying atmosphere of openness and honesty. He gets a more accurate view of his world, which cannot but be therapeutic; and his respect for his parents is increased because, by admitting their defects, they are acting in a more respectable manner.

I do not, in such situations, insist on the parents' revealing their every fault—only those that directly pertain to the child and come up naturally in the context of the child's therapy. The parents' lives need not be an open book to the child, for they have a right to their privacies. For example, a father's impotency or a mother's frigidity are not problems that would generally come up in interviews in which the child is present.

I once treated a child who had a school phobia as well as many other fears, such as ghosts and visiting the homes of other children. The child's father was afraid to fly in airplanes, and the mother was claustrophobic. Both were overprotective and feared letting the child cross the street alone, ride her bike, and swim in deep water—when other children her age were doing so. The parents' own fears plus their admonitions to the child regarding neighborhood activities made her world a dangerous place indeed. The parents were able to follow my advice to let the patient engage in the same activities as her peers, and this was helpful in reducing some of her phobias. However, their own phobias were of many years' duration and were deep-seated. I could not, therefore, remove significantly this contributing element to the child's phobias. In order to reduce its affects on her, I advised the parents to discuss their phobias with the patient. I encouraged them to communicate to her their realization that their fears were exaggerated and unrealistic as well as their helplessness to change themselves in spite of their wishes to do so. I felt it was important for the patient to hear directly from them that their thinking was distorted.

The parents were hesitant to follow my advice, lest the child lose respect for them. I convinced them that it was important for the child's therapy for her to gain an accurate view of the world and that they were contributing to her distortions by not confronting her with their awareness that they themselves had symptoms that were, in part, the result of false notions about reality. Furthermore, I convinced them that their daughter was already aware of their phobias and that the very process of their hiding them from her was causing her to lose respect for them. They hesitantly agreed to follow my advice; and their doing so, I believe, played a role in the child's improvement. It is important for the reader to appreciate that all psychiatric symptoms are complex and are not merely the result of distorted ideas about reality. But the correction of false notions is a central and vital aspect of psychiatric treatment.

The question of a child's using profanity to a parent is related to the respect issue. The parent, if he is properly caring for his child, must inevitably frustrate him at times—thereby evoking angry feelings and thoughts. In such situations it is natural for the child to come out with a few vulgar epithets. Presently, most still consider it unacceptable for a child to curse at his parents. However, enlightened parents recognize that it is important to allow the child appropriate anger expression, without guilt. If a parent suppresses his child's use of profanity toward him, he may feel that he risks inhibiting him and inculcating unnecessary guilt. The dilemma is not really as great as it may initially appear. One can suppress the use of profanity toward a parent without necessarily making the child feel inordinately guilty about anger expression in general. A parent can say, "I can see how that makes you angry. Be as angry as you want. But you're not going to talk that way to me. Think such things all you want, but you just can't talk that way to parents. Talking that way to your friends on the street is another story." Responses such as these do not make the child feel loathsome or guilty about his anger, but at the same time they teach him restraint and socially acceptable practice.

"You're not old enough to understand things like that." Many parents, with the justification that they are protecting their children from psychological trauma, lie or evade rather than answer their children's questions directly. Most parents no longer give the old stork story when a child asks questions about his origin, but many still couch their responses with euphemisms or other patent prevarications. Many are

careful to avoid discussing in front of a child the impending death of a person well-known and possibly even loved by the child. When the child is finally told, only he is shocked by the news—everyone else has had the time to slowly accustom themselves to the loss. He may then be told that the deceased is now "living in heaven" and leading a very enjoyable life—even when the parent has absolutely no belief himself in an after-life. A child may not be told about an impending divorce until the actual day of separation. Again, he is deprived of the opportunity to desensitize himself to the trauma. Similarly, he may not be told about a hospitalization until the actual day that he is to go. And then he may be told all sorts of absurd things about its purpose, for example, that there will be no pain, and even that there will be no operation—when the parent knows that this is not the case.

In all of these examples the parents operate under the misguided notion that the disclosure of the unpleasant news will be psychologically deleterious to their children. Actually, children are far less fragile in this regard than most parents appreciate. Most are well able to tolerate all of the aforementioned painful situations. What they are not able to handle (and they do not differ very much from adults in this regard) is the anxiety that comes from being kept in ignorance. The child usually senses that something "bad" is taking place. When his questions are un-answered, avoided, or answered euphemistically, he senses the duplicity. He knows that he is not being given the full story and can only think the worst. From his vantage point, the issue is one that is "too terrible to talk about." Then, he may become preoccupied with all sorts of fearful fantasies—fantasies far more horrible than the event that is not being disclosed to him. Such children would adapt far better to the trauma if they were given direct and honest explanations—at a level commensurate with their age and ability to understand.

Some parents take advantage of the child's naiveté and credulity and consider it the grandest joke to fool him. They gleefully watch the child squirm as they tell him stories about "the bogey man" and other malevolent creatures. Or, they may threaten the child with horrible punishments in order to discipline him—punishments that are totally impossible or that the parent has absolutely no intent of implementing. Others lie to their children by covering every possible deficiency—lest the child lose respect for them.

The child whose parents lie to him in the ways I have just described are doing him a serious disservice. Under the guise of protecting him from pain, they are causing him more problems than he would have had were he told the truth. They are causing their child to lose trust in them—and that is one of the most devastating things that can happen to him. If his own parents cannot be relied upon to tell him the truth, who, then, can he believe? This problem may become acute when the child's lack of trust may extend to the teacher, and he may consequently be seriously compromised in his ability to learn in the classroom. In addition, such parental duplicity squelches the child's natural curiosity. If one's important questions are continually incapable of being answered, one's curiosity is dampened. And by the time such children reach school, they may have lost the interest in and the hope of learning anything from anyone.

"Mother knows best." Many of the drawbacks of this comment have already been described in the previous section. If believed by the child, this kind of remark tends to provide him with a distorted view of parental assets. If disbelieved, it lessens the child's respect for the parent because of the intrinsic duplicity of the statement. However, this kind of comment has additional implications. Generally, the parent who professes it means well and hopes that the child's adherence to the principle will serve him well. It is usually true, that when there is a difference of opinion between a mother and an infant or very young child, the mother's position is the more prudent one. However, some parents continue to imbue this concept into the child long after it is appropriate. As a result, the child may continue to rely solely on his parents' advice beyond the age when he should be making many decisions on his own and when his own opinions about what is best for himself should, at least, be given serious consideration and may, indeed, be better-advised than those of his parents.

In addition to fostering dependency, such comments also tend to undermine the child's self-esteem. Implied in the notion that mother is always smarter, is that the child is always dumber. Resentment toward the parent inevitably arises in response to such implications, and continual advice from an omniscient person cannot but lower the child's self-esteem even further.

For the very young child, absolute decisions by the parents are probably the best. The child cannot appreciate the subtleties and shades of meaning or the arguments for and against a particular decision. Even for controversial subjects, such as whether or not to allow thumb-sucking and pacifiers, the parent should weigh the pros and cons in his own mind, come to some decision himself, and then follow through with the approach he has chosen. Benevolent despotism, I believe, is the best form of government for children and other primitive peoples.

As the child grows older, however, he can appreciate more of the complexities of life and should be told, in a controversial situation, whether or not the parent is certain about his decision. If *some* course of action is warranted, it is best taken, even if ambivalently; but the parent's lack of certainty should be communicated to the child without shame or hesitation. For example, "I don't know whether you'll be better off at Camp A or Camp B. They're different kinds of camps. Let's try Camp A this summer. If it doesn't work out, we'll try Camp B next summer." Such an approach helps the child appreciate that his parents are fallible and not omniscient. It does not undermine respect because, as already mentioned, admitting occasional deficiencies and fallibilities enhances, rather than detracts from, the child's respect for a parent.

"I don't know what I would do without her." This comment, which is made to enhance a child's self-esteem by praising her for her usefulness, can be a cover-up for exploitation. Although a certain amount of helping with household chores is a maturing experience for the child, the parent who excessively uses an older child to help care for the younger one(s) is exploiting the older and probably depriving the younger of proper parental attention. Children who are so used respond with anger and hostility.

Other parents, as a manifestation of an extreme dependency problem, may use the child as a confidant. The child is generally ill-equipped to provide a parent with genuine consolation, advice, etc., but may try to comply in order to avoid the parents' disappointment and rejection. Children of such parents are being deprived of the strong protecting parental figure so necessary to a child's healthy growth and development. Although some children respond with a spurious maturity, others become insecure, anxious, and generally poorly equipped to function in society because their parents have not provided them with the wherewithal and knowledge to cope with life's problems.

"Where did we go wrong, doctor?" The reactions of parents who learn that a child has developed psychiatric difficulties can be divided into two categories: those who believe that any parent can be unlucky enough to have such a child and those who consider the parents, and especially the mother, to be the invariable cause of children's psychiatric disturbance. Unfortunately, we in the field of child psychiatry and psychology have provided strong support for the latter group. Unless the child is obviously suffering from organic disease of the brain, we try to learn what things did go wrong, what mistakes the parents did make, and what psychological disorders the parents have had that may have contributed to the child's disturbance.

To the best of my understanding, psychological disturbances are the result of a combination of factors, both hereditary and environmental. And the environmental factor includes not only the parental influences, but also those of teachers, neighbors, peers, the mass media, and events of the world at large. I have seen many parents who have been essentially loving and devoted to their children, who have made no significant mistakes, who did not have significant disturbances themselves, but whose children are in trouble. The causes in such cases lie, in my opinion, in the genes and in environmental influences having little, if anything, to do with the parents. But even when parental factors have played a role in bringing about the child's disorder, one still cannot appropriately say (in the vast majority of cases) that the disturbance was "the parents' fault." Generally, the parents have tried to do everything that they have considered to be in the child's best interests. At any given point, most parents do what they think will benefit the child. Unfortunately, they may be misguided or blinded by their own psychological disorders and, in this way, contribute to the child's difficulties. In a sense then, the parents are "at fault" in that their behavior did play a role in bringing about the child's illness. Had they not acted the way they did, the child might not be as sick, or even sick at all. However, their "guilt" is not intentional, and accordingly they are less blameworthy.

I often describe this important distinction to the parents of children I see in my practice (most of whom feel quite guilty about having to bring their child to a psychiatrist) by using the analogy of a man driving an automobile. If, while driving, a defective part causes the car to swerve out of control and hit a child on the sidewalk, the man is in a sense "at fault." Had he not been driving his car at that time, in that place, the child would probably not have been injured. He is guilty, however, by accident. If he had purposely driven his car up on the sidewalk in order to hit the child, the law would have treated him quite differently. He would have been considered to have committed a crime; he would be guilty by intent. From the child's point of view, he still suffers the same injuries, and it probably matters little to him in which way the driver was at fault. From the driver's point of view, whether or not the guilt is appropriate depends upon whether the child's injuries were the result of an unfortunate accident or purposeful malice.

Some parents of emotionally disturbed children automatically consider themselves the malicious perpetrators of a crime rather than innocent sufferers. They flagellate themselves for having contributed to the child's disorder, while at the same time exclaiming that they always did what they thought was best. These people may have grown up in an environment where each person believed that he had responsibilities to others that went far beyond what most would consider realistic. The good person, they were taught, not only willingly takes on the responsibility for the happiness and comfort of all, but also feels ashamed if he fails in his duty to those around him. Believing that humans can rise to any exigency can provide a feeling of control over the uncontrollable and lessen the fears we all have about the unpredictable calamities that may befall any of us.

The parent who lives with an inordinate sense of responsibility for his child's welfare only ostensibly provides him with loving care. What he is really providing is overprotection, as he anticipates the child's every need lest he has to blame himself if anything goes wrong with the child. In an environment where his parents assume so many of his responsibilities the child tends to become less capable of making his own decisions and providing for himself. When things go wrong he tends to blame others since his experiences have always been that others have assumed responsibility. Such parents often expect others to be critical of them if they fail to rear a perfect child—every one of whose needs is provided for. This excessive dependence on the opinions of others may cause the child to become dependent as well on others' opinions and cause him to someday himself live under the same overwhelming burden of responsibility.

"When I studied psychology in college . . . " This introduction is generally used to justify many unhealthful interactions with and approaches to the child. It is most unlikely that the stated approach was in any way suggested by the instructor, but the parent has distorted what was taught or recalls what was never said or even implied to justify the particular childrearing approach.

One mother I knew, would allow her child to crawl all over her naked body because she recalled being taught in college to allow the child to "express himself." When he was about four, she began to notice that he got erections while crawling on her, and that became the point at which she would stop the game—only to play again another day. When he was referred to me at seven with severe anxiety and tics, she was still doing what she had "learned in college." The child, of course, was being excessively aroused and then not permitted release. His symptoms related primarily to tension and repressed anger toward his mother.

Some parents become excessively indulgent from what they have learned in college while others become punitive. Some overprotect, and others become inordinately cautious. In fact, most of the pathological manifestations I describe in this book have been justified, at one time or another, by people who claim that they are only doing what they were taught in college.

THE EFFECTS OF PSEUDO-LOVE AND DEPRIVATION OF LOVE

Most psychological disturbances that therapists deal with are, in part, the result of difficulties in the parent-child love relationship. Although many factors are involved in bringing about the various types of psychological disorders, most share in common the deprivation of parental affection.

The parent-child relationship serves as the model for all of the child's future involvements; and since the child tends to generalize, he will anticipate from others the same kinds of responses he received from his parents. If his relationship with his parents has been basically gratifying, he will tend to seek and anticipate similar such gratifications from others. On the other hand, if one or both of his parents profess affection but, either overtly or implicitly, reject the child each time he reaches out for it, he will come to distrust assertions of love and become anxious when they are offered. The psychiatrist Harry Stack Sullivan referred to this phenomenon as the "malevolent transformation." Ostensible benevolence becomes transformed into malevolence for the child has become conditioned to experience pain when affection is allegedly being offered. In extreme forms of rejection, where the parent is more overtly rejecting or abandoning, the child develops even stronger feelings of antipathy and alienation from people. Once again, he generalizes from his experiences with his parents and assumes that others will react to him in a similar manner. The parent-child relationship, therefore, determines a whole range of possible degrees of involvement with others—from the intensely intimate to the very distant.

Although it is impossible to chart here the whole range of effects that deprivation of love in childhood can have on the individual, we can safely say that the ability to relate fully to others will be strongly impaired. Some people will be able to see relationships only in terms of a particular personality trait or a special ability (such as athletic prowess) and thus take the part for the whole of a person; in extreme cases these people will only find certain anatomical traits, such as breasts, interesting and take this as the focus of a relationship. Other individuals, disillusioned with their parents and, consequently, with other people, turn to themselves for gratification. Still others will be able to relate only to pets or will at least find these the most satisfying and least demanding involvements, while others may turn to their work or hobbies to the exclusion of all else.

What is significant here is the extent to which a basic inability to engage in personal relationships shapes an entire life. Anyone, at some point in his life, may find other fields of experience or interest more satisfying than a total relationship with another person; but abnormality, or disturbance, is present when one of the limited relationships described above excludes all other human interaction. The child significantly deprived of parental love may be forced into being open only to one of these limited forms of relationship.

2

Self-Esteem

The most important element in bringing about psychological disorder is deprivation of parental affection, though other factors may contribute. And low self-esteem is one of the earliest and most significant effects of this deprivation that the young child develops. Having no guidelines of his own, he derives his self-image from what the psychiatrist Harry Stack Sullivan called "reflected appraisals"; that is, from his parents' opinion of him. Later, when he makes friends, enters other homes, and goes to school, new criteria are introduced, and distortions in his self-image, which may have been derived from the parents, can be modified. In healthy development, two main processes take place: (1) increased experience and further modifications produce greater accuracy and realism in the self-image; (2) decreased reliance on the environment and increased respect for inner convictions cause one to determine his self-esteem less by the capriciousness of external events and more by the tried and tested internal criteria for ascertaining self-worth.

However, this earlier experience of "reflected appraisal" is so deep and lasting that the child whose parents are significantly rejecting may never be able to gain a full feeling of self-worth and, as a result, may spend his life futilely utilizing a variety of neurotic and even psychotic mechanisms to bolster his low self-esteem. The following sections provide examples of how parents influence the formation of a child's self-image and suggest ways in which parental behavior and attitudes can modify —positively or negatively—the child's self-esteem.

"Johnny called me stupid." A three-year-old runs to his mother crying, "Johnny called me stupid." The mother replies, "You're not stupid. He's silly," and the child stops crying. Hopefully, as he grows older, the child will consider, as well as what others say of him, his own ever-growing inner repertoire of criteria for self-worth, for failure to do so leaves him at the mercy of all who might criticize him. Since he can never be completely acceptable to everyone, he must invariably be exposed to disapproval; but indiscriminately accepting all criticism can only result in his chronically detesting himself. The parent must help the child understand that he is not exactly what others may consider him to be and help him appreciate that, no matter how hard he tries, there will always be those who will dislike him.

The parent must help the child enrich his set of criteria for judging his self-worth. He must help the child look to his own opinions, to those of his parents, and to those of others outside his home. The child should learn to consider with receptivity, but not with gullibility, the opinions of those he respects; he should learn to accept what seems reasonable to him and reject what does not. He must be helped to see his parents' own distortions and their fallibility: "Your father is disappointed in you because you aren't too good in sports. To your father, sports is the most important thing in the world. There are many others who don't think that any single thing, like sports, is all that important, and they don't put down someone just because he isn't good at sports."

"We have great respect for his natural inclinations." Many parents, in their desire to avoid the child's over-dependence on those around him, go too far in their "respect" for the child's opinions and behavior and their wish that he achieve "self-actualization." The child who is unduly allowed to realize his "true self" may develop, I believe, a variety of difficulties. He may become excessively anxious because he is not being taught the controls and limits that are so important if he is to function well with others. He may become distrustful of others and attempt to rely on only himself in situations he is ill-equipped to deal with adequately.

The parent who takes the attitude, "If he says it or does it, it must be good," does not ultimately produce a child with a valid sense of his own self-worth but someone with the delusion that he can say and do no wrong. Such an attitude will hardly win the child much affection from his peers, and the rejection and alienation he is exposed to cannot but lessen his self-respect.

"This *is my daughter*." The sense of pride a loving parent has for his children is generally appreciated by them and contributes to their own feeling of self-worth. The healthy parent is *slightly* delusional about his children and tends to distort his perceptions of them so that he somewhat minimizes their deficiencies and exaggerates their assets. In moderation the child profits from this distortion because it provides a counterbalance for the unfair criticisms that he, like all humans, is subject to. The person who loves us is esteemed, in part, because of his benevolent blindness to our faults and his readiness to see admirable qualities that others seem to be oblivious to. The child whose parents do not have this sense of pride in him will be less likely to have it in himself and will, as a result, fall very low in his own esteem.

"*Can't you do anything right?*" A certain amount of parental criticism is necessary and desirable if the child is to make an adequate adjustment to the world. Criticisms do not necessarily lower self-esteem. In fact, by sharpening the child's discrimination about what the world expects of him, and by enriching his sophistication of the world, they play an important role in enhancing his ultimate sense of self-esteem. Useful knowledge is esteem-enhancing. The ignorant man cannot feel good about himself.

However, when criticism is given with malevolent, rather than benevolent, intentions, problems may arise. This may occur when the parent generalizes and communicates to the child that rather than an isolated defect, his error is proof of total inferiority. To call a child "clumsy" when he spills his milk may be a little harsh, but it relieves the parent of his irritation and is basically a valid criticism. To tell him, "You are one of the biggest slobs I have ever seen and if you keep up this way I don't know how anyone is ever going to tolerate you," may express the anger the parent feels; but it also conveys to the child that, in addition to being clumsy, he has other qualities that will predictably alienate all who have the misfortune to come in contact with him. Doing one thing wrong does not warrant the generalization : "Can't you do anything right?" Failing one subject does not justify the condemnation : "You'll never amount to anything." Parents who believe that such invectives are corrective are misguided indeed. What they may accomplish is to bring about the very personality patterns the parents fear will result. In addition, such comments have a devastating effect on the child's self-esteem.

"How will my children respect me if I admit my faults to them?" Although some of the implications of this comment have been discussed earlier, I will focus here on its possible effects on the child's self-esteem. If a parent feels so insecure that he cannot admit occasional defects to his child and if the child does not come to appreciate his parent's deficiencies himself, then the child may come to view his parent as someone who is either perfect or very close to it. Even when a parent does reveal his deficiencies, most children still tend to see their parents as more powerful, wise, effective, and efficient than they really are. From the child's vantage point, parents are giants. His inferiority to them in practically all areas is painfully apparent to him and contributes to feelings of inadequacy. Under the best of circumstances, therefore, the child will develop mechanisms to compensate for these feelings of comparative inadequacy. The parent who needs to present himself as flawless to his children increases the painful disparity between himself and them and adds to this source of the child's feelings of inadequacy. The healthy child will use genuinely compensatory mechanisms (such as the development of talents, skills, and traits that provide real ego-enhancement), whereas the disturbed child may use specious maneuvers (boasting, stealing, and grandiose thinking, for example) to make up for this relative inadequacy.

In addition, if the child grows up still believing his parents are perfect (or close to it), he cannot but be disappointed with everyone else in life who has flaws. He will either suffer continual disillusionment in his relationships or involve himself only with those who, like his parents, are "flawless." Relationships with "perfect" people, maintained as they must be by denial of deficiencies and delusions of faultlessness, are at best unstable and generally short-lived.

"I'm proud to be American (black, Jewish, Irish, Italian, etc.)." A sense of pride, if it is to be genuinely ego-enhancing, must be based on an attribute acquired through some effort. The fewer such sources of pride one has, the more likely he is to attempt to gain such feelings from qualities he has inherited or otherwise effortlessly come to possess. But it requires a certain degree of self-delusion to consider the easily acquired attributes to provide the same sort of esteem-enhancing gratifications as real accomplishments.

For example, to say, "I'm proud to be an American," is not a very effective way of enhancing one's feelings of self-worth, since the person born in the United States did absolutely nothing to become an American.

To say "I'm proud I'm Jewish because Einstein, Freud, etc., were Jewish" is an inane comment. The speaker is obviously trying to gain some prestige himself by association with great Jewish men. He is trying to delude himself into thinking that he is somehow a better person because he is of the same religious background as these great contributors. Einstein and Freud have justification for feeling proud of their accomplishments (and possibly their parents and teachers for the roles they played in their growth and development), but not everyone else in their synagogue. Similarly there is nothing to be either proud or ashamed of in being black, Irish, Italian, Afghanistanian, Timbuktuian, or anything-else-ian. We are what we are (regarding national and ethnic origin) because of how, where, and when the genetic dice fell for us.

However, distortions about one's heritage are usually communicated to the child in the earliest stages of his life. They teach him to utilize specious maneuvers to enhance his self-esteem and divert his efforts from endeavors that can genuinely enhance his sense of self-worth. They teach him empty boasting and false pride—qualities that are intrinsically ego-debasing.

"I wish her nose wasn't so big." Those whose body parts or features, although completely normal physically, do not conform to what is considered ideal by their particular culture may find themselves at a significant disadvantage. For example, in modern America, the breast has been subject to a succession of changes in this regard. In the 1920's, flat-chested women were all the rage, and well-endowed females did all they could de-emphasize their bosoms. Since that time, bustiness has been in vogue, and it is now the less-endowed who feel inadequate. Many techniques have been devised to correct their "defect": injection of silicone, surgical implantation of plastic material, and even transplantation of fatty tissue from the buttocks. As young girls approach puberty, they eagerly await the development of these particular organs with an interest that goes far beyond their involvement in other bodily changes that are simultaneously taking place. "Practice bras" may be purchased in anticipation of the great day when breasts will appear, and wearing "falsies" may be the only way the youngster feels comfortable in public if her peers develop earlier or more abundantly.

"Nose jobs" are also in vogue at the time of this writing. These are especially common among Jewish girls who are led to believe that there is something intrinsically ugly about Jewish noses and that to have one like a Gentile girl cannot but enhance one's popularity. Short men wear "elevator shoes." Tall women slouch and wear flat shoes. Adolescent boys compare penises to see whose is larger, and the less "well hung" may avoid locker rooms to protect themselves from the humiliations they anticipate there.

There is nothing innate about any of these feelings of shame and dissatisfaction with one's own body. All are culturally determined and transmitted through the parents from one generation to the next. All reflect an inappropriate dissatisfaction with one's body and contribute to a person's feeling of low self-worth. All start in childhood. Happily, there has been a recent trend among youth to counter these insidious and hypocritical attitudes. Because they have a greater sense of pride in their bodies, there is less shame, less covering, and less artificiality. Sadly, there are other youngsters who use the same new sense of freedom of dress and grooming to justify the most slovenly appearance. These individuals have little basic pride in themselves. In general, however, there is more pride in the body one is born with and less concern with how it compares with the average or with some supposed ideal. Although the ideal is being within the normal human range and there is still some stigma attached to being extremely different, the accepted range of normality has been broadened. "This is my body," the young people boast. "If you don't like it, there is something wrong with you." "There is no part of me that is shameful to expose," they claim. They do not wear bras to change the natural shape of their breasts. (I have no doubt, however, that this practice serves seductive purposes as well.) They do not try to straighten naturally kinky hair, change the color of their skin, or de-emphasize the thickness of their lips.

"I was swimming champ at my summer camp." Some children may attempt to compensate for their feelings of inadequacy by exaggerating their competence or boasting about exploits that never took place. Recognizing that the child who excels enjoys the admiration of others, the unpopular child may try to gain similar prestige. These are the children who describe themselves to their classmates as having been champions in various activities at summer camp. These are the ones who boast that they "never crack a book" or they "never have to do homework" when, in fact, they may be studying quite hard to get good or even passing grades. Such children, through their descriptions of interesting and unusual exploits, may enjoy some ego-enhancing attention at first. However, they live with the fear that their prevarications will be disclosed—and such feelings invariably lower their feelings of self-worth. In addition, if they have any conscience at all, they cannot but have less inward respect for themselves for lying. And when others discover that they have been taken in (and they inevitably do) then such children may suffer even more rejection than when they had been unpopular but truthful. This increased alienation from others produces even further feelings of worthlessness. Here again, the principle is well demonstrated: the neurotic symptom, which is in part derived to enhance self-worth, usually ends up by lowering it—its other "benefits" notwithstanding. Although other factors may contribute to this kind of lying, the attempt to enhance self-esteem is central.

The parents of such children would do well to impress upon them that they will invariably end up being less liked rather than better liked when others realize they are being lied to and that they can be liked for themselves without being "the champ." In addition, parents do best to help such children develop traits and abilities that will genuinely attract others so that duplicity as a way of gaining affection will be unnecessary.

The class clown. Most classes seem to have at least one clown. He is the child who basically feels unloved and dupes himself into believing that the laughter of his classmates is a sign of their affection for him. He seems blind to the fact that the children are more often laughing *at* him rather than *with* him and deludes himself into thinking that their enjoyment of his antics reflects respect. However, he is still not the one who gets elected to class offices, who is invited to birthday parties, or who is selected early when teams are being formed. In response to this further rejection (and loss of self-respect), he may resort to even more harebrained escapades in the futile attempt for acceptance. What results, of course, is even further alienation—and the vicious cycle may continue.

If the parents can impress upon such a child that his antics are losing him friends, rather than gaining them, and that children are still not seeking him out in spite of the fact that they laugh at his jokes, they may be able to reduce the likelihood that the child will resort to this ego-debasing maneuver. However, again the parent must help him develop genuinely attractive traits that will draw people to him if he is to give up the clowning pattern and not substitute equally self-defeating forms of relating to his peers.

The briber. Children whose behavior is such that their peers do not voluntarily seek them out may find that "philanthropy" can gain for them an amazing degree of popularity. Doling out candy, money, small toys, and other gifts may make the difference between standing on the sidelines and being one of the team, if only as a pinch hitter. The "gifts" may make the difference between spending a lonely afternoon in the house and being one of the gang, if only as a follower. The child may resort to stealing money from parents and siblings to support his charitable enterprises. Although purchasing friends in this way may temporarily relieve the child's loneliness and its associated feelings of worthlessness, he inwardly knows that his friendships are specious, that they are dependent upon continual bribery, and that he is being exploited. Such awareness inevitably lowers his feeling of self-worth.

Again, the parents of such a child must try to impress upon him that he is being taken advantage of and that those who play with him only for a price are not true friends. More important, they must help the child rectify those patterns that are alienating his peers in the first place and replace them with modes of relating that will enhance rather than detract from his feeling of self-worth.

The cheater. The cheater does not have, or does not believe he has, the competence to be successful in the activity in which he cheats. He does not seem to appreciate that reaching a goal dishonestly cannot provide the same degree of satisfaction or the same sense of accomplishment as coming by it honestly. He does not seem to appreciate that the gratifications he may derive from the attainment are generally more than counterbalanced by the inner feeling of shame that the accomplishment was not genuinely earned. The child who cheats on school examinations can be told, "You really can't feel good about having gotten this high mark by copying." In addition, he can be reminded that it is likely that his classmates have observed what he has done and that this certainly is not going to enhance his popularity.

Generally, when a child tries to cheat when he is playing a game with me, I tell him that it is no fun for me to play when he cheats and that I will only continue to play as long as he follows the rules. Having the living experience that his cheating may threaten the continuation of an enjoyable experience, as well as lessen the affection he enjoys from someone he esteems, can serve as an effective and realistic deterrent. In addition, I generally ask him whether he plays the same way with his peers and if so to consider the possibility that this may be one of the reasons he has trouble keeping friends.

The reader should note that in such situations I do not appeal to higher ethical and moral principles when attempting to modify a child's behavior, but rather to the child's sense of expediency and to other considerations relevant to his everyday experiences. In my philosophy of things the cheater is not being watched by someone up there who is keeping a careful record and will see to it that someday he will be punished for all his transgressions (either in this life or after death). I therefore cannot use such appeals to help the cheater see the errors of his ways. I can, however, appeal to more immediate considerations that are not only more effective in helping the child with the problem but that also avoid the additional difficulties introduced, I do not believe in appealing to the

Almighty for help in solving the child's problems. To be reminded that cheating makes you feel lousy about yourself and may lose you friends is honest, direct, and relevant to the child's life in the present. To invoke the wrath of God, hell's fires, and other forms of eternal damnation may scare the child out of cheating, but it may scare him into other things far worse.

"*I never heard anyone say such terrible things.*" Some children are made to feel that they are the first persons in the history of the world to utter certain thoughts and feelings. Believing that the ideas that spontaneously and uncontrollably appear in one's mind are among the most abominable in the history of mankind invariably makes one feel terrible. Such attitudes are particularly common over sexual and angry feelings, and I will discuss these issues in greater detail in Chapters 4 and 6. The lowered self-esteem, which is part of the guilt children feel over certain ideas and urges, is primarily the result of parental attitudes, although it can be modified by the child himself or external influences.

The healthy parent recognizes that there is no thought that is foreign to any human mind. He helps the child accept the most heinous ideas as natural and understandable under certain circumstances. He teaches the child to express them when appropriate and to suppress them when not, and he teaches the child effective and civilized expression, not inappropriate self-censorship and self-denigration. He reassures his child that not only do many children have similar thoughts and feelings, but that he himself has also had, or still has, the same kinds of ideas and emotional reactions. In this way he can counterbalance some of the widespread social and cultural attitudes that engender unnecessary and inappropriate guilt and the lowered self-respect intrinsic to it.

"*Nice boys don't fight.*" Inhibition in asserting oneself is another source of low self-esteem. The child who is smoldering with pent-up hostilities over not having stood up for his rights has little respect for himself. He derogates himself because of his passivity, and his suppressed anger in itself interferes with a feeling of self-satisfaction. The parent who discourages a child from fighting his battles, who tells him that "Nice boys don't fight," and who advises him to keep away from boys who are rough or use profanity fosters repression of anger, which interferes with the feeling of well-being that is necessary to a strong sense of self-regard. Encouraging the child in asserting himself, in not letting himself be taken advantage of, and in appropriately expressing his resentment can be most helpful in alleviating feelings of inadequacy that stem from repressed anger. Winning a well-fought battle does, after all, enhance one's feelings of competence.

"Boys don't cry." The notion that it is unmanly to cry is a deep-seated one in our culture. Although the proscription is less rigid for women, the woman who cries is still considered more immature or hysterical than the one who can hold back her tears. The tradition, I believe, is an unfortunate one, for it does not properly respect innate responses. Those who adhere to the principle unnecessarily deprive themselves and their children of an emotional outlet, the inhibition of which contributes to the formation of psychological disorder. One of the effects of the prohibition against crying is that the child who spontaneously bursts into tears is made to feel humiliated, and consequently his self-esteem is lowered.

The crying prohibition is frequently extended even to a child whose parent or grandparent has just died : "Be brave, don't cry," or "Big boys and girls don't cry." And even if the child is not exposed to such gross and misguided admonitions, he may very well be exposed to subtler remarks : "Mary is taking it so well," or "He's holding up beautifully." Mourning involves a piecemeal desensitization to the pain one feels over the loss of a loved one. Each time one thinks of the deceased the pain becomes a little more bearable. Each time one cries one feels a little less pained over the loss. To inhibit these reactions (which I believe to be innate) is to prevent a healthy psychological restoration. The persistence of such pent-up emotions prevents the sense of well-being necessary to feeling good about oneself. In addition, if the child feels humiliated and embarrassed over his tears, an even further lowering of his self-esteem is suffered.

Every child does well, therefore, to see his parents, especially his father, cry in appropriate situations. The parent who runs into another room so his children will not see him cry makes it less likely that they will have a healthy attitude toward crying. Our children learn much from their imitation of us. If the adult is free to cry when the situation warrants it, the child is more likely to act in a similar way.

"She criticizes herself mercilessly." Depression, in the adult sense, is not common in childhood, though it certainly does exist. Children are generally happier, more optimistic, and less weighted down by the responsibilities of the adult world. One element, however, that can contribute to depressive symptoms by severely lowering self-esteem is that of turning hostility, which should be externally directed, inward toward the person himself. The child feels so guilty over his anger and so fearful of directing it to its proper object that he unconsciously turns it toward himself to provide some release of his pent-up feelings, often in the form of self-deprecatory preoccupations.

Such children have learned (primarily from their parents) that anger is an unacceptable emotion to express. They turn their anger inward against themselves (a safer target), and their self-flagellation and self-disparagement result in a significant lowering of self-esteem. The parent should help such a child direct his hostility toward the appropriate source so the irritations that are producing the anger can be more effectively dealt with.

"Look ma, no hands!" Of all the things I have ever heard uttered by a child, this is one of my favorites. These four short words beautifully epitomize some vital psychological principles. The boy who exclaims, "Look ma, no hands!" as he rides his bicycle is clearly proud of his accomplishment: not only can he ride his bicycle, but he can do so without using his hands. His hard-earned skill in so delicately balancing his bike is a genuine source of ego-enhancement to him. Real accomplishments and genuinely desirable attributes are the bedrock upon which feelings of self-worth are built. Without this foundation, feelings of security are at best shaky and are more likely pretense and delusion.

An additional element of psychological import in the boy's boast relates to his need to communicate his accomplishment to his mother and to the implied anticipation of her praise and admiration. The long-sought-after attainment, the ego-enhancing deed, no matter how great a source of satisfaction it may be, cannot provide us with full gratification unless we can share the accomplishment with others and win some praise or other positive feedback. And mother is the prototype of all future praisers.

In my opinion, the ideal attitude toward potential admirers should be to appreciate that one's primary source of pleasure and ego-enhancement can only be derived from the productive act itself. We should recognize that the praise of others can be only of incidental importance in this regard. It should not be our primary concern, it should not be our primary motive for initiating the activity, nor should we need praise so much that we are willing to engage in odious pursuits to attain it. Rather the admiration and esteem of others should be the fringe benefit of our accomplishments. We need expertise in bike riding (and the adult derivatives of such childhood accomplishments) to provide us with genuine self-worth, and we need an admiring mother (and her surrogates in adult life) to give us further support, encouragement, and ego-enhancement. The boy who first said, "Look ma, no hands!" has told us much. We are fortunate that someone overheard him and passed his comment on.

"What a beautiful picture. What is it?" A repeated theme in this book is that honesty to the child is generally in his best interests and that

dishonesty (even though well-meaning) often causes more problems than it is designed to prevent. However, there are times not only when parental dishonesty is better for the child, but also when honesty in such situations could be deleterious. For example, when a child proudly displays a picture he has drawn, it would be cruel for a parent to comment on its artistic merits in accordance with adult standards or his own lack of understanding of what he is looking at. To say, "It's beautiful," is, in a sense, untruthful. But in another sense it is not. What is beautiful is the total experience of the child proudly showing his picture and the warm glow emanating from him. What may also add to the beauty of the scene is the adult's warm pleasure in response. If the adult's enjoyment and pride is added, the child will generally not be bothered by the illogicality of the added question, "What is it?" Similarly, a five-year-old girl's older sister has just proudly announced that she has lost a tooth and that she is going to put it under her pillow to see what the "tooth fairy" will leave her during the night. The younger girl, after a short period of pouting and squelched tears, pulls each of her teeth to see if one of them might possibly be loose. She then goes over to her mother and, while tugging one of her teeth, imploringly asks, "Is this tooth loose?" Only the most inhumane would not answer, "Well, a *little* bit."

When used judiciously and in moderation, our children's self-esteem grows on such fabrications. To deprive the child of them is to undermine his self-confidence as well as his relationship with his parent.

"You'll be a great engineer someday, and we'll all be proud of you." The two-year-old who builds a tower of blocks beams over his accomplishment. His sense of mastery is ego-enhancing. The mother who says, "What a beautiful tower you've built!" directs her compliment to the product of his labors and thereby further raises his feelings of self-worth and increases the likelihood that he will build again. In contrast, the mother who responds, "You're going to be a great engineer someday, and we'll be proud of you; the family will be famous," uses the child's accomplishments for her own self-aggrandizement, lessens his pleasure and feelings of competence, and makes it less likely that he will derive ego-enhancing gratifications from building.

The general principle that the most meaningful praise directs itself to the product of the child's labors is an important one. It genuinely says to the child: "You have every right to feel good about yourself for what you have accomplished." The parents who try to use their child's attainments for their own ego-enhancement rob the child of some of the gratifications of his attainment. Such a parental attitude may be a contributing factor in some children's loss of incentive to work and learn.

"Dad, can you help me with my homework?" The parent who, under the guise of helping his child with his homework, actually does it for him or points out his mistakes so that the child can be assured of handing in perfect papers, is seriously undermining the child's self-confidence. The child cannot possibly enjoy a feeling of mastery if he has not indeed "mastered" his subject. A few poor grades do far more for such a child than all his A's in homework. The low marks may mobilize him to learn on his own, whereas high marks, essentially obtained by his parents, may cripple him educationally. The preferable attitude for the parent is to view the child's homework as a matter between the child and his teacher. If the child does poorly, he will have to deal with her displeasure. The parent should be available to help the child, but in ways that stimulate his efforts and encourage enthusiasm. He helps the child figure things out rather than figure things out for him. His aim is to help the child learn how to help himself. The principle is best described in an old Icelandic proverb that goes something like this: "If you give a man a fish, you have provided him with a meal. If you teach him *how* to fish, you have provided him with a meal for life."

Similarly, the father who makes models for his son so that they "look better" is sabotaging the child's attempt to gain a feeling of self-confidence. The mother who cannot allow her daughter to cook her own rather mediocre cookies and intrudes so that they "come out better" robs the child of an important growth experience. Such children become psychologically paralyzed; they become incapable of performing up to their age level in many areas; they cannot help but compare themselves unfavorably with their peers; and they inevitably suffer from feelings of inadequacy.

"The other kids probably cheated." Parents frequently contribute to a child's feeling of low self-esteem by disparaging those who are successful. When the child does not compete successfully, he is told that others' rewards are undeserved, that they are due to good luck, or that they are the result of special favors and influences. The teacher is described as having "pets," and little Jamie never seems to be one of them. Or Sarah has the worst string of bad luck with her teachers. Joey's primary problem in school is that he's too honest—the others cheat on examinations and he wouldn't stoop that low. In all of these explanations for the child's failures or deficiencies, his own inadequacies, which may have contributed to his poor standing, are not even considered. The psychiatrist Harry Stack Sullivan describes the consequences of such parental attitudes:

If you have to maintain self-esteem by pulling down the

standing of others, you are extraordinarily unfortunate in a variety of ways. Since you have to protect your feeling of personal worth by noting how unworthy everybody around you is, you are not provided with any data that are convincing evidence of your having personal worth; so it evolves into "I am not as bad as the other swine." To be the best of swine, when it would be nice to be a person, is not a particularly good way of furthering anything except security operations [loosely: a constellation of psychological mechanisms that protect one from anxiety and feelings of low self-worth].[2]

The parent, then, who protects his child from justifiable criticisms by deprecating others does not orient the child toward looking to his own deficits as possible contributing factors to his difficulties. The child, thereby, becomes less equipped to function adequately and so becomes even more insecure.

"What a nice boy." Compliments not ultimately associated with concrete accomplishments can be ego-debasing. "What a fine boy," or "Aren't you a nice girl," stated when one cannot think of anything specific to compliment a child on, makes many children squirm. They sense that they are being "buttered up"; and they are insulted as well, because the comment implies that the speaker thinks they are stupid enough to be so taken in. At some inner level the child responds: "The only reason he calls me a 'nice boy' is that he can't think of anything *really* good to say about me." But, "What a good cake you baked," or "Great, a home run," makes a child stand a few inches taller.

It behooves parents, then, to encourage their children to develop their interests and talents, for without proficiency in genuine skills, feelings of competence can, at best, be unstable. The child must, however, be discouraged from pursuits in which he has demonstrated particular ineptitude (if he hasn't avoided them himself). The asthenic child cannot feel good about himself with a father who expects him to be an athlete. The child who has limited scholastic aptitude feels far worse about himself if his parents have inordinately high academic aspirations for him. Children who have not developed areas of genuine competence do not feel better about themselves by being patronizingly flattered; it only makes them feel even worse.

The feeling of being needed. Feeling genuinely needed contributes to one's sense of self-respect. One of the criteria I use to determine if a

[2] Sullivan, Harry Stack, *The Interpersonal Theory of Psychiatry*, New York: W. W. Norton and Co., 1953.

seriously depressed person is suicidal is whether he has the deep conviction that no one in the whole world would miss him were he dead. Although children are, for the most part, dependent and need their parents far more than their parents need them, if the child is to have a healthy feeling of self-esteem, he must still feel that his loss would be painful to his parents. (The healthy child in a loving home doesn't think about his parents' reactions to his loss; this is often a source of concern to the emotionally deprived child.)

The child's feeling that he is a source of pride to his parents—that he can engender in them a warm inner glow—contributes to his feeling needed. The younger child feels elated over the fact that he can make others laugh. (Those who lose this quality completely as adults are sad people indeed.) The girl who, as "mother's helper," sets the table and the boy who helps father change an automobile tire are filled with pride by the knowledge that they are contributing members of the family team. When playing games with a child, the adult does far better for both himself and the child if he selects one that is enjoyable to both. When an adult finds a game tedious, but continues to play through obligation, the child is aware, at some level, that he is not really needed as a challenging adversary. He senses the adult's boredom and lack of interest through the latter's impatience and easy irritability, and the game becomes a trying and oppressive ordeal for him. The sham can be ego-debasing. On the other hand, when the adult genuinely enjoys the game, the child appreciates that he is needed and enjoyed. Sensing the adult's involvement and pleasure, the child feels useful and desirable, and winning a hard-fought game can provide even further ego-enhancement.

The aforementioned sources of feeling needed apply to the child in a relatively affluent culture. The child in an economically deprived culture or in a society where he is *actually needed* to contribute to the economy may derive additional gratifications in this area (provided the labor is not excessive and the economic deprivation not significant). In many Israeli Kibbutzim, for example, children of five are already members of the labor force. They are required to perform light tasks in accordance with their age. These are not token assignments but active and meaningful contributions. Although child labor laws have protected children against shameful exploitation (and I am not suggesting their repeal), they do deprive children of the opportunity to gain ego-enhancement from work that is genuinely needed in the society. There are very few opportunities in affluent Western societies for children under fourteen to work in jobs in which their contributions are genuinely needed. Newspaper delivery and baby-sitting are hardly vital but can provide the child with a small measure of the enhanced self-respect that comes from playing a useful role in one's society. Children as young as nine and ten can perform many useful jobs at home and can often participate meaningfully (in a limited way, of course) in many parents' occupations. Children of this age are capable of delivering messages, transporting light packages, stacking, sorting, and performing many other simple jobs. Parents who encourage, stimulate, and require such participation provide their children with a healthy experience indeed.

"I didn't get the job because. . . ." The story is told about the stuttering man who enters an elevator in a New York City skyscraper and says to the operator, "S-S-S-Seventy-t-t-two, p-p-please." The elevator operator replies, "Going up to RCA?" "Y-Y-Yes," answers the man, "I'm ap-p-p-plying f-f-for a j-j-job as a r-r-r-ra-d-d-dio a-a-a-n-n-nouncer." Fifteen minutes later the man reenters the same elevator. The operator asks, "Well, did you get the job?" "N-N-No," answers the man. "Th-Th-They f-f-f-f-found ou-ou-ou-t I w-w-was J-J-Jewish."

The story demonstrates its point quite well. To explain a child's failures and rejections as resulting from prejudice or other irrational animosities may certainly be the case in certain situations—and it is the parents' job to define these clearly when they occur. There is a tendency, however, on the part of those who are the object of prejudice to believe that all rejections result from discrimination rather than from personality defects and thereby to avoid painful confrontation with their personal deficiencies. The preservation of self-esteem by such avoidance is specious. Blinding the child to his deficiencies may protect him temporarily from the esteem-lowering effects of such confrontation; but a heavy price is paid for this benefit. He is deprived of the opportunity to take courses of action that might rectify the defect and thereby truly enhance his sense of self-worth.

This kind of displacement mechanism need not be confined to prejudice. The adolescent girl who attributes her lack of popularity to her large nose is generally disappointed after the operation when the telephone doesn't start ringing. Other youngsters may attribute their interpersonal difficulties to acne, tallness, shortness, father's income, location of their home, birthmarks, minor blemishes, etc. And although it may be true that the particular "defect" is alienating to a small fraction of those they encounter, it is rarely as loathsome a quality as the youngsters believe. They have exaggerated its importance to avoid coming to terms with what may be more significantly estranging qualities. If the youngster considers his unpopularity to result from minor skin blemishes, there is no reflection on his qualities as a person; he was born that way, and he is being discriminated against through no fault of his own. Only the irrationality of others is the cause of his failure to have friends; and because he takes none of the blame himself, he can preserve his self-respect. However, to come to terms with the fact that he may be selfish, egotistical, or disrespectful of the rights of others, would make him think less of himself. In addition, it would involve him in the possibly long and arduous process of trying to rectify these deficiencies. The former attitude provides only ostensible self-respect; the latter promises genuine feelings of self-worth if the child can pursue it—and it is the parents' job to help the child have the courage to do so.

"He keeps talking about how lousy he feels about himself." When a patient tells me, "I feel lousy about myself," I generally ask, "Are you doing anything that would make anyone else feel lousy about himself if he were doing the same thing?" Often, after some thought, I get an affirmative answer. The child may be cheating on tests, stealing, or lying excessively; and if he has anything approaching a normal conscience, he will feel guilty about these acts. Intrinsic to guilt is self-hatred: "What a terrible person I am for doing all these horrible things." The child in such a situation might be told, "As long as you do those things you're going to find that you'll feel lousy about yourself. I think you'll see that if and when you can stop, you'll feel better about yourself." If the child can be encouraged to take positive action and restrain himself from engaging in the guilt-evoking behavior, then one of the elements contributing to his low self-esteem will have been eliminated. However, since the elements contributing to low self-esteem are many and complex, their alleviation is generally not brought about through simple maneuvers or words alone. Rather, action in a number of areas over a period of time is usually necessary if meaningful changes are to take place.

"He has such high standards." Perfectionism is, in part, an attempt to compensate for feelings of inadequacy. By doing things better than others one can feel superior and more competent. To a point, such an attitude is valid because we cannot fully judge the worth of our efforts without comparing them to the successes of others. When, however, the individual sets up unrealistically high standards, he can never be satisfied with his performance and so will suffer with chronic feelings of inadequacy.

The oldest child tends to be more perfectionistic than his younger siblings. In the early years of his development, he has only adults to identify with and will, therefore, primarily take their standards for his own. All subsequent siblings have partial identification with children—

their older siblings(s)—and so are likely to be looser regarding what they expect of themselves.

One common contributing element to a child's perfectionistic attitudes is parental perfectionism. The parent who basically believes that A is the only passing grade sets the stage for his child's development of perfectionistic problems (as well as other possible difficulties, such as total withdrawal from the academic scene). Very successful parents may, by the very nature of their success, produce very high standards in their children. However, my experience has been that when the children of such parents become unduly perfectionistic—when they strive not merely for good performance but for perfect performance—and when they become exaggeratedly frustrated at failing to achieve perfection, other factors are operative. For example, in the pursuit of his own success the parent may have neglected the child. Or the parent may have been actively competing with the child or instilling in him unrealistic standards of excellence. In all these situations, it was not the parental success alone that caused the child to be unduly perfectionistic, but additional contributing factors were operative. Parental success, however, need not produce difficulties for children—in fact, it can serve as a stimulus for the child to achieve equal or even greater competence.

Some children, however, seem to be "naturally" perfectionistic and do not appear to have been exposed to any of the influences I have described; but in all but the most severe cases, altered parental attitudes toward performance can sometimes help such perfectionistic children. Children tend to see their parents as omniscient and omnipotent; they generally try to emulate them; and this may contribute to their being perfectionistic. Appreciation by the child that the parent himself is fallible can be helpful, and it is important that parents take frequent opportunity to confront their children with their own frailties. One need not resort to artificial or contrived situations, since life inevitably provides enough natural, ordinary failures. For example, if mother leaves the cake in the oven too long, she could tell her perfectionistic daughter, "You see, it's just what I've been telling you; everybody makes mistakes at times." If father dents the car, he can say to his perfectionistic son, "This is an example of what I've been telling you. No one is perfect." Other comments that may be helpful to these children include the following: "As long as you think that any grade below A is unacceptable, you'll feel lousy about yourself"; "As long as you feel you have to be the best basketball player in every single game in order to be acceptable, you'll feel terrible about yourself"; and "As long as you keep thinking that the only way to be happy is to win every class election, you'll be miserable." Although many factors contribute to perfectionistic attitudes, the aforementioned approaches—if utilized over a period of time by parents who themselves are not unduly perfectionistic—can be helpful to many children in reducing their perfectionism and thereby enhancing their sense of self-worth.

"Virtue is its own reward." When I use the word *virtue*, I refer to thoughts and deeds that the individual's culture considers admirable. The person who has accepted these values, who has the deep conviction that they are estimable, will feel good about himself when he conforms with them and bad about himself when he does not.

For example, giving to others is an activity that most children learn is a "good" thing to do. Children, however, are not famous for their spontaneous generosity. As they grow older, however, they can gradually come to incorporate this value if they see that their parents genuinely get pleasure from giving (not merely preaching it). If the parents have been successful in engendering this value in the child, giving in itself can then provide him with great feelings of satisfaction about himself and thereby contribute significantly to the enhancement of his self-esteem. This does not mean that his inner gratification in performing the act itself cannot be heightened by the praise of others—a totally natural desire. However, if the need for praise and external appreciation is the main motivation, then the giving is done for purposes of self-aggrandizement, and the self-esteem produced is specious. Or if the person gives because he feels he must suffer to be appreciated, there is little chance that he will derive any enduring sense of self-worth from his giving.

Living, then, in accordance with the values of one's culture can provide an individual with deep-seated feelings of self-worth, and giving is only one of many such values in our culture and each society has its own. This is what I believe is being referred to by the "Virtue is its own reward" concept. Although the proverb is considered cliché and trite to many, it has great validity nevertheless. The basic tenets upon which these values rest are laid down in childhood. For it is then that parents, through example and word, can impart principles that can provide the child with important ego gratifications and a heightened sense of self-worth if he adheres to them as he gets older.

"All I want is that my children should be happy." There is hardly a schoolchild who has not been asked to memorize these lines, which Thomas Jefferson wrote in the Declaration of Independence:

—We hold these truths to be self-evident, that all men are created equal, that they are endowed by their Creator with certain unalienable Rights, that among these are Life, Liberty and the pursuit of Happiness—

Yet there is hardly a person who thinks seriously of the significance in this passage of the word *pursuit*—a word that is vital to its meaning. Jefferson might well have written Life, Liberty and Happiness, but he was wise enough to know that no man can be guaranteed the right to happiness, something that exists at best, only for short periods of time and under very special circumstances.

Dr. Geoffrey Osler, a New York City neurologist and a gifted teacher, once suggested that Jefferson should have written "Life, Liberty and the happiness of Pursuit." Osler's position, which I support, was that the *process of pursuit* of a goal provides our greatest happiness. In the *attaining* and in the short period around the time of *attainment* we enjoy the greatest happiness in life. Although life may allow us, therefore, many periods of happiness it cannot provide us with a chronic state of happiness. For the sake of completeness (but not, by any means, for the sake of poetic beauty), one could combine what Jefferson and Osler said and guarantee to all men the right to Life, Liberty, the pursuit of Happiness and the happiness of Pursuit. In short, all should be given the freedom and opportunity to enjoy the happiness that can come from pursuing one's goals.

We live in a world where this basic truth is not widely appreciated. People are led to believe that life can be continually happy and that there actually are people who are completely happy. Although no one has ever actually met such a person, everyone has read about them in books and magazines and seen them on the movie and television screens. We talk of wanting our children to "be happy." Marriage is supposed to provide us with "happiness." The state of chronic happiness can be obtained, we have come to believe; it's just that something always seems to come along that interferes with it. And we may die with the feeling of dissatisfaction that life has somehow passed us by and has not given us the degree of happiness that, under better circumstances, we might have enjoyed.

Such an expectation from life, an expectation laid down in childhood by both parents and society at large, helps produce feelings of disillusionment, frustration, and lack of satisfaction with oneself. This was effectively stated in the recent film *Lovers and Other Strangers*. A young married man returns to the home of his parents to inform them that he has decided to get a divorce. His distraught parents naturally ask him why. "What has happened?" they imploringly ask. (This and the remaining quotes in this vignette are approximate.) "Nothing special," answers the boy, "I'm just not happy in my marriage, and I want to be happy." In response to this his mother shouts, "If you're going to spend your whole life trying to be happy, you'll be miserable!"

We do best for our children to impart to them that life is never perfect. Life inevitably has its frustrations, its struggles, and its grave disappointments. It can also provide, for those who are willing to work for them, intense periods of gratification and even happiness. If we are successful in imparting this view to our children, we will lessen the likelihood that they will suffer with ego-debasing disillusionments about themselves and others.

I close this chapter with a comment once made by a three-year-old girl that epitomizes much of what I have said in this chapter. She was sitting between her parents, pointed to each of them in turn and said, "Mommy, I love you! Daddy, I love you! And I love I, myself!"

3

Eating and Other Oral Gratifications

Probably the first thing we do in life, after we start breathing, is eat. It should be no surprise, then, that eating assumes tremendous psychological importance throughout life, and problems around it are common. Cultural patterns vary, of course; but there are more similarities than differences among parents regarding the kinds of problems that arise from misconceptions about food.

Although distortions play a role in the formation of psychological problems related to eating, my focus here is on the milder problems, which have some chance of being corrected by instruction and appeal to reason. The severer forms generally require more intensive approaches and changes in one's life—changes that may sometimes be brought about by psychotherapy.

"I would never think of bottle feeding my child." There is probably some truth to the theory that the mother who breast-feeds her child is more maternal than the one who chooses not to. Women who consider the practice "primitive" or "disgusting" are generally inhibited in

expressing not only their maternal feelings, but other feelings as well. Many of the women whose breasts "dry up" or "don't give enough milk" psychologically resist the process. The paucity of milk is not so much the result of physical impairments in the milk-producing mechanisms as an inhibition of these processes by psychological factors.

Some women who are fundamentally quite unmaternal, but have learned about this important criterion for judging maternal capacity, breast-feed to prove to themselves and others that they are strongly maternal. They may become obsessed with breast-feeding and take every opportunity to talk about and even demonstrate it—all in the service of compensating for basic impairments in their maternal expression. Their condescending attitude toward women who bottle feed may be another manifestation of their own basic desire to do so. (We condemn most vociferously those who do what we would basically like to do but cannot allow ourselves to.) Women with healthy attitudes toward breast-feeding do not advertise it. They appreciate (as even many psychologists do not) that breast-feeding is only one of many manifestations of maternal expression and that cuddling, tenderness, dedication, pride, worry, physical care, and a host of other factors—both physical and emotional—contribute to maternal feeling.

Whether misused or not, feeding from the breast is one of the most important psychological experiences of infancy. But even when the child is not breast-fed, eating takes on such great psychological import that infantile reactions may become lifelong. I am not referring to the psychological reactions associated with the awareness that food is necessary to survival but rather to the symbolic significance that food takes on in this early period. In brief, it often becomes equated with mother's love—for both the infant and the mother. One of the child's most important expectations from the mother is that she provide him with food—food that alleviates the pangs of hunger and produces feelings of relaxation and well-being. The most content and satisfied human being in the whole world is the infant with a full belly of mother's milk. His is the euphoria that follows the gastronomical orgasm. Since it provides the child with such deep gratifications, it is not surprising that food can become for him synonymous with mother's love. And the mother, appreciating the power of food as a provider of satisfaction for the infant, comes to give it meaning beyond its survival value. She too sees it as one of the manifestations of her love and may come to use it to compensate for deficiencies she may have in her affection for the child. The more inhibitions she may have in maternal expression, the more she may resort to food to compensate for and hide her defects. To equate food with love is to ascribe to food a quality that is not intrinsically a part of it, to give it a power beyond itself.

"She's a very stubborn baby. She keeps grabbing the spoon and making a mess." The growing-up process is a continual conflict between dependence and independence. While satisfying his dependency needs the child is deprived of the enhanced sense of self-esteem and competence that comes from asserting himself. When he does act independently, he cannot allow himself the pleasures of being dependent, so he goes back and forth between the two. The one-and-a-half-year-old child runs a few yards ahead of his mother to prove to himself that he doesn't need her support in walking and running. But he periodically looks behind him—just to be sure she is there. And the infant who grabs the spoon and wants to feed himself is trying to gain the same sense of independence and competence. The mother who battles the child on this issue, in order to prevent the mess he inevitably will make when he feeds himself, suppresses an important growth experience. In order to save a few cents' worth of food and to avoid a few minutes extra work, healthy and productive forces within the child are squelched.

"I would never let my child use a pacifier." It is a well-accepted fact that the need for oral gratification goes beyond the nutritional, and the lips and tongue are a source of sensory gratification at all ages. When an infant is given a bottle whose nipple has a large hole, he will quickly satisfy his nutritional needs, but he will continue to suck in order to gain his oral sensory gratifications because the milk has flowed so rapidly that these have not been fully satisfied. Thumb-sucking is another manifestation of the need for oral satisfaction in the child. For the adult, kissing is an important source of sexual gratification, and there is no doubt that the same needs contribute to the pleasure of smoking.

Some parents freely indulge their own oral sensory gratifications but deprive their children of the same opportunities. Not permitting their children to use pacifiers is one example of this phenomenon. Many such parents will allow the child to gain such non-nutritional oral satisfaction from the breast or bottle, but the pacifier is *verboten*. Some claim that it is the artificiality of the pacifier that they dislike; that there is something unnatural about it; that the child should have the real thing or nothing at all. This position appears totally illogical to me. The infant's oral sensory needs are, after all, greater than the adult's. Since the bottle and breast are not continually available to him, why then shouldn't he be allowed to suck on a pacifier? Some of these same parents will allow the child to go around sucking on the nipple of an empty bottle, but not on a pacifier. Such an attitude may contribute to the child's turning to other methods of oral gratification, the most common of which is thumb-sucking.

"Take your thumb out of your mouth." Thumb-sucking often occurs in utero. There are babies whose fists, at birth, reveal the fact that they have spent a significant amount of time in the fetus's mouth. To attribute this behavior, then, entirely to psychological problems is to stretch the concept of such disorders somewhat ludicrously. Thumb-sucking enables a child to gain oral sensory gratification beyond those he can obtain from merely eating. It is probably as important to the infant as genital sexual satisfaction is to the adult and to deprive him of this gratification is as frustrating as depriving the adult of sex. The child who is deprived of the opportunity to suck on the nipple of his empty bottle or to suck on a pacifier is more likely to suck his thumb. This, however, is not always the case since children differ in their need for oral gratification. Some need a great deal; others very little.

Like many other forms of sensory gratification, thumb-sucking can alleviate tension. When it persists beyond the age of four or five or when it is obsessively engaged in, it is likely that the child is abnormally tense. To force such a child to refrain from thumb-sucking is to deprive him of an outlet for his tensions, and he may become even more tense—thereby increasing even further his need to suck his thumb. Only by removing the underlying tensions can one hope to lessen the overuse of this natural tranquillizer. Or, if one is successful in suppressing the thumb-sucking, the child may develop other ways to reduce tension, such as excessive masturbation, rocking, temper tantrums, and tics.

One justification that parents often give for their prevention of thumb-sucking is that it introduces germs into the mouth and can cause infection. However, as I have already discussed, the most important factor in determining whether a child gets an infection is not whether he is exposed to disease-producing organisms but the strength of his own body resistances. Keeping a child's thumb out of his mouth removes only a small fraction of potential sources of infection. He will invariably put other germ-carrying objects into his mouth, and many of the foods mother feeds him also contain germs. We can't get away from them; they are practically everywhere. Prohibiting thumb-sucking, therefore, is futile as a way of avoiding infection, but the power struggle involved in the attempt to get the child to stop his thumb-sucking and the tension build-up that results if one is successful contribute to the formation of psychological difficulties for the child.

Another argument often given for justifying forcible removal of the child's thumb from his mouth is that the practice can cause "buck teeth" and other malformations of the teeth and their bony supports. Most dentists agree that thumb-sucking, when engaged in during the period when the child has his deciduous teeth (milk teeth or baby teeth), will not cause malformations of the permanent teeth. When the child sucks his thumb below the age of six, the baby teeth may be pushed forward a little; but the supporting bony structures are generally not, so the permanent teeth usually grow in correctly. Most children stop their thumb-sucking by this age. Entering school, where thumb-sucking is looked upon as something done only by "babies," often results in a dramatic discontinuation of the practice. If the thumb-sucking does persist into the period when the permanent teeth are growing in, then dental malformations may, but will not necessarily, occur. Even in such cases, one does best to try to alleviate the underlying tensions rather than to try to force the child to stop, which usually increases the problem. All things considered, I believe that the most prudent course is to gently try to discourage the practice while trying to alleviate suspected underlying tensions. If one is not successful in doing this, I believe that one still does better by risking ultimate corrective orthodontic work than to subject the child to the psychological trauma of being hounded over his thumb-sucking and deprived of this important tension-alleviating device.

"Finish your spinach or you can't have dessert." Some mothers, as a manifestation of psychological problems, compulsively force their children to eat; others do so primarily because they are misguided. They believe that if the child does not eat three full meals a day, he may not get his minimal daily requirements of various nutriments and may then suffer from a variety of nutritional deficiencies. They have little or no respect for the child's internal mechanisms that monitor his eating, cause him to be hungry when he needs more food, and produce a feeling of satiation when no further food is physiologically warranted. As early as the 1920's it was demonstrated that if children of weaning age were given the opportunity to freely choose from an assortment of foods that contained a variety of necessary nutriments they would, on their own, satisfy all their nutritional requirements. In probably the best-known study,[3] done by Clara M. Davis at the Children's Memorial Hospital in Chicago, children who had just been weaned were presented with a wide assortment of food three times a day. Each child had his own small table and could eat as little or as much of any food he wished. Empty dishes were quickly refilled. No mention of food was made during the eating

---

[3] Davis, Clara M., Self-Selection of Diet by Newly Weaned Infants. *American Journal of Diseases of Children,* 36:651–679, 1928.

sessions. There was no encouraging or discouraging the child about what to eat. Although a child might show a particular preference for a certain food, this would generally be short-lived, and he would then favor other foods that provided him with the nutriments lacking during the period of limited variety. None became obese (even one boy who drank a quart of milk at each noon meal), and none became undernourished. And not one of the children developed digestive disturbances.

Although we know very little about these regulatory mechanisms, we do know that they are there and that they can be relied upon to guide our eating habits and satisfy our nutritional needs. The parent's job is to make available the necessary assortment of food and to respect the child's inner cravings regarding which foods and how much of each he wants to eat.

I am not suggesting that the home be a twenty-four-hour restaurant where the child can, at any time, order anything he wants and have the parent provide it. What I am suggesting is that the child be offered three meals a day and that if he knows in advance he will not be eating a certain food, it not be prepared for him. (I would be very cautious about preparing substitutes on a routine basis, lest the mother becomes enslaved by the restaurant concept.) If the child does not wish to finish a particular food he should not be forced to. Rather waste a few cents than engage in games and power struggles. Games like "One for you and one for me. One for Aunt Jane and one for Uncle Dick" are a wasteful drain on the parent's time and energies and are psychologically deleterious to the child. Threats like "If you don't finish your spinach, you can't have dessert" are also unnecessary. There is no good reason why the child should have to finish his spinach in order to have dessert. If the child has demonstrated a dislike for spinach, there are plenty of other foods of similar nutritional value that the mother could have prepared. Or if he generally does like spinach but just doesn't feel like finishing it that day, he will not die of iron deficiency anemia if he is allowed to skip it. He should not be deprived of the nutritional value of his dessert because he has not availed himself of other nutriments. Threats like "No television if you don't finish" or "You're not leaving this table until you finish your supper" invite unnecessary power struggles. There are enough unpleasant tasks in life without adding unnecessarily to them, and forcing a child to eat is doing just that.

I am not suggesting either that the child be allowed to freely ingest anything he wants at any time of the day. A chocolate bar eaten fifteen minutes before dinner will suppress a child's appetite, and then the mother's preparations will have been in vain if she allows the child to refrain from eating. If she forces the child to eat, she risks his developing unhealthy attitudes over food and may contribute to psychological problems over it. Accordingly, reasonable attempts should be made to prevent the child from ingesting food shortly before meals.

Some parents believe that breakfast is the most important meal of the day and that one needs vast amounts of energy on awakening in order to have the strength to function adequately, both physically and intellectually, throughout the day. Many children, however, may get along quite well eating little or nothing at breakfast time but may want to satisfy the bulk of their nutritional needs at some other time of the day, while their parents fret lest they die of malnutrition by lunchtime. Other parents have firmly imprinted in their minds some chart about basic categories of foods. They believe that there will be dire consequences if the child does not ingest certain amounts of food from each of these categories; like the Chinese restaurant menu ("One from group A and two from B"). Still others have special hang-ups about particular foods. For example, only freshly squeezed orange juice is good enough for little Benjamin. The canned variety is looked upon as practically poisonous, and no good mother would ever give such swill to her child.

My experience has been that such beliefs are deep-seated, and attempts to alter many parents' attitudes regarding feeding their children are often quite difficult. Parents frequently consider me heartless or crazy when I make recommendations along the above lines. They ask me if I really practice what I preach with my own children. Although I reassure them that my own children, as well as all the others I have known who have been reared in accordance with these principles, have never suffered from rickets, beriberi, pellagra, scurvy, or any other deficiency disease, they do not really believe me. And so they go on hounding their children and expending their energies in wasteful power struggles.

"Milk: the perfect food. Bread: the staff of life." In my grade school days I was taught that milk was "the perfect food." I remember as a youngster coming into the house—sweating profusely after a few hours of playing baseball on a hot summer day—going to the refrigerator and gulping down, directly from the bottle, two or three glasses of good, cold milk. As that nectar poured down my esophagus into my stomach I reveled in cool euphoria. And on occasion, I thought about the distillate of concentrated health I was ingesting. A quart a day was the prescribed amount. Drink that and, as far as health was concerned, you had it made. In those days milk was not homogenized so the cream usually rose to the top of the bottle. The newly opened bottle, then, offered an even richer dose of the salubrious concentrate—even though it wasn't as tasty. When

I think back now on those days, my blood curdles. I am not speaking entirely figuratively; that stuff practically curdled my blood. Although the fats and fat derivatives I introduced into my bloodstream may not have actually coagulated into curd, they deposited themselves along the walls of my arteries and arterioles. The deposits are there to this day, in my brain, my heart, my aorta, and everywhere else.

Competent physicians today recommend that after the weaning period, generally during the second half of the first year of life, children not be given whole milk. Rather, they suggest that skim milk be used and then only in small amounts. This is suggested not simply because of the relationship between fat ingestion and arteriosclerosis, but also because obesity does not go along with longevity. And drinking milk is a good way of getting fat. This is another one of the theories I espouse that results in parents thinking I'm rather mad. The notions instilled within us in childhood become deeply imbedded and render us unreceptive to different ideas. This particular attitude about milk may be particularly resistive to modification because of its psychological import— milk being mother's first and most important food and, therefore, not something one readily deprives one's children of. But I hope that the time will come when parents will take a saner attitude toward milk.

Another maxim from my early school days was that bread was "the staff of life." Since ancient times, I was taught, bread has been the mainstay of the human diet. Wheat, a relatively ubiquitous plant, is highly nutritious and has served as one of mankind's favorite staples. All this is irrefutable. The problem for us, in affluent Western society, is that we have too much of a good thing. We still retain attitudes toward food that were held by our ancestors in the days when one's whole life may have been spent in the quest of it, when everyone lived under the threat of starvation, and when wasting food was a sin. Now that we have more than ample supplies we still act like we can't get enough of it. We eat too much bread and other high caloric foods. We eat far beyond the amounts necessary for health—to the point of overweight and ill health. Children are taught that there is something wrong with leaving food on their plates. They cannot leave the table until they finish eating. They have to stuff themselves if they are to be "good." As adults we are told that there is something impolite in not eating everything our hostess serves us—even if we have to choke on something we don't like. And the hostess, in order to avoid the humiliation of saying, "I'm sorry, we're all out of such and such," stocks up on three times as much food as her guests could possibly consume. In restaurants, since we are paying for the food, we feel we are cheating ourselves if we don't eat everything. We use our stomachs as garbage cans—stuffing into them a lot of excess refuse. But unlike the garbage can, we hold onto the food. We carry it around with us—taxing our hearts with the excess load, clogging our arteries with fatty substances, and generally shortening our lives.

The best attitude that we can transmit to our children about food is that it is necessary for the maintenance of life and that it can be a source of pleasure as well. But, as with many of the pleasures in life, excess can be dangerous. We do our children a disservice if we do not communicate to them the dangers inherent in over-eating.

"Martin, don't forget to take your vitamins." A few years ago, a mother I was interviewing in association with her son's psychiatric evaluation described what I considered to be an exaggerated interest in her children's nutrition. She was highly preoccupied with giving them vitamin supplements, wheat germ, and other foods she considered particularly nutritious. When I tried to explain to her that all this was not in the best interests of her children and that they would do quite well if allowed to eat naturally, she didn't take me seriously. So I dropped the matter, as I usually do in such situations, because of my recognition that people who are so obsessed do not change through mere discussion.

About a year after the boy's treatment terminated, she called me in an agitated state. On routine physical examination their doctor had found changes in the retina of one of the child's eyes that suggested that he might have a brain tumor. The doctor recommended immediate hospitalization. The parents were naturally grief-stricken and called me to advise them on how to handle the situation with the child. After a week of intensive evaluation in the hospital the doctors were quite puzzled. They could find no evidence for a brain tumor or any other disease. Yet the eye findings were unequivocal. On reevaluation of the problem, they learned of the mother's exaggerated involvement with diet. With this lead, new tests were done and the diagnosis quickly established. The child had a case of hypervitaminosis A—a disorder due to excess ingestion of vitamin A, which can directly affect the retina of the eye, the spleen, the liver, and the blood. Needless to say, the mother was instantly cured of her preoccupation.

The absurdity of the principle that if a little is good, a lot is even better is well demonstrated with vitamins. We need minute amounts of vitamins each day—and no more. If we ingest more than we need, the excess is not utilized by the body but generally excreted. To take an excess of most vitamins is the same as throwing them directly into the toilet. (In fact, to do so would get rid of the "middle man.") Three vitamins, however, (A, C, and D) when ingested in excess can cause diseases that are not inconsequential. Drug manufacturers and their henchmen on Madison Avenue have perpetrated a myth about vitamins that has made them fortunes and created, at times, misfortune for those who were credulous enough to be taken in. And when I speak of misfortune, I am not confining myself to those who have suffered with hypervitaminoses. I am referring to the far larger group who have wasted their money, been seduced into fears and preoccupations of perhaps life-long duration, and have handed these down to their children as well.

"We never let our children eat candy and other junk." Some people believe that the corn they serve their children at home is perfectly healthy but that popcorn bought in a store has mildly lethal ingredients. Fried potatoes served at home or in a restaurant is a perfectly respectable food, but potato chips are to be avoided. Apples and oranges, as sources of sugar are fine, but chocolate bars and ice cream contain mysterious and indefinable noxious substances. Cheese, tomatoes, flour and spices are excellent sources of nutriment, but put them together into a pizza pie and you have a food that will have harmful effects on the child's system.

Most of these notions have little or no validity. Changing corn into popcorn in no way introduces deleterious substances. By the time potato chips are absorbed from the digestive tract, they are indistinguishable from mother's homemade french fries. Sweets can play a role in tooth decay (especially those that stay in the mouth, like caramel and sour balls), but the sugar in apples is just as likely to do this as the sugar in chocolate bars. Sweets will depress the appetite and so are best not ingested before meals. But the sugar in an orange will do this as effectively as the sugar in ice cream.

I do not claim that the grades of meat used in the hot dogs sold in certain places of amusement are the highest. And I do not deny that there are pollutants, additives, and preservatives that may be harmful to all of us. I know, as well as anyone else, that each time one eats in a restaurant one may be ingesting food with rat droppings in it. And I know that food handlers are not particularly famous for their cleanliness. However, these are dangers facing all of us. There is no need to add unreasonable prejudices about nutrition.

4

Childhood Sexuality and the Oedipus Complex

The oral phase. Freud used the term *sexuality* in a broad context and roughly equated it with sensuality. He used the term *psychosexual* to refer to phenomena with both sexual and psychological components. Observing the infant's great interest in eating and sucking, he considered that function to be the primary source of psychosexual gratification in infancy and called the first year-and-a-half of life the oral phase of psychosexual development.

Although oral functions are certainly a source of pleasure during this period, there are other equally important drives necessary for survival that also strive for sensual gratification during this phase of the child's life. The infant craves bodily contact for the cutaneous gratification it offers, and satisfactions associated with rocking and moving also appear to be indispensable for healthy development. The child cries out not only when it is hungry, but also when it wants to be held and rocked. (Of course, it cries out as well when it is suffering physical discomfort,

94

but such cries are not related to demands for sensual pleasure.) Considering these other drives, the time in which the infant eats and fantasizes about eating presents a relatively small, albeit important, fraction of the time spent in fantasy about and gratification of indispensable needs. The term *oral phase* is therefore, in my opinion, an unfortunate one because it emphasizes only one aspect of the child's physical and psychological life during this period.

The anal phase. Freud designated the ages from one-and-a-half to about three-and-a-half as the anal phase of psychosexual development because he considered the pleasurable anal sensations associated with the retention and expulsion of feces to be the primary sources of sexual (again in the broader sense, meaning sensual) gratification during this period.

There is little question that Freud's was a culture in which the preoccupation with bowel function was exaggerated, and it is for this reason that many of his patients exhibited what he referred to as "anal" problems; i.e., neurotic disturbances that were ramifications of difficulties arising in that period of life when toilet training is an important developmental and psychological consideration. Freud considered the training situation to be the central psychosexual issue for the normal child in this period and assumed that the Victorian Viennese preoccupation was a universal one.

In my opinion, the normal, well-adjusted child learns to control his bowel functions with a minimum of difficulty. Praise for acceptable performance and mild reprimand for "accidents," plus emulation of parents and older siblings, seem to be enough for the healthy child to accomplish his training. If, however, the child is exposed to a parent with exaggerated concern over this function, then a situation conducive to the development of neurosis is present.

For example, there are parents who try to train the child before he is physiologically capable of voluntarily retaining his feces. (This generally coincides with the time the child begins to walk.) Others have some preconceived notion about how often a child should move his bowels; and if he does not comply with their expectations, he is given enemas and laxatives. These parents may believe that their failure to get the child to evacuate his bowels will result in the build-up of various toxic substances in his system and will cause headaches, cramps, and other bodily disturbances. It is often very difficult to get such parents to leave their children alone and let them have their bowel movements when they want to. Other parents think that enemas are an important part of the treatment of most illnesses, that the noxious agents that produce and are produced by disease can be removed from the body only through bowel catharsis. Still others are concerned with providing the child with an assortment of foods that have specific effects on the consistency of the child's stool. Such parents may very well bring about the kinds of psychological problems that Freud called anal—problems that not only center specifically on bowel difficulties, but also relate to certain personality characteristics such as compulsivity, perfectionism, excessive orderliness, obstinacy, and frugality. In addition, the parent who is preoccupied with bowel training is most likely exposing his child to a host of other deleterious influences that may contribute to the formation of neurotic symptomatology.

American parents today are not nearly so compulsive about bowel training as were the parents of Freud's patients, but ours is still a society where there is an excessive interest in bowel training and in hiding the products of excretion. That the organs of excretion are hidden as well invites a certain exaggerated curiosity on the part of the child. The healthy child, from the age of three on, occasionally verbalizes about the excretory function and indulges in scatological humor. But in my opinion, it is only in the child with neurotic problems that such fantasies become a significant part of his inner mental life.

Louise Bates Ames,[4] a psychologist at the Gesell Institute in New Haven, did an excellent study of the fantasies of 270 children (135 boys and 135 girls) as revealed by the spontaneous stories they told. It was found that in children two to five years of age the predominant theme at every age for both sexes was that of violence. The number of stories revealing some kind of violence ranged from a low of 63% for boys of two to a high of 88% for boys of three-and-a-half. Of the fifteen two-year-old boys (mean age 2.5 years), 60% of the stories dealt with violence, and for the girls the figure was 68%. Other themes in the two-year-old group were food and eating, sleep, good and bad, possible sibling rivalry, possible castration, and reproduction. None of the group of thirty two-year-olds described stories overtly concerned with anal functions.

Pitcher and Prelinger,[5] psychologists at Yale University, in their study *Children Tell Stories* also attempted to learn about children's fantasies through their story telling. A group of 137 children (70 girls and 67 boys) ages two to five told 360 stories. Eight main themes were found:

[4] Ames, Louise B., Children's Stories. *Genetic Psychology Monographs*, 73:336–396, 1966.

[5] Pitcher, E. G. and Prelinger, E., *Children Tell Stories*, New York: International Universities Press, Inc., 1963.

aggression, death, hurt or misfortune, morality, nutrition, dress, sociability, and crying. One or more of these eight themes could be found in each of the 360 stories. Aggression appeared most often—124 times. Hurt or misfortune was the next most frequent theme, appearing 89 times.

Classical Freudian psychoanalytic theorists would consider many of these violent themes to be psychological anal derivatives. I consider them to be related to a host of frustrations and repressed hostilities, only a small segment of which relate to anal functions. In either case, these studies well demonstrate that the *overt* fantasies of the child in this period do not concern themselves specifically with anal sexuality.

The phallic phase and the Oedipus complex. Toward the end of the third year of life, Freud believed, the primary source of sexual gratification shifted to the genitals. Important areas of sexual interest in this phase, which lasts until the age of five or six, are said to be voyeuristic and exhibitionistic, as well as urethral-erotic. In the phallic phase, sexual interest is said to be strong and is primarily directed toward one's own genitals and expressed through masturbation, whereas in the genital phase, which begins at puberty, the sexual focus becomes externally directed.

During the phallic phase, Freud believed, both normal and pathological children *universally* develop what he called the Oedipus complex. The term *oedipal* was derived from Oedipus, the hero of the Greek tragedy *Oedipus Rex*, written by Sophocles about 430 B.C. In the play, Oedipus, through a series of fateful events, actually consummates the oedipal act; namely, he kills his father and has sexual intercourse with his mother. The term *complex* in psychology refers to a constellation of thoughts and feelings centering on a particular theme. Briefly, then, the child with an Oedipus complex manifests a genital-sexual attraction to the parent of the opposite sex and an associated feeling of envy and hostility toward the parent of the same sex. The urges are considered to be genital-sexual, although not necessarily specifically associated with heterosexual intercourse as the primary source of genital gratification. Oedipal fantasies, according to the classical Freudian school, may include a variety of misconceptions regarding the exact nature of the parents' sexual life: the child may fantasize that the parents get pleasure by looking at one another's genitals; by engaging in oral-genital contact; by rubbing themselves against each other; or by going to the toilet together. Included also are fantasies of marriage and the desire to give the mother babies or to bear the father's children. In each case, the child fantasizes himself or herself in the role of the rival parent. In addition, the boy may fear that his hostility toward his father will result in the latter's retaliation, especially by castration, and this produces what Freud called castration anxiety.

Freud considered the Oedipus complex to be part of normal human psychosexual development and regarded the failure to resolve or come to terms with it to be the central element in the etiology of all neuroses.

His explanation for the development of the Oedipus complex in the male was far simpler than in the female. The boy's possessive love of his mother and murderous rage toward the father is a natural extension of the loving relationship the mother has always provided him. The resolution of the Oedipus complex involves resigning himself to the fact that he cannot totally possess his mother—a resignation made easier by his fear of castration by the father. Observing the female's absence of a penis confirms for him that his own penis can be removed. In addition, through identification with his father, the boy incorporates the latter's dictates against incest and patricide. Such "identification with the aggressor," further assists him in repressing his oedipal impulses. He develops a contempt for all who could have slept with his mother, be it himself, his father, or anyone else; the "mother-fucker" is considered most loathsome. Lastly, Freud considered biological maturation to be operative as well: "The time has come for its [the oedipus complex's] dissolution, just as the milk-teeth fall out when the permanent ones begin to press forward."[6]

For the girl, things are more complicated. When she first observes that the little boy has a penis, she considers herself to have been deprived of a most valuable organ. Her mother, who bore her this way, is blamed, and the little girl turns to her father for love. (Because the mother also lacks this invaluable part, the girl's respect for her markedly diminishes.) The father, as the possessor of a penis, is looked upon as a more likely source of gratifying the little girl's desire to have one herself; and through fantasied sexual intercourse with the father, the female child hopes to incorporate a penis. The adult female, by bearing a male child, can satisfy her desire to produce a penis of her own. Even if the baby is a female, it can still symbolically represent the longed-for penis. Other factors that contribute to the transfer relate to the girl's anger toward her mother. The mother becomes an object of hostility because she inhibits the little girl's masturbation and because she refuses to give up her affection for the father in order to devote herself totally to the child.

---

[6] Freud, Sigmund, The Passing of the Oedipus Complex, translated by Joan Riviere, Collected Papers, Vol. 2, New York: Basic Books, Inc., 1959.

In the female's oedipal resolution too, the child resigns herself to the fact that her mother's love for her father is such that she can never have him completely to herself. Rebuffed by her father, she renounces and represses her oedipal wishes. Since her father will not provide her with the penis she so desperately wants, getting one symbolically through childbearing is the best she can hope for, and she must turn eventually to other men for this purpose.

Freud's emphasis on the Oedipus complex was deep and extensive, and its ramifications pervade his writings. His supporters and detractors have commented on it at length. Before presenting my own views of the Oedipus complex, however, I will present the theories of some of Freud's followers because some of their opinions have influenced and contributed to mine.

OTHER THEORIES OF THE OEDIPUS COMPLEX

Carl Jung. Jung also considered the Oedipus complex to have innate elements. He, however, believed in the *inheritance* of psychological experiences and regarded contributions from the inherited collective unconscious of mankind to be significant. Primordial images (psychic legacies of the past history of mankind) are operative in the formation of the complex. "The Mother Archetype"—the inherited psychic image of the prototypical mother—serves as the basis for the child's deep attraction to his mother. The actual mother, in turn, activates the archetypal mother—the "composite image of all pre-existing mothers, a model or pattern of all the protecting, warming, nourishing influences man has experienced or man will experience."[7] The child would want to remain at the breast of the "Eternal Mother" but reality requires him to separate from her. He is "driven by the eternal thrust to find her again, and to drink renewal from her."[8] To Jung, however, the attraction toward the mother has little to do with sex but rather involves the child's desire for protection and food. The attraction is also an ambivalent one, for she represents both the archetypal "Good Mother" and the "Terrible Mother"—the latter being the one who denies and frustrates the child.

To Jung, the child in a healthy household does not have significant difficulty resolving his oedipal ties and becoming independent of his family. It is only in a home where the child is exposed to deleterious

---

[7] Mullahy, Patrick, *Oedipus Myth and Complex*, New York: Grove Press, 1955.

[8] Jung, Carl G., *Psychology of the Unconscious*, New York: Dodd, Mead and Co., 1949.

psychological influences that he develops neurotic oedipal fears and guilts. In spite of Jung's emphasis on past factors contributing to the formation of the Oedipus complex (factors not only from the child's own early life, but also from the past history of mankind), his approach to its resolution focuses mainly on the present and the future. He attempts to work through the present problems that perpetuate the oedipal ties and considers behavioral manifestations and dream symbols to have future implications as well; that is, the patterns that exist in behavior and in dreams tend to persist into the future; and therapy, by focusing on these present patterns, attempts to alter their future repetition.

Alfred Adler. To Adler, the infant, by virtue of his size and realistic inadequacies, cannot but feel inferior in comparison to the adults around him. One way in which he can compensate for these feelings of inadequacy is to predominate over his parents. Normally the child has no particular preference as to which parent he would like to dominate. However, if the mother is overprotective, the child's excessive demands become gratified and an Oedipus complex develops. The excessive availability and, often, seduction of the overprotective mother stimulate the child's sexual attraction to her. Receiving so many intense satisfactions from the mother, the boy tends to turn away from the father. He may feign helplessness or use physical illness to gain extra attention and control. As he grows older, the pampered child becomes increasingly ill-equipped to cope with the real world and withdraws even more into the mother's outstretched arms, further strengthening the oedipal tie.

For the girl, the Oedipus complex develops similarly when the father is overprotective and seductive. According to Adler, in both sexes the sexual and dependent gratifications are subordinate to the life goal of domination, possession, and exclusive control in the service of compensating for feelings of inferiority.

Otto Rank. For Rank the most painful experience of life is birth, which removes one from the most blissful state of intrauterine existence. Throughout life one tries to recapture this lost paradise, for birth anxiety is the "primal anxiety" and the basis for all other anxieties of life. All childhood fears and anxieties are derivatives of primal anxiety, and their expression allows a gradual catharsis of the primal anxiety. Weaning is the second great trauma in the child's life. It, too, involves a painful separation from the mother, but it derives a significant part of its traumatic effect from the prior birth trauma.

The "primal wish" is to return to the womb, and sexual intercourse appears to be the most likely way of accomplishing this reunion with the mother. The mother's genitals, however, as the site of the original birth trauma, are extremely anxiety-provoking. The healthy boy turns, therefore, to other women, whose genitalia evoke less fear. But the boy with an unresolved Oedipus complex obsessively tries to reenter his mother and desensitize himself to her genitalia by repeatedly exposing himself to them. The repudiation by the mother is seen as another enforced separation similar to the birth trauma. The healthy boy accepts the rejection and seeks substitutes; the neurotic persists in his attempts to achieve the goal of reentry. The girl may attempt to gratify the primal wish by identifying with her own clitoris and attempting to gain partial entrance into her own vagina, which symbolizes her mother's; and she may identify herself with her own intrauterine child and consider herself to be her own mother.

The healthy person is satisfied with partial, substitutive, and symbolic gratifications of the primal wish. The neurotic will settle for nothing less than a real return to the intrauterine state; and since this is impossible, he is doomed to disappointment and frustration.

Rank's concept of will also enters into his explanation of the Oedipus complex. Rank uses the word *will* to refer to one's innate drive toward self-realization, individuality, and creative expression. In the oedipal conflict between the father and the son, each is trying to impose his will on the other. The father tends to rob the son of individuality by trying to mold the boy in his own image. The son, to protect his individuality, may withdraw from the father, out of the fear of being overwhelmed by him, and turn to the mother. A similar conflict exists between the girl and her mother. The conflict is primarily one of "wills" rather than sexual prerogatives. Rank points out that, in the Sophoclean play, Laius, Oedipus' father, fears that a son would vie with him for power. Therefore, hesitant to father a child, he has to be seduced into the sexual act by Jocasta, his wife; and when Oedipus is born, the boy is abandoned, only to return as a young man to engage Laius in the power struggle which he most feared.

Karen Horney. Horney did not consider biological elements to play a role in the formation of the Oedipus complex. She regarded it as the result of two specific family conditions, the first of which is parental seduction. The child has the biological potential for sexual interest in the parent of the opposite sex, but the urge is inconsequential unless there has been actual seduction—overt or covert, physical or psychological. The second and most common factor is parental deprivation of affection. This produces in the child a conflict between his desire to approach his parents for gratification of his dependency and other needs and his wish to express the hostility he feels toward them for the rejection. The latter arouses anxiety because the expression of anger could bring about even further alienation from the already depriving parents. An attempt is therefore made to assuage this anxiety by drawing even closer—thus the obsessive "love" of the Oedipus complex. The attraction has little to do with sex, but rather is toward the parent who appears more likely to offer protection and security.

For Horney, oedipal reactions can intensify problems relating to more fundamental processes. The child normally feels somewhat alone and helpless in a world that, no matter how benevolent, must frustrate him at times and thereby appear hostile. The fears and anxieties he experiences in such a world are referred to as his "basic anxiety," and the hostility he perceives as "basic hostility." The guilt and fear he may feel over his basic hostility may result in his projecting it in order to deny its existence within himself. This projected hostility adds to the basic hostility, which in turn makes his world even more anxiety-provoking. These basic anxieties and hostilities and their intensifications can be experienced by normal children. When there is real parental rejection, the basic anxieties and hostilities increase. In this way rejections that engender the Oedipus complex also produce other difficulties, which in turn add to the child's oedipal problems.

Harry Stack Sullivan. Sullivan made little direct reference to the Oedipus complex in his writings, for he did not consider there to be a significant sexual element in the normal parent-child relationship. The predilection of the child for the opposite-sexed parent, he believed, is fostered by the parents and is in no way related to biological determinants. Each parent feels familiar with the same-sexed child and somewhat strange with the opposite-sexed. In addition, each tends to use the same-sexed child for vicarious gratification more frequently than the opposite-sexed. Fathers pressure their sons to achieve goals that may have eluded them, and mothers similarly encourage their daughters. These factors result in the tendency by the parents to be more authoritarian with the same-sexed child and more permissive and indulgent with the opposite-sexed. The child then responds to the more affectionate parent and becomes alienated from the more coercive one. The resulting behavioral manifestations are those that Freud referred to as the Oedipus complex. Sullivan agreed that one could observe these intrafamilial attractions but did not consider them to have much importance in the basic etiology of psychogenic disturbance.

Erich Fromm. Fromm believes that the Oedipus myth is best understood as the rebellion of the son against the father's authority in a patriarchal family. Feeling coerced and overpowered, the son develops hostility toward his father, the expression of which helps him gain his independence. The domineering father is an intrafamilial reflection of an authoritarian society, and the son's rebellion is symbolic of his antagonism against a coercive social structure. Fromm claims that in societies where patriarchal authority is weak, the Oedipus complex does not develop. Childhood sexual interests are normally present, but he considers them to be generally satisfied autoerotically. When the mother is overprotective or otherwise fosters excessive dependency, then the fixation on her develops as seen in the Oedipus complex.

THE OEDIPUS COMPLEX AS I SEE IT

All of the preceding theorists were adult analysts, and their concepts of the Oedipus complex were derived from data gathered from the analyses of adults, many of whom were neurotic and some probably even psychotic. (Some of Freud's cases would certainly be diagnosed psychotic by today's criteria.) The data provided by adult patients regarding their childhood must be suspect considering that distortions caused by fallible memory and the passage of time, as well as by pathological processes, are inevitably present. Although Anna Freud, Melanie Klein, and many other classical child analysts have had extensive experience with children, most of their writings indicate that they have not questioned the basic tenets of Freud's formulation of the Oedipus complex. They have been, I believe, selectively inattentive to clinical material suggesting that alterations and modifications might be appropriate.

My concept of the Oedipus complex is based on careful and receptive consideration of the theories already discussed, as well as on my own observations of children in both normal and clinical situations. My concept borrows much from my predecessors but also relies heavily on my own clinical experiences.

First, I believe that there is a biological sexual instinct that attracts every human being to members of the opposite sex. From birth to puberty this drive is not particularly strong because during this period the child is not capable of fulfilling the drive's primary purpose of procreation. Although weak and poorly formulated during the pre-pubertal period, it nevertheless exhibits itself through behavior that I consider manifestations of *oedipal interest*. The normal child may speak on occasion of marrying the parent of the opposite sex and getting rid of his rival. These comments may even have a mildly sexual component, such as "and then we'll sleep in bed together." Instinctive impulses for territorial prerogatives may also be operative here. But I do not believe that psychologically healthy children have the desire in this period for genital-sexual experiences with the parent, nor do I believe that their sexually tinged comments are associated with strong sexual-genital urges. Rather, what the healthy child may on occasion want is a little more affection and attention, undiluted by the rival.

In a setting where the child is not receiving the affection, nurture, support, interest, guidance, protection, and generalized physical gratifications (such as stroking, warmth, and rocking) that are his due, he may, in his frustration, become obsessed with obtaining such satisfactions and develop the kinds of sexual urges, preoccupations, and fantasies that Freud referred to as oedipal. The instinctive sexual urges, which are normally mild and relatively dormant, have the *potential* for intensive expression even as early as birth. Getting little gratification from his parents, the child may develop a host of fantasies in which the frustrated love is requited and the rival is removed. Such fantasies follow the principle that the more one is deprived, the more one craves and the more jealous one becomes of those who have what one desires. Such manifestations can appropriately be called *oedipal problems* in the classical sense. Thus, the foundation for the development of neurosis is formed not, as Freud would say, through the failure to resolve successfully one's sexual frustrations regarding the parent of the opposite sex, but through the failure to come to terms with the more basic deprivations the child is suffering.

Whereas Freud considered the sexual preoccupation to arise in the child automatically, I believe that this mode of adaptation to parental deprivation is only one of many possible adjustments and that family and cultural factors play an important role in determining which one is chosen. Parental seduction is only one factor that tends to foster the oedipal adaptation. This seduction need not be overtly physical; it can arise through verbal provocations and titillating exposures. Without parental seduction the child is less likely to involve himself in a sexual adaptation to parental deprivation and is more likely to utilize non-oedipal mechanisms. Seduction enhances the likelihood, but is not essential to the development, of oedipal difficulties. (I have seen oedipal problems arise without parental seduction.)

I also believe that family and cultural factors that tend to foster the child's rivalry with the same-sexed parent can also be instrumental in bringing about the complex. I agree with Fromm that the authoritarian father in a patriarchal household may be a contributing factor in the formation of the Oedipus complex in the boy and with Sullivan who postulates that the parent's stricter attitude toward the same-sexed child fosters oedipal rivalry. Once again, however, I have seen children utilize the oedipal mechanism in the absence of significant rivalry-engendering behavior by the parents.

The classical paradigm of sexual attraction to the opposite-sexed parent and hostility toward the same-sexed seems to me an oversimplification of what one observes clinically. Most often there is great ambivalence toward both parents. The boy with a depriving yet seductive mother has good reason to be angry. He is deprived of basic affection and provided with seduction as a substitute. Clinically the anger may be revealed directly, but more commonly it is handled by a variety of defense mechanisms that repress or displace it or allow for its discharge in symbolic fashion. If any of the anger remains in conscious awareness, the child may become fearful of his mother's retaliation. To protect himself, his avowals of love may increase since they serve to deny his basic anger. Or his hostile impulses may take the form of his fearing that his mother will die, and this too may be handled by obsessive concern for her welfare. A variety of other possible mechanisms as well may come into play to assist the child in handling his basic ambivalence. A boy may still harbor, in addition to his rivalrous hostility toward his father, deep-seated loving feelings and dependent longings toward him. The hostility may cause anxiety that he may lose the father. And this may result in obsessive protestations of affection. Anyone who has observed what is sometimes referred to as a childhood "oedipal panic," whether in the boy or in the girl, will readily confirm that intense feelings of love, hate, and fear regarding *both* parents dominate the clinical picture.

THE UNRESOLVED OEDIPUS COMPLEX AS A SOURCE OF PSYCHOLOGICAL DISTURBANCE

Neuroses, most would agree, are the result of many factors acting in various combinations: cultural, social, familial, psychological, and biological. For Freud, the psychobiological (especially the psychosexual) factors were crucial and he considered the unresolved Oedipus complex to be at the root of all neuroses. In my opinion, whatever cultural, social, and biological factors may be operative in the etiology of neurotic symptoms, parental—and especially maternal—deprivation is essential to their formation. All neurotic symptoms are in part an attempt to cope with this basic deprivation; and the way in which the child chooses to adapt is determined by biological, cultural, social, and familial influences. One deprived child becomes overdependent, an adaptation elicited and perpetuated by his overprotective mother. Another reacts by withdrawing, an adjustment with which his neglectful parents are comfortable. Another discharges in sports the hostility he feels toward his rejecters—sports being, in addition, an activity of premium value in his milieu. Another takes drugs or becomes a juvenile delinquent because that's how kids on *his* block adapt. Another uses his symptoms to enjoy compensatory attention. And so it goes. One could cover the gamut of psychogenic symptoms and find the common element of deprivation in each of them. I am fully aware that symptoms are most complex and many factors contribute to their formation, but the adaptation to emotional abandonment is central and omnipresent. The well-loved child is generally relatively free from psychopathology.

I use the term *oedipal* then to refer to those mechanisms by which the child, in the attempt to compensate for early emotional deprivation, obsessively craves for and tries to gain the affection of the opposite-sexed parent and exhibits concomitant jealous rivalry toward the same-sexed parent. Oedipal problems are likely to arise in a situation of parental seduction or paternal authoritarianism, but they can appear in other family settings as well.

The range of psychological reactions to parental rejection is broad; and many, if not most, contain elements of more than one stage of psychosexual development. Rarely does one see purely oral, anal, or phallic phase symptomatology. When the predominant theme appears to involve obsessive attempts to gain the love of the opposite-sexed parent or excessive rivalry with the same-sexed parent, then one can conveniently apply the term *oedipal*. The homosexual, whose obsessive "love" of males is a thinly disguised attempt to deny an underlying hatred of men and who fears women because they too closely resemble his forbidden, seductive mother, could be considered to have oedipal problems because his difficulties fundamentally reflect the oedipal paradigm. When a patient's adjustment to the privation involves, for example, compulsive eating, the term *oedipal* is not usually used even though the food may be a symbolic representation of the mother's love. The more remote the overt symptom is from the themes of mother-love and father-hate (or vice-versa), the less likely it will be labeled oedipal. However, if the compulsive eater (who is considered to be suffering with "oral" difficulties) has a dependent, thinly disguised sexual relationship with his mother, his problems would more likely be considered oedipal.

Thus, the term *oedipal* is misleading because it purports to describe a symptom complex that rarely, if ever, exists in pure form. Most often, if not always, there are elements of other stages of psychosexual development. In addition, to use the term *oedipal* is equivalent to naming pneumonia "cough" or encephalitis "headache." Just as cough and headache are the superficial manifestations of the more general underlying diseases, pneumonia and encephalitis, the Oedipus complex is only one possible symptomatic manifestation of a whole class of symptom complexes resulting from the basic disorder of parental deprivation. Also, the term is restrictive because it tends to focus undue attention on the sexual elements in the adaptation while disregarding the more important non-sexual aspects. It suggests that the primary problem is sexual, which it isn't.

My comments on the Oedipus complex here in no way constitute a total theory. Nor do I wish to suggest that parental deprivation of love can successfully explain all oedipal problems or indeed all neuroses. There is still much in this field that requires reexamination and clarification. My intent is merely directed to correcting widespread distortions and making Freud's basic concept more directly applicable to contemporary society.

FURTHER COMMENTS ON CHILDHOOD SEXUALITY

"We believe most sexual differences to be artificially induced by male chauvinistic attitudes." These words, of course, are those of the new "liberated" woman, the woman who is throwing off the shackles of female servitude, the woman who is refusing to accept her second-class status as a human being. There is much, I believe, that is healthy in this movement, and the world will be a better place because of it. Like all movements, however, there are a wide variety of opinions—from fanatic to sober—being expressed under the same aegis. I therefore appreciate that the criticisms I make here do not apply to all members of the movement, but only to those who, I believe, have gone to some excess in their enthusiasm to promulgate their cause. In addition, it is my purpose here to discuss only the issue of sexual identification and its specific relationship to child rearing. (It is not within the scope of this book to even touch upon the many other problems to which the members of this group are turning their attention.)

To begin, there are obvious differences between the sexes that are undeniable. Let us refer to these, for the sake of this discussion, as the *primary sexual functions.* In the female this function is childbearing and breast-feeding. Although the female may choose not to bear a child herself or not to breast-feed the one she does give birth to, she cannot relegate these activities to the male. The male's primary sexual function is that of fertilization. He cannot transfer this function to the female. So much for the obvious and irrefutable.

Now to the speculative. I believe that there exists within each woman a *maternal instinct* that is part of the primary sexual function.

I believe it to be innate and psychobiological; that is, it has both psychological and biological components. It includes the physical urge to copulate in order to conceive. That the female, if healthy, will want to have sexual intercourse without the goal of conception in no way weakens my argument. The primary biological purpose of copulation is fertilization not orgasm. Bearing the child within her and having the physical capacity to nourish the child from her own body contributes to the formation of a kind of psychological tie with the child that the male cannot fully develop. I believe all women to be born with this capacity, which, like many other physiological functions, varies in intensity in different people. When there is little or no expression of the maternal instinct, repressive psychological factors are operative; even the most mannish lesbian, somewhere deep down, wants to be a mother.

I believe also that the male has a *paternal instinct*, which is also psychobiological. It includes a biological desire to copulate and thereby bring about the birth of a child. Again, that he may want to have sexual intercourse without fatherhood as a goal does not in itself refute my point; he still has within him the deep-seated urge to have children at some time in his life. In addition, I believe that there is a psychological tie that the healthy man develops with the child he has fathered—even when it only exists *in utero*. This interest in its welfare is a manifestation of his paternal instinct. These urges, which go beyond the procreative, manifest themselves in his desire to provide the mother and child with food, clothing, and shelter and to master whatever technical skills are necessary in his society to achieve this end. Being physically stronger enables him to perform many of these functions more efficiently than the female—and this was especially true before the invention of machinery.

Speaking teleologically, these inborn maternal and paternal instincts serve the purpose of perpetuation of the species. In the service of this goal, they include not only the urge to participate in the reproductive process (each sex in his or her own way) but also the innate desire to rear the child so that he or she can become a functioning member of society and thereby further ensure the survival of mankind.

Each sex, in addition to the primary sexual function, has the innate capacity and the desire to gain gratifications in the other's primary area. For the sake of this discussion, I will call these the *secondary sexual functions*. The female, as a secondary and ancillary interest, has the desire to involve herself in the traditionally masculine activities and to enjoy the many satisfactions they can offer. These, of course, vary from age to age and society to society and run the gamut from the most ancient traditionally masculine pursuits, like hunting and building shelter, to modern professions and skills. The male likewise has deep-seated instinctive urges to involve himself in the details of his child's care that have been traditionally the mother's function.

Each sex has been denied the opportunity to obtain gratifications in his or her own area of secondary sexual functioning. The examples of discrimination against women are legion. However, men have been subjected to a similar, but more subtle, form of prejudice. They have been enslaved by the tradition (more of their own making, than of women's) that it is unmasculine to involve oneself in the particulars of child rearing. Hugging and cuddling one's baby, feeding it, cleaning it when it wets and soils, dressing it, and so on are activities that men have been led to believe are unmanly and engaged in only by the weak and effeminate. The goal we should strive toward (and we have made definite headway in recent years) is that women be given opportunities to gain gratifications in traditionally male areas. This will necessitate not only great flexibility on the part of social institutions to accommodate her childbearing and child-rearing involvements but also an alteration of social attitudes regarding the male's involvement with his children. Such changes have to be laid down in the earliest years of life, both in the home and in the schools, if they are to be meaningful. The ideal is not, I believe, a 50–50 split—half the time the mother is with the children and half the time the father—as many Women's Liberationists propose. Rather, I believe, that when the children are in their earliest years they do best with the greatest amount of time being given by the mother, who, as I have said, is instinctively more involved with and capable of caring for them during this period. This is not to say that the father should not be around. Every encouragement should be given him and every opportunity provided him to satisfy his paternal needs without embarrassment or the fear that he will compromise his masculinity. As the child grows older, mothers should be given more and more time and opportunity to satisfy their interests in their secondary area of functioning.

In line with this view, I do not agree with those parents who try to minimize sexual differences in their children in order to prepare them for a future world that will allegedly not recognize such differences. I do not believe that boys and girls in childhood should be dressed alike. (That teen-agers are doing so in the early 1970's is not, in my opinion, significantly affecting their sexual orientation. By that time sexual identity is pretty well established and will not be significantly altered by such a superficial thing as clothing.) Nor do I believe that boys should be given dolls and girls trucks *as primary presents for important occasions*, such as birthdays and Christmas. I do believe, however, that such presents might be given in an ancillary fashion, or on less important occasions, to strengthen interest in each sex's secondary area of functioning. In the traditional game of house, the girl should still be encouraged to play the role of "mother" and the boy that of "father." However, I would also encourage the "father" to come home from work early a couple of days a week or to give over his Saturdays to take care of the children while mother is out taking courses or working at something she is interested in. These are the kinds of identifications that I believe are healthiest for parents to foster and it is on this concept of maleness and femaleness that my ensuing discussion is based.

"*We never undress in front of the children.*" Freud's misconceptions about childhood sexuality are, I believe, responsible for central errors in his oedipal theory. In addition, they have fostered some unfortunate attitudes in parents regarding their children's sexuality.

First, concerning the child's attitudes toward his genitalia, there can be little doubt that unnatural social attitudes produce in the child a curiosity that might not otherwise have occurred. One unfortunate outgrowth of Freudian teachings was the warning that parents, by undressing in front of their child—even at ages as low as six months to one year—could produce sexual fantasies and frustrations that might contribute to the formation of oedipal problems. In my opinion, the healthy home atmosphere is one in which the child (up to the late pre-pubertal period—ages ten to eleven) is permitted to occasionally observe his parents in the nude, in casual and natural situations. In my opinion, it is psychologically deleterious to strictly hide one's body from the child, because such an attitude fosters the development of unnatural curiosities and excessive cravings, which then contribute to neurotic attitudes toward the opposite sex. In such an environment the family serves to lessen and counteract the pathological attitudes that are produced by a culture in which the ubiquitous use of seduction, in the mass media and elsewhere, fosters neurotic sexual preoccupations. On the other hand, nudity in the home should not be taken too far. It is just as inappropriate to artificially expose the child when the situation usually does not call for nudity. If the child is excessively exposed to parental nudity, then the kind of seductiveness Freud spoke about may very well be occurring. Sexually stimulating verbalizations or titillating physical contact when clothed may be equally seductive. In our culture, which strictly prohibits parent-child sexuality, such seductive behavior can lead to frustrations, guilts, and other neurotic manifestations. What is to be avoided is seductiveness, not nudity. The two do not necessarily go together.

Another reason given by classical psychoanalysts for avoiding exposing the child to parental nudity is that the comparison of the adult's sexual organs to those of the child is said to contribute to the formation of feelings of insecurity and inadequacy in the child. The boy cannot but unfavorably compare his own penis to that of his father, and the girl is said to feel inadequate regarding her own breast development when she sees her mother. I believe that feelings of inadequacy have far more to do with other factors in the parent-child relationship than with genital size differences. The child who is receiving adequate affection, protection, and guidance in a stable home will certainly wish to be an adult, with all the privileges and gratifications that that entails. He will not single out his parents' genitalia for particular emulation, nor will he consider his own small organ as a painful deficiency. The neurotic child may do so, but it will not be because he has seen his parents naked but rather because of defects in his relationship with them—defects having little or nothing to do with the dressing situation.

In the pubertal and post-pubertal periods, because the child has become sexually-genitally oriented, the same dressing criteria should be used as with non-family adults. This applies for both the parent and the child of the opposite sex. For either to undress in front of the other cannot but produce stimulations leading to anxieties and conflicts because of our cultural taboos against incest. However, parents and same-sexed children should continue, in my opinion, to undress in front of one another in appropriate situations—such as in locker rooms or when changing clothing when opposite-sexed family members are not in the immediate vicinity. Such occasional exposures can add to their sense of relaxation and intimacy with one another.

The position I have taken on parental undressing in front of children is based on the prevalent mores in the early 1970's. There is good evidence that changes are taking place in the direction of a greater sense of freedom regarding nudity and less shame of the human body. If these trends, which are now primarily confined to those in their teens and twenties, are to ultimately become the standards subscribed to by the majority, then what I have said will have to be modified. In such a world there will be less pathological curiosity about the human body, less equating nudity with seductivity; and consequently less guilt and frustration will be produced in the child who sees his parents naked.

Although I consider such potential changes to be healthy, I have a lingering doubt. Part of the fun in sex is related to the fact that one has the opportunity to see things one has been prohibited from viewing since the earliest years of childhood. If all the "sights" become freely available, perhaps some of the fun will be taken out of sex. Perhaps man will have to devise new prohibitions in order to enhance curiosity. Man is, at the same time, a most strange and creative creature. If these changes regarding nudity take place and if my doubts prove to be valid, he can be relied upon, I am sure, to devise new ways in which he can play games with himself.

"*We never let our kids come into our bed in the morning.*" We cuddle infants and toddlers, and practically everyone recognizes that such contact is healthy for them. Until Freud came along many parents continued to cuddle their children even when older, though to a lesser extent. But it was Freud's view that during the phallic period (ages three-and-a-half to five or six) the child is quite a sensuous little animal and wants nothing more than to "sex around" (not necessarily to have intercourse, though) with the parent of the opposite sex. Parents are warned, therefore, about the dangers of such "seduction"—particularly because it can contribute to the formation of oedipal problems and difficulty in resolving one's Oedipus complex. The child "seduced" in this way will become so involved with the parent of the opposite sex that he or she may have difficulty breaking away and forming meaningful relationships with opposite-sexed peers. Or a variety of neurotic and even psychotic symptoms (fears, compulsions, obsessions, etc.) may arise that may be manifestations of oedipal problems.

I do not believe that the child is as "sexed up" during this period as the classical Freudian psychoanalysts would have us believe. There is however, a desire for generalized physical-cutaneous gratification such as cuddling, stroking, and scratching, which is only mildly sexual for the normal healthy child. To deprive the child of the satisfaction of these desires during this period is more likely to produce the kinds of difficulties Freud talks about than to prevent them. Of course, true seduction, in which the child is strongly aroused genitally on frequent occasions can bring about psychiatric disorder.

During this period the healthy child loves to cuddle with his parents and this should not only be allowed but encouraged. Before going to sleep at night and upon arising in the morning seem to be the child's favorite times for such activities. Fifteen minutes or so of hugging, cuddling, or just lying together not only does the child no harm but can do him a lot of good. It makes him feel loved, wanted, and enjoyed. To deprive him of these simple and innocent pleasures cannot but make him feel unloved, unwanted, and rejected—and it is feelings such as these that are at the roots of most forms of psychological disturbance. During the day as well, a few short periods of cuddling, wrestling, and horseplay (regardless of the sex of the parent and child) can be salubrious. Fortunately, most healthy parents ignored Freud's (and their doctor's) advice and satisfied their instinctive desires to have some degree of physical contact with their child. Many of those who did (and still do) follow it are people who are basically cold and unaffectionate and use Freud's advice to justify their rejection of their children.

"Last night Billy came into our bedroom while we were having intercourse." Freud used the term *primal scene* to refer to the child's imagery of his parents having sexual intercourse. The images can arise from actually seeing the parents having sexual relations or, more commonly, from spontaneous fantasies without ever having observed them. Freud believed that such fantasies, when they arose without an actual observation to stimulate them, were *inherited* memory traces from ancient times when all children probably observed their parents having sexual intercourse. Such fantasies, according to Freud, serve as the basis for oedipal and masturbatory fantasies and are, therefore, of fundamental (or prime) importance in the formation of the Oedipus complex. (The term *primal* refers not only to the fantasy's basic importance in the Oedipus complex but to its ancient heritage as well.)

Freud acknowledged that most patients did not actually observe parental intercourse but found that *all* ultimately recollected such fantasies if the analyst probed long and hard enough. Many of his patients recalled overhearing their parents having relations, and such memories were uniformally emotionally charged. He considered the analysis of such memories and the alleviation of problems that stemmed from them to be of vital importance in the psychoanalytic treatment process.

One of the outgrowths of all this focus on the primal scene is the widely-held notion that the child's actual observation of his parents having sexual intercourse is just about the worst thing that can possibly happen to him, that if anything can produce oedipal difficulties it's seeing one's parents copulating.

I do not think it is an exaggeration to say that most children in the world, both in the past and in the present, have seen their parents (as well as possibly aunts, uncles, older siblings, and other adults) having sexual intercourse. Most of the children in the world grow up living in the same room (or area, since many don't even have a room) as their parents. Although the adults may cover themselves, there is still a significant amount of observation of the activity. It is doubtful that most of these children suffer with the kinds of difficulties Freud described as stemming from such fantasies and observations. In cultures, however, in which the sexual act is given great meaning, in which the child is instilled with the notion that it is sacred, secret, or shameful, then unnatural curiosities and emotional reactions may result. I do not believe, then, in any inheritance from our ancient ancestors of psychological reactions to such observations nor do I believe that excessive reactions to the act are universal. Rather, I believe that in Western and in certain other societies the act has been invested with such special meaning and has become associated with such high emotional charge that all sorts of complicated and maladaptive reactions can become associated with it. Freud assumed that what was psychologically true for Victorian Vienna at the turn of the century was true for all of mankind (a very sweeping generalization, to say the least).

One could argue that many social attitudes about sex are unhealthy and that the most natural thing would be to make love openly. However, people who have involved themselves in various types of group sex experiences often find that jealous reactions arise and that the group's activities must be carefully structured if these are to be kept in bounds. One could then argue that these jealousies are socially conditioned and that "healthy" people would not have them. They could be considered manifestations of neurotic dependency and overpossessiveness. Others would argue that the jealous reaction, although not innate, inevitably arises when someone else has what one wants very badly. The group sex situation, then, can only be tolerated by those who have little or no strong interest in anybody in particular. None of the liberated or radical sexual experimentation that has flourished in the last few years—communal living where partners are shared, group sex, transient sexual encounter for both men and women with no non-sexual attachment tied to it—has significantly altered the values that many in our society place on the one-to-one male-female relationship in which sex is a significant, but not sole, component. It is in light of the intrinsic value that I place on sex within a deeply intimate relationship that I make the following comments on the child's observance of the primal scene.

First, I believe that one does better for the child to impress him with the fact that certain things his parents say and do together are "private." This includes sexual as well as non-sexual matters. As he grows older he will come to better appreciate the particulars. One does not have intercourse in front of one's child because it is an act of such great pleasure for both parents that the child cannot but want to join in and gain similar gratifications (just as he or she does when mother and father hug). If one is willing to provide the child with these satisfactions (to the degree that he is physiologically capable), then perhaps there will be less jealousy. However, the social reactions to incest are so strong and the stigma so great (and the child cannot but ultimately be affected by them) that the child will certainly get into difficulties outside the home. The parent who is not willing to engage in an even partially incestuous relationship with his or her child does well to impress upon the child that the sexual act is a highly private and personal act that one shares only with a limited number of people—and then only under special circumstances. In order to protect the child from intense jealousy and other reactions (such as fear), one should take significant precautions that the child not hear and preferably not even know exactly when the parents are having relations.

Now to the question of the child's observing the primal scene. First, it is important to realize that no single event or trauma causes chronic emotional disturbances. Only longstanding or repeated exposure to troubling experiences causes them. Observing parents having sexual intercourse on one occasion is an *event*. Only the parents can turn it into a trauma. If the child does happen to come in, either for a moment or throughout the complete act, and actually observe his parents having intercourse, nothing terrible, I believe, is going to happen to him— nothing terrible so long as it doesn't become a pattern; and nothing terrible so long as the parents handle it reasonably. If it happens often, the parents have to ask themselves whether they might be setting things up so that the child will be an observer. There are parents who do this; and though to delve into the reasons why they do is beyond the scope of this book, such behavior is a manifestation of psychological disorder on their part and can contribute to the child's development of various untoward psychological reactions.

More commonly, the child's observance of the primal scene is a rare occurrence. Although one must tailor his approach to the particular situation and the particular child, there are some general principles that I have found helpful on those occasions when my advice has been sought on this problem. One common reaction is for the child not to wish to talk about what he has seen. The parents should then encourage him to discuss it in order to learn what distortions, if any, he may be entertaining and to help him to deal with his reactions. Some children conclude that the act is a violent and hostile one and that the various noises are manifestations of pain that the father is inflicting on the mother. The parents should impress upon the child that it is an act of love and affection and that great pleasure, not pain, is experienced. They should communicate also that it is done in private and that he was, therefore, sent out of the room when he came in. Since the child is not in a position to appreciate all the psychological and philosophical considerations as to why he cannot watch, it's best left at "It's private" and "That's the way the world is." The child should be told that it is a natural and wonderful experience that he will enjoy himself someday when he is older. It is best that the parents be as matter-of-fact as they can (as hard as that may be considering the circumstances) and that the discussion be short and simple. If the parents get unduly excited, if they make an issue of it over a long period of time, then problems may arise. Under such circumstances the child may develop various distortions and emotional reactions to sex that may contribute to his developing problems in this area.

If the child refuses to talk, he may still be receptive to hearing some of the things I have just mentioned. The parents should select those that they think will be most meaningful for the child—taking into consideration his age and the total situation. Whether or not the child does ask questions, whether or not he listens silently or receptively, it is a good idea to close the discussion with the invitation to the child that he be free to ask his parents any questions at all about what has happened. It is the parents' openness and honesty, more than anything else, that will determine whether or not the child will develop adverse psychological reactions.

"Penis envy" and "castration anxiety." Freud says that the female child, when she first realizes that boys have penises and she does not, considers herself to have had a penis but to have lost it, possibly because she was "bad." She may then develop what he called "penis envy." The male child is also said to view with horror the lack of a phallus in the female because its absence implies that his penis can easily be removed, especially if he is "bad." This phenomenon is said to contribute to "castration anxiety."

I do not believe that castration anxiety is present as a significant concern in the normal boy, nor is penis envy a preoccupation in the well-adjusted girl. The healthy girl may, on occasion, express the desire to have a penis, but this, I believe, is related to the general feeling of jealousy any child has when someone has what he or she hasn't. The healthy child accepts his sex and has pride both in the sexual and non-sexual aspects of himself. If, however, the boy is raised in a home where he has been actively threatened because he touches himself or engages in other activities unacceptable to the parents, then, of course, he may readily develop castration anxieties. Or if the female is conditioned to believe that being a male is infinitely more desirable, then the ground-work for penis envy is certainly being laid. In general, I believe that unhealthy psychological symptoms centering on the genitalia more often than not pertain to non-sexual difficulties for which the genitals are being used as a symbol. The penis usually symbolizes masculinity in general with both sexual and non-sexual connotations—the non-sexual including such attributes as self-assertion and productivity in the world. The vagina and breasts may symbolize not only sexuality but also the broader context of femininity—including physical attractiveness, the capacity for bearing and rearing children, and homemaking ability.

Masturbation. In moving from the symbolic aspects of the genitalia to actual genital self-stimulation in children, some clarification of terms is necessary. When the term *childhood masturbation* is used, no distinction is usually made between occasional touching of the genitalia, which almost all children engage in for the mild pleasure it affords them, and more intensive masturbatory practices obsessively engaged in and often culminating in orgasm. Frequent genital self-stimulation by the child, whether or not it is associated with orgasm, is pathological and reflects psychogenic difficulties. Occasional mild stimulation is normal.

According to Freud, in the phallic stage the child masturbates primarily in response to overt or symbolic fantasies of sexual involvement with the parent of the opposite sex. Masturbatory guilt is primarily the result of oedipal guilt: the child is said to feel guilty about his sexual desires for the forbidden object, his or her parent. In my opinion, the masturbating child is essentially communicating to the parent this message: "I must turn to myself for pleasure because you don't provide me with the love I need." By prohibiting the act, the parent is protected from this painful confrontation. This is not to say that other factors do not contribute to masturbatory guilt, but what I have just described is, I believe, central. Parental deficiency in providing the child with adequate affection is a most significant element in bringing about obsessive masturbation. The child whose environment is essentially a giving and rewarding one does not obsessively resort to this compensatory concentrated pleasure.

Generally, the normal child does not have specific fantasies associated with his occasional genital stimulation. He just touches himself because "it feels good." With regard to those children who do masturbate obsessively, I have found that generally children below the ages of seven to eight do not have specific fantasies. Beyond that age, from eight to twelve, children describe a variety of fantasies, both sexual and non-sexual. In such children, when the sexual fantasy is associated with a member of the opposite sex, it does not usually, in my experience, involve sexual intercourse but rather looking, rubbing, and caressing. More pathological, but nevertheless seen in this older group of children, are occasional sadomasochistic masturbatory fantasies, which might include whipping and being tortured, as well as homosexual fantasies, although the latter are most often confined to the caressing type. Occasionally the child's masturbatory fantasies will include animals (most often dogs), and sometimes this is associated with actual experiences in which there has been sex play with animals.

The already described study by Ames, as well as one by Pitcher and Prelinger, confirms what I have said regarding the sexual fantasies of children in the oedipal period. Ames found that only 1.8% of all stories of children from two to five related to reproduction. Among the children studied, no fantasies regarding sensual-sexual experiences with parents were described. The primary theme for the three- to five-year-old child was violence. Pitcher and Prelinger found that the main themes in the three- to five-year-old group were aggression, hurt, and misfortune. In the stories in which the child described his relationship with the parents, sensual-sexual involvements were rare. Instead the whole gamut of other possible modes of interaction, both friendly and hostile, were present.

My own clinical experience is consistent with the findings of these studies; that is, the conscious fantasy life of the normal child at the three- to five-year-old level contains little overt sexual material. One might interpret some of the fantasies to have a latent sexual content. However, most of the fantasies and dreams of children, both normal and neurotic, are more meaningfully interpreted non-sexually, despite the fact that a small percentage of children with psychogenic disturbance are preoccupied with sexual activities, urges, and fantasies, either overt or symbolic.

Sexually exciting dreams, moreover, are extremely rare in childhood. If there were such strong sexuality in childhood and it were not being directly revealed in fantasies (as shown by Ames, Pitcher, and Prelinger), it could be expected to manifest itself occasionally in the dream. For the dream, although it may disguise, is closer to the primary drives and can be expected, as in the adult, to provide occasional gratifications of repressed instinctive impulses. In the disturbed child, the kinds of fantasies described by the Freudians may indeed be present; but such fantasies are best understood in a broader context, with sexual material representing both sexual and non-sexual elements in the child's mental life.

In order to counteract the strong social forces that can evoke guilt in the child over masturbation, it is important for the parent to be particularly careful to be non-punitive in his reactions to the child's masturbation—whether it be excessive or not. Generally, I suggest that parents tell the child that it is perfectly all right to touch himself or herself but that such things are done in private. Again, one cannot go into all the reasons *why*. The main reason is simply that, given the way the world is at the present time, anyone who masturbates in public is subjected to the most dramatic and often punitive responses. If a child, he may be ignored; he may be made an outcast; his parents may be notified; he may be sent to a psychiatrist; other parents may not want their children to associate with him; etc. If an adult, he would generally be considered so far removed from reality that the label *psychotic* would be applied and institutionalization seriously considered. The child whose parents do not advise him to masturbate privately may be lessening the likelihood that he will feel guilty, but they will not be preparing him to adjust well to the world.

The child who masturbates excessively (with or without orgasm), who generally prefers masturbating to involvement with peers and other forms of recreation is usually a disturbed child. He is generally a child who has suffered deprivations (either overt or covert) in his relationships with his parents and who is compensating by turning to himself for pleasure because so little is forthcoming from his environment. Some kind of work with a professional in the mental health field is often necessary to help such children enjoy other gratifications and to help them with some of the other problems that are usually present.

"You show me yours and I'll show you mine." This is probably the most popular game played by children since the invention of clothing. From early life the child is taught that he is to cover certain parts of his body. In addition, he is prevented from seeing these same areas in others—especially those of the opposite sex. The rules may be somewhat lax around the home, but they are rigidly enforced in his encounters with outsiders. Such restrictions cannot but produce curiosity and excitations that would not have otherwise arisen. If you tell a child (and most adults, for that matter, as well) that he can read any book in the house except a certain one with a red cover, one need not ponder long which book will be read when the adult is out of sight. Forbidden fruit *is* sweeter—there is no question about it. Nursery school children (girls as well as boys) find looking up the teacher's dress, while they lie on the floor during rest period, a most exciting game. Little Carl finds the genitalia of the little girl next door far more fascinating to examine than his sister's. Sally and Joan spoke for days about the time Jimmy left his fly open. The penis they saw that day was definitely, but undefinably, different from their brothers'.

The exhibitionistic and voyeuristic games children play in this period serve primarily to satisfy the child's curiosity. The main emotional responses are giggling and feelings of awe. Genital-sexual excitation, if present, is usually minimal. Often the focus is on the bowel and bladder functions—which are even less likely to produce sexual excitation. In the neurotic child, however, for whom other gratifications may not be forthcoming, there may be excessive interest in such play; and there may be associated sexual excitation, masturbation, or fantasy preoccupation.

Most parents are not happy to permit their children to engage in sex play. They tend to believe that sexual activities follow the principle that the more one gets the more one wants. Early exposures and stimulation, they reason, may result in excessive involvement in the teens—with its specters of promiscuity and pregnancy. I agree that it is not in the child's best interests to allow sexual play with other children. Perhaps the time will come when there will be total freedom of sexual activity between (and even among) all consenting parties. But, the so-called sexual revolution notwithstanding, that day is far from here; and whatever hypocrisy exists in our society regarding sex (and it is ubiquitous), it is this society to which the child will have to make some degree of accommodation and adjustment. The child who is given free rein to engage in sexual activities is not being prepared to function in a world that still does not sanction such freedom.

Another reason for stopping children from sex play is the possibility that the sick child, who is obsessed with sex, may seduce a healthier child into excessive interest. Probably a *very* healthy child would not be easily involved, but the child who is borderline can be drawn into an obsession he might not have otherwise had. The problem, then, is not whether the child should be stopped, but rather, how one can do it without instilling too much guilt.

Generally, I suggest that parents say something along these lines: "I can see how you and Mary want to see what the other one looks like. All children like to play such games. However, it's not permitted. When you are grown up, you'll be able to do such things." I am aware that no child ever responded to such a comment with anything but resentment. To tell a child that he can do something when he is grown up is like saying he can do it twenty million years from now. But it's better to say that and provide some hope, than to omit such reassurance and imply that he'll *never* be able to do that sort of thing. The other comments are clearly made in the service of guilt alleviation. I say alleviation, because the very nature of the situation, the very prohibition of the act, must engender *some* guilt. However, one can still try to lessen the amount of guilt by accepting the impulse as natural and normal—and clearly stating so. Again, I recommend the simple statement: "It's not permitted." The child is not sophisticated enough to appreciate all the subtleties involved in the reasons why; and even if he were, he would probably not be in agreement that his activities should be stopped.

The Resolution of the Oedipus Complex

The normal child, according to Freud, resolves his Oedipus complex by the age of five-and-a-half to six. He then enters a six-year period of sexual quiescence—the latency period—which terminates at puberty. There is, indeed, little sexual interest in this period but not, I believe, because of repression of oedipal drives and resolution of the Oedipus complex, but rather because, as I have described, there is relatively little genital-sexual urge to be repressed in the first place. It is not until puberty, with physiological genital maturation, that sexual urges of adult intensity are normally present. The child has the potential to exhibit such interest and achieve such gratification, but to do so would be, in my opinion, pathological.

In spite of this low level of sexual activity during this period, there is probably more sexual interest and fantasy than in the preceding phases of life, not less as Freud indicates. Because of the child's greater experiences with those outside his home, he is more likely to have encountered arousing sexual stimuli.

The word *resolution* is generally used to refer to the cure or dissolution of the Oedipus complex, but I prefer to use the term *alleviation* because oedipal involvements and interests are never completely resolved. At best oedipal problems can be alleviated. My therapeutic approach to oedipal difficulties reflects my concept of the Oedipus complex itself: the problems to be alleviated are not the result of parental sexual seduction but rather of more generalized emotional deprivation. Therefore, I consider the improvement in the parent-child relationship crucial to the alleviation of oedipal problems in the child. The boy who has obtained little gratification from his mother may become fixated in the effort to secure it. His entire life may be devoted to this futile pursuit. It is as though he reasoned that there is no point in moving on to seek satisfaction from others. If his own mother does not provide him with enough affection, how can he expect strangers to offer it? A therapeutic attempt is therefore made to improve his relationship with his mother so that he will obtain some of the gratifications that are his due in childhood. Gratification at this time will make him more confident about his ability to obtain similar satisfactions from others in the future. The same rationale holds for my attempts to improve the girl's relationship with her father. The father plays a significant role in the girl's development of a healthy sense of femininity, and the girl who lacks a salutary paternal experience is likely to develop pathological oedipal adjustments.

To accomplish an improvement in the parent-child relationship, the child must come to terms with the fact that there are problems in his involvement with his parents that have to be worked on. I attempt to help the child change those elements in his behavior that might be contributing to the difficulties. I try to help him gain a more accurate picture of his parents, their assets and their liabilities, the areas in which they can provide him with meaningful gratifications and those in which they cannot. He is helped to accept the fact that he cannot completely possess either of his parents and that the affection and attention of each of them must be *shared* with other members of the family. This sharing concept is an important one to impart. The child must be helped to appreciate that no one can possess another person completely : his father shares mother with the children ; his mother shares the father with the children ; and he has no choice but to share his mother with his father and siblings. In the context of sharing, however, *he must be reassured that, although he may not get as much as he might want, he will still get something.*

He is encouraged to seek satisfactions from his parents in the areas in which they are genuinely capable of providing them at such times that they can be provided. And he is encouraged to pursue elsewhere those gratifications that his parents are incapable of giving him. I try to impress upon the child the fact that just because there are deficiencies in his parents' love does not mean that he is unlovable and that no one else, either in the present or future, can love him. Deeper involvement with peers is encouraged to help him compensate, and he is consoled with the hope that as he grows older he will be increasingly able and free to enjoy meaningful relationships with others. For boys, identifications with assertive men are fostered so that their future chances of obtaining a desirable mate are enhanced. Identification with a male therapist, teacher, camp counselor, or scoutmaster can be helpful in this regard. Identifications and behavioral attitudes that will increase the likelihood of the girl's attracting a mate in the future are also fostered.

Whereas for Freud the resolution of oedipal conflicts comes out of fear of castration, resignation, and natural biological processes, in my approach the child is given something in compensation for his loss and is, therefore, more likely to give up the obsession. The child with oedipal problems has not pursued these alternatives on his own and must be helped to do so. I cannot imagine true resolution without such substitutes.

Attempts are also made to diminish the guilt the child may feel over his sexual or hostile thoughts and feelings and to correct misconceptions that contribute to such guilt. He is repeatedly told, for example, that his impulses in these areas are shared by most, if not all, children. He is reassured that hostile thoughts, as such, cannot harm. He is encouraged to use his anger constructively to bring about a reduction in his frustrations and resentments. I try to encourage his entry into situations where he may have the living experience that the expression of anger does not generally result in the dire consequences he anticipates. Little direct attention is given to penis envy, masturbation, castration anxiety, childbearing, and sexuality in general. Even when the child's symptoms are overtly sexual, emphasis on the relatively non-sexual approaches I have described is more therapeutically effective. As I have said, the sexual is most often a symbolic representation of more basic non-sexual problems that are more directly dealt with in my approach.

In addition, I work closely with the parents and attempt to correct any misguided approaches to the child that might be contributing to the schism in their relationship with him. If the parents are motivated for, or receptive to, psychiatric treatment for themselves, I help them arrange for it, either with me or with another therapist. If, from such therapy, they can provide the child with more affection, there will be a greater likelihood of his alleviating his oedipal problems.

Regarding the resolution of oedipal conflicts, one final point should be made. The term *resolution* implies a final working through, a complete solution, a coming to peace with one's Oedipus complex. I think that the more one has been deprived, the less the likelihood that one can fully resolve his reactions to early deprivations. All patients, I believe, regardless of their pathology and the length and success of their treatment, never completely give up the attempt to get one more drop of milk from the empty breast. Often, the breast has been far more freely flowing than the patient realizes. The child ill appreciates the efforts of his parents and the time and energy involved in his upbringing. He more often recalls the frustrations and deprivations. The child's hypercritical attitude toward his parents is further intensified by his projection of his own hostilities onto them. Because of this projection he perceives them as far more malevolent than they really are. Even when he becomes a parent himself, after he has had the opportunity to view the parent-child relationship from another vantage point, he tends to maintain and preserve his own childhood distortions.

What about the so-called normal people (whoever they are and whatever that means); those out there whom therapists never see; those whose life adjustments are good? My guess is that they too never completely cease trying to please their mothers and fathers and gain their approbation. In their minds' eye, even when they are old and *their* parents have long since died, thoughts like "My mother would have been proud of me for this" or "I'm glad my father wasn't alive when that happened; he would have never forgiven me" still persist. For the first five years of life, children endlessly seek their parents' approval, and for the next ten to fifteen they are still significantly dependent on it. I do not believe that such "programming" can ever be completely erased.

5

Guilt

Conscience refers to the mental mechanisms that guide and assist the individual in inhibiting himself from performing acts that are unacceptable to significant figures in his environment. The feeling an individual experiences when he performs, or is tempted to perform, such unacceptable acts is guilt. This chapter will discuss the basic principles of the origin of guilt and some of its primary manifestations.

Stages in the development of guilt. I propose three stages in the child's development of the capacity to experience guilt. During the first phase, which I refer to as the Pain Stage, the parents prevent the child from participating in unacceptable behavior by the direct infliction of pain. A two-year-old child who runs into the street will not be deterred from doing so again by lectures on the dangers of automobiles. A slap on the backside, not-so-gentle removal from the street, or strong castigation is much more effective. The child learns to restrain himself because he says to himself, in essence, "If I run into the street, my mother or father will hurt me or yell at me. I'd better not." Living for the moment, as he does, he cannot at that age be expected to say, "I'd better not run into the street because someday I might get hit by a car."

In the next stage, the Shame Stage, the child's primary deterrent is the fear that significant environmental figures will discover him performing the prohibited act and will reject him. Of importance here is the child's fear of being *seen* by parents or their surrogates, and thereby rejected. He envisions himself standing in the center of a circle of critical adults all of whom are crying out, "Shame on you!" At this stage, the deterring forces are still externalized; when the important individuals are no longer in the immediate vicinity, the child cannot be relied upon to deter himself.

In the final stage, the Self-Blame Stage, or Guilt Stage, the child has incorporated the parental values. Here, the inhibitions have been internalized, and the inner rather than the outer voice deters. Alone and unobserved, the child suffers the admonition of the internalized words of authorities. The child deters himself because he would despise himself were he to perform the unacceptable act. It is as if he said to himself, "How terrible it would be if I did that. What a terrible person I would be if I did that. I won't do it." Once this phase has been reached, the parents can relax their vigil. The child can be trusted to behave because the mechanism is powerful—so powerful that it is apt to function with exaggerated severity and even lend itself to the formation of neurotic and psychotic mechanisms.

Guilt. Each stage contains two essential elements: (1) ideas, feelings, and acts of wrongdoing and (2) parental punishment. The latter, be it in the form of rejection, withdrawal of love, castigation, chastisement, or any of the commonly used disciplinary measures is the original punitive element in guilt. As the child develops, he encounters an ever-growing horde of figures, each empowered to punish him for his transgressions. Although punitive fear may be repressed or unrealized, it is never completely lost in the guilt reaction. Even in adult guilt there is the fear of retribution from some authority—real or fantasized. Anxiety may become a concomitant of this aspect of the guilt reaction if the punishment is vague or if it is not known whether it will be administered. The individual then finds himself under a sword of Damocles, never knowing when or if it will fall.

Appropriate guilt. If an act or thought is considered "wrong" in the opinion of the majority of significant individuals in the guilty person's environment, then the guilt is considered appropriate. The normal, healthy child develops his sense of guilt according to the stages I have described. It is not merely fear of various authorities that contributes to the formation of the guilt mechanism but also identification with important individuals in the child's milieu. The qualities exhibited by parents, teachers, ministers, scoutmasters, admired relatives, and famous people the child has come to admire are incorporated. The child wishes to grow up and be like a particular individual because he has learned that acquiring that person's characteristics enables one to enjoy certain social benefits. In the process of emulating these models the child internalizes their standards and ideals, and these become the guidelines by which he will ultimately judge his own behavior.

As I will discuss in detail in Chapter 8, in play the child can practice and reinforce the parental dictates that contribute to the formation of his conscience. In playing house, for example, children can be observed reiterating all the *do's* and *don't's* they have learned from their parents, and much time is spent practicing and repeating these principles of behavior. When alone and fantasizing, the child can sometimes be heard repeating various parental admonitions. One mother described overhearing her four-year-old daughter murmuring to herself, "Nice girls don't say shit. Nice girls don't say shit." Younger siblings can also be useful in this process. Vehemently castigating a younger brother or sister for the most minor indiscretion can serve to ingrain the particular admonishment in the reproacher's own psyche.

If the guilt is appropriate there is often a simple relationship between punishment and the assuagement (and even removal) of the feeling of wrongdoing. For the child, punishment—even in the form of parental displeasure—can be effective in alleviating guilt. The crime has been committed, punishment suffered, and the slate is clean. Some children will even ask for the punishment to alleviate the guilt feeling and may become distraught if it is not forthcoming. (For the adult who feels appropriately guilty, remorse and self-denigration usually provide sufficient punishment.) However, such a simple relationship does not exist between punishment and guilt alleviation for the inappropriate forms of guilt now to be discussed.

Exaggerated guilt. In exaggerated guilt the individual suffers a degree of remorse and self-recrimination far above what the significant individuals in his environment consider reasonable. Many children in therapy suffer with such hypertrophied consciences. They feel excessively guilty over feelings that other children can accept with relative equanimity. This is especially true for hostile thoughts and feelings. Such children may fear that their angry thoughts may actually harm the person at whom they are directed. Or they may anticipate violent repercussions to their expressions of hostility. Their anger, therefore, may find substitutive and symbolic expression in a variety of symptoms such as compulsions, nightmares, and phobias.

Parents of such children, although often somewhat inhibited in expressing anger, are rarely as punitive in their reactions as the child envisions. Parental inhibitions have a way of becoming exaggerated when they are transmitted from parent to child in ways that are not very clear. Perhaps the great difference in size and strength between the parents and the child contributes to this. Perhaps the child's natural tendency toward primitive and dramatic thinking plays a role. Projection of the child's own repressed hostilities onto the parents is often a factor in his seeing them as more castigating than they really are.

Firstborn, in my experience, are more prone to exhibit excessive guilt than their subsequently born siblings. This is due, in part, to their having only adults to identify with and thereby developing higher standards for themselves. The younger siblings form partial identifications with the older ones and so have less rigid figures to emulate. Another family constellation that may be conducive to the formation of rigid consciences is one in which there is a significant gap between the youngest and his elder siblings. A child born into a home where his siblings are all in their teens is generally pampered and overindulged. In addition, he may develop a very rigid conscience in an attempt to keep up with all the "adult" figures who surround him. Early in life he learns that if he is to be allowed to join the family in various activities he must "act grown-up" and inhibit himself from expressing not only his natural playfulness and rambunctiousness but possibly alienating hostility as well. Without a rigid conscience, he may find himself left behind when the others go off to enjoy themselves.

The rejected child may become excessively inhibited in expressing anger. He is already suffering abandonment; he cannot risk further alienating his parents with expressions of hostility. He had better be particularly good if he is not to lose entirely the little affection he is receiving. Also the child who is exposed to religious teachings that induce guilt over anger or sexual expression, regardless of the degree or situation, may become exaggeratedly fearful of expressing himself.

Since complex neurotic factors contribute to the guilt of such children, there is no simple relationship between punishment and the alleviation of their guilt. One thing that can be said for most of them, however, is that although they may want more punishment for their "transgressions," they generally do better receiving less.

Fantasized guilt. Another form of inappropriate guilt is fantasied self-blame: the child fancies himself to be responsible for an event he is in no way responsible for. Associated with the ideas of wrongdoing are profound feelings of worthlessness: "What a terrible person I am for what I have done."

Whereas in the previously described form of inappropriate guilt there is indeed a "transgression" (but the individual magnifies the gravity of it), in this form there has been no actual "wrong" (but the individual fantasizes that there was one). Here delusional elements of varying degree are operative. For example, the child who believes that his parents got a divorce because he was "bad" believes this, in part, because implicit in the idea "It's my fault" is the notion of control. Such a child will often promise that he will "be good" in order to effect a reconciliation. The guilt then is a delusion; a belief of responsibility when there is none. That the child may have been "bad" at times is certainly true. But that there is a cause and effect relationship between his being bad and his parents' divorce is not. In depressions (much more common in adults than in children), the self-denigration in the individual's guilt may be a manifestation of hostility that is displaced from someone else to himself. The masochistic person may develop fantasies of guilt in order to get punishment—that being the only way he feels he can get others to involve themselves with him.

As the reader can appreciate, fantasized guilt mechanisms are complicated and often require psychotherapy if they are to be alleviated. Since the feelings of wrongdoing have little or nothing to do with any real transgression but stem from other sources, punishment may not only not alleviate such guilt but may cause a perpetuation of the guilt and its associated psychological disturbance.

Diminished or absent guilt. Some children do not develop consciences in accordance with the phases I have outlined. They may have a deficiency or even an absence of guilt in many areas of functioning. In determining whether a child has such a deficiency, consideration of behavior appropriate to his age is essential. The normal seven-year-old child is expected to be restless in the classroom, to occasionally lose things, and to be somewhat sloppy. However, when he exhibits these characteristics with a frequency and to an extent that interferes with his learning (and possibly that of his classmates as well), a defect in the self-regulating inhibitory mechanisms may be present. (I say *may* be present because identical behavior may be exhibited by a child with a normal or even rigid conscience who is so overwhelmed with anxiety that he cannot control himself, although he feels quite guilty about his transgressions.)

The problem of identifying guilt defects in children is further complicated by the fact that there is no such thing as uniform and simultaneous development of guilt functions. A child, for example, may be quite aware of social proprieties when visiting the homes of others, but in his own house he may exhibit almost total disregard for the rights, feelings, and property of others. He may mercilessly taunt a sibling close to his age, but show tenderness and sensitivity to a much younger child.

When deficiencies in the guilt mechanism are present in adult life, the individual is referred to as a psychopath; in adolescence, he is called a juvenile delinquent; and in childhood, the term *adjustment reaction* or *behavior disorder* is applied. This multiple terminology is misleading because it implies different disorders when, in fact, there is a constant and primary diagnostic element: a failure in the development of internalized mechanisms that can inhibit the individual from performing acts that are considered unacceptable by significant figures in his environment.

As mentioned, the child develops a healthy guilt mechanism primarily through his identification with and emulation of his parents. If they have deficiencies (either overt or covert) he is likely to exhibit them as well. The parents, however, can, and most often do, play a more active role in inducing guilt in the child. Their aim should be that the child form an autonomous, but not overzealous, guilt system—neither too harsh nor too lenient. The balance is a tenuous one and reaching a stable middle point is difficult and probably rarely achieved. But at least the parent should have some concept of the ideal balance and attempt to attain it. For example, in my opinion, the ideal grade for a child to get in conduct is a B (or whatever his school's equivalent is for moderately good, but not perfect, behavior). Although the child with an A may be perfectly fine and free from psychopathology, he may be an overly inhibited and excessively guilty child. The child with a B is probably exhibiting a certain amount of normal rambunctiousness, natural playfulness, and a healthy (but not excessive) degree of defiance of authority, a quality vital to the advancement of civilization.

To help instill a normal degree of guilt the parents should react with a certain amount of surprise and indignation (even if it is a little bit put on) when the child exhibits such forms of antisocial behavior as stealing and lying. The most effective deterrent for the child's repeating the unacceptable act is the feared loss of parental affection. Appeals to God, the police, and other authorities (either real or fabricated) may produce excessive fear and guilt, as well as lack of trust in the parents when their duplicity is discovered. Ideally, the child should be brought to the point where he is "good" because it makes him feel good about himself and because it also makes significant figures in his milieu feel good toward him. In other words, he is good for the sake of expediency rather than adherence to some higher ethical principles. Although I believe there may be such principles, the young child is not intellectually equipped to appreciate them; and when he does appear to be reacting in compliance with them, he is usually responding to more mundane considerations (such as fear of punishment). He may be taught, for example, that it is "wrong" and cruel to hurt others. His deterring himself from doing so is not usually related to his sympathy for or empathy with the person upon whom he might inflict pain, nor is it usually related to his conviction for the validity of the "Golden Rule." Rather he refrains because if he hurts others they, or some adult authority, will hurt him in return. Although the parents should expose their children to the higher principles, they should do so in the hope that someday in the future they will be "heard" and appreciated but in the knowledge that at present the child can, at best, only *appear* to be acting in compliance with them.

6

Anger

ANGER, HOSTILITY, AND AGGRESSION

Anger—which I use synonymously with *hostility*—has two components: the psychological and the physiological. The former includes both thought (what the brain is thinking) and affect (what the brain is feeling). The physiological factor includes concomitant body reactions such as changes in blood pressure, respiratory rate, and pulse rate. The physiological constituent is certainly innate, and identical responses can be seen and measured in many animals. *Aggression* can, on the one hand, be used in a complimentary sense when it means "assertive," as in "This organization is looking for aggressive young men." On the other hand, when such aggression results in insensitivity to the feelings of others or when people are hurt, the word is definitely pejorative: "He's so aggressive, he doesn't care whom he pushes aside to get what he wants." At other times *aggression* is used as if it were synonymous with *anger* or *hostility*. Because of the confusion that this word sometimes creates, I try to avoid it and instead use *assertive*, or *self-assertive* for desirable aggression and otherwise use *anger or hostility.*

ANGER, RAGE, AND FURY

Anger has survival value in that it enhances our capacity to deal with irritations and dangers. We fight harder and more effectively when we are angry. Anger builds up when there is frustration and helplessness, and it is reduced when the irritants are removed. This same anger can help to remove noxious stimuli; but as long as the painful stimulus remains, anger will be provoked and increased—resulting in even more intense emotional reactions. This can best be described with an example and associated paradigms:

A man gets a splinter in his finger and removes it quickly. He feels better.

Noxious stimulus + Removal

↓

Pleasurable relief of pain

If the splinter is too deep for him to remove it with his own fingernails, the man feels frustrated.

Noxious stimulus + Inability to remove it

↓

Frustration

The frustration serves to stimulate increased efforts to remove the noxious stimulus. He gets a pair of tweezers, takes out the splinter, and then feels all right.

Frustration + Early removal of noxious stimulus

↓

Pleasurable relief of pain + Cessation of frustration

If he cannot find a pair of tweezers, his frustration increases and he gets angry: "This God-damn splinter is painful. Where the hell's a pair of tweezers?"

Frustration + Continual inability to remove noxious stimulus

↓

Anger

So angered, he is mobilized to act further. He goes next door, borrows a pair of tweezers from his neighbor, and takes out the splinter.

Anger + Removal of noxious stimulus
↓
Pleasurable relief of pain + Cessation of anger

Suppose his neighbor has a pair of tweezers, but refuses to lend them. The pain and anger continue, and now there are additional feelings of helplessness. His anger changes to rage—the feeling that comes with profound impotence over removal of a chronic noxious stimulus.

Anger + Prolonged impotence in removing a noxious stimulus
↓
Rage

The rage reaction has a purpose. It's a last ditch stand. With it, irrational things are done that are in the service of removing the noxious stimulus, but that are often misguided. He rants and becomes abusive. Even if the neighbor then gives him a pair of tweezers, he suffers consequences such as embarrassment and the need to make apologies. The anger reaction is coordinated and directed toward a specific goal. The rage reaction is more chaotic and is less likely to be effective. Even when it is, the slate is usually not then wiped clean. There are often untoward side effects after its utilization.

Rage + Removal of noxious stimulus
↓
Pleasurable relief of pain + Untoward side effects

Fury is sometimes used to describe a degree of rage in which the inappropriate reaction reaches psychotic proportions, whereas rage is more typically neurotic. The enraged man with the splinter, who then rampages through his neighbor's house attacking and possibly even killing his neighbor, would be considered to be in a fury. The rage has been so deranging that he has become psychotic.

Rage + Prolonged exposure to noxious stimulus
↓
Fury

We do best for our children by teaching them to remove noxious stimuli at the earliest possible time. The more disturbed the child, the greater the likelihood that he is not effectively dealing with noxious stimuli early enough and that he is harboring unexpressed anger, rage, and even fury.

ANGER INHIBITION

Since life inevitably exposes us to noxious stimuli, anger is ubiquitous. However, the survival of society depends on a significant degree of anger inhibition. Over the millennia man has evolved various systems for protecting himself from those whose unbridled expression of anger would endanger him. The most widely efficacious system is guilt. It is very efficient because the individual deters himself from performing the hostile act, and others need be less guarded. Shame and punishment have also been utilized, with varying degrees of success, in inhibiting angry expression.

Since murder, the extreme expression of hostility, is such an irreversible destructive act, society has had to utilize the most powerful mechanisms to prevent its unbridled expression. Religions have long been of service in providing ways to help man inhibit emotions and actions that are potentally dangerous to himself and others, and religious methods have relied heavily on the guilt mechanism. Yet however helpful the guilt deterrent has been, I believe that it has been misapplied, misdirected, and overused. Since anger can lead to rage, then fury, and then murder, many religions have interdicted all the milder forms of anger as a safety measure against the expression of the violent forms. This is somewhat like banning the use of fire because it can get out of hand or prohibiting the production of electrical power because occasionally someone gets electrocuted. Fire and electricity are certainly useful and so is anger. It need not be lethal.

Anger must be harnessed and used to help deal with life's frustrations. Children must not be taught that there are good folk somewhere who are never angry. Nor must they be filled with guilt over the angry feelings that they inevitably have.

The children I see in my practice are products of this heritage, and it is no surprise that problems involving the expression of anger are common, if not the most common. My experience has been that children's stories and fantasies are concerned more with anger than any other theme. The previously discussed studies of Ames, Pitcher, and Prelinger [4,5] of the Gesell Institute (see Chapter 4) similarly found anger to be the predominant theme in the stories elicited from schoolchildren.

Such findings are not surprising. The child is continually exposed to frustrations. He is bombarded with "Don't do this" and "Don't do that" "Don't touch this" and "Don't go there." No surprise then that he suffers many frustrations and resentments. Yet he cannot overtly express these feelings for fear of invoking even further criticism from his parents, especially if they believe that he should not be having any angry reactions to their restrictions. He can neither flee nor fight, and so he develops one or more maladaptations : he denies and represses his anger (with the help of his minister and Sunday School teacher); he sublimates it, *i.e.*, channels it into socially acceptable outlets (plays "war"); he displaces it (hits his brother); he releases it vicariously (watches horror stories on television); and he mentally projects it onto others ("It's his fault." "Kids always pick on me."). His dreams and fantasies symbolically allow release of his anger and are a powerful and effective form of substitutive gratification because no one can stop him from having them. They are things he truly has all to himself.

THE NIGHTMARE

The analysis of a nightmare can serve as a useful model for understanding many of the child's hostility fantasies and stories. In the typical nightmare the child is fearful that a malevolent figure (a robber, a monster, etc.) will enter his room. Usually the intruder comes in from a window or closet or from under the bed. I believe that the interloper is the incarnation of the child's unacceptable angry impulses that have been relegated to the unconscious. At night, when other distracting stimuli are removed, the pent-up hostilities of the day, which continually press for expression, are attended to. Daytime activities such as sports, sibling fights, and television, which have provided some release of hostility, are no longer available. At night, residual hostility from unresolved daytime frustrations pressure for release. In the nightmare, the symbolic derivatives of the child's anger (the robber, etc.) press for expression into the child's conscious awareness (symbolized by the child's room). The greater the child's guilt over his anger, the more it will be repressed. The urgency for release becomes correspondingly greater, as does his fear of the anger symbols when they threaten to erupt into conscious awareness. Up to a point, the more guilt-ridden the child, the more frightening the nightmare. When the guilt is extremely great, however, even the symbolic incarnations will be repressed, and the child will be "protected" from his nightmares—and this vehicle for release of anger will then no longer be available to him.

In addition, the malevolent figures can represent the child's hostility projected outward (they are outside his room), or they can symbolize hostile elements within significant figures (such as his parents). When the frightening figure threatens to abduct the child, then the dream may reflect separation anxieties. The nightmare, like all dreams, is rich in meaning, and many elements contributing to its formation are beyond the scope of this book to discuss in detail. Central to it, however, are the child's *own* repressed hostilities; and the fears the child experiences during the dream are most commonly of his *own* anger.

MALADAPTIVE EXPRESSION OF ANGER

In seeking to dissipate his anger, man often employs maladaptive mechanisms. This is especially true of the anger-fight reaction. When confronted by an enemy, for example, he may drop to his knees and pray to unseen forces for help. Or he may direct his anger at friends who could be of assistance to him in defending himself. Sometimes he displaces his anger upon inanimate objects (such as a nearby tree or wall), or he may totally deny the existence of anger within himself by repressing it and pretending nothing is threatening. He may direct it toward symbols of the enemy (voodooism), or he may sublimate his anger and discharge it through sports and artistic endeavors if the danger is not immediately life-threatening. He may in some cases direct his anger toward himself and commit suicide.

One of Freud's important contributions was to define the relationship between repressed emotions and psychiatric disturbance; and, partially because of the widespread awareness of his work, sophisticated adults today appreciate the importance of expressing their feelings, both positive and negative. However, in spite of our new insights, many still have a somewhat misguided attitude about anger. Psychiatrists and psychologists have, unfortunately, played no small part in bringing this about. The problem, basically, lies not so much in encouraging the *expression* of anger, but in our failure to direct attention to its *aim*.

In recent years the advice to express anger when one feels it has become so widespread that it is almost a cliché. Presumably, once the angry feelings are released, one will no longer feel angry. The account executive whose client is making his life miserable is encouraged by the members of his encounter group to hit pillows. If there is any discussion about his working out the problem with the client directly, it is usually of minor consideration. "Shout . . . scream . . . rant," he is told. "Let it out! More! More ! More!" As he nears exhaustion, the group expects that he has "gotten it out of his system" and that his loving feelings are now free to reveal themselves. Little is said about the fact that within a few hours he will once again be in exactly the same situation that provoked the anger in the first place.

It is far more constructive, in my opinion, to direct anger toward more specific goals. As I have said, anger is best expressed in its early phases, before, through the process of continued suppression, it builds up into rage. My advice to the beleaguered account executive would be to stop wasting his time and energy hitting pillows and instead confront his client in the earliest stage of irritation, or at least at a time when he is not so angry that he can't think clearly. He should express his feelings with a single objective in mind : changing the situation that angers him. The changes he requests may not be feasible; he may even have to turn the account over to someone else as a last resort. But in either event, he will then genuinely no longer be angry about that particular situation.

Not all noxious stimuli are external, however. When the source of frustration, for example, is a low feeling of self-worth that a situation produces in an individual, then expressing the anger externally is futile. If A feels worthless because B inappropriately deems him so, the problem will not be resolved by A getting B to change his opinion, but rather by A coming to appreciate that he is not necessarily what B considers him to be. These internal noxious stimuli are often more complex and difficult to remove than the external and may require intensive treatment if they are to be effectively dealt with. But the same principle still holds regarding their relationship to frustration and anger.

One of the purposes of therapy is to help the patient avoid utilizing maladaptive reactions to anger. He is encouraged to use his anger efficaciously to deal with threatening situations and noxious stimuli. In a similar manner we owe it to our children to teach them effective and appropriate utilization of their anger—both by instruction and by personal example. We must teach them to remove irritants at the earliest possible time. We must help them appreciate that there are times when their efforts will be successful, and then they will no longer feel angry. There will be times, however, when they will not be successful. Then, they must be taught to resign themselves to their failures and to seek substitutive gratifications. W. C. Fields is said to have put such advice admirably : "If at first you don't succeed, try, try again. If after that, you still don't succeed, Fuck it ! Don't make a damn fool of yourself." The message is a wise one and is the kind of advice most of us do not follow as much as we should.

PARENTAL ANGER TOWARD ONE ANOTHER OR OTHER ADULTS.

"We never fight in front of the children."   Parents who subscribe to this theory believe that displays of hostility toward one another will frighten the child and may undermine his security. A facade of marital bliss must be maintained if the child is to be psychologically stable. Some believe that the child must not be privy to parental discord

lest he interpret the fighting to mean that his parents will break up. Others hold that the child will respect his parents less if he observes them to be engaged in battle.

It is hard to imagine two people living together whose needs so dove-tail, whose desires toward one another are so predictably met that they never experience frustration and irritation with one another. My experience has been that when a couple states that they have been married a number of years and have never had a fight, inquiry invariably reveals either significant inhibitions on the part of one or both in the expression of anger or such uninvolvement with one another that the term *marriage* is hardly an appropriate name for the relationship. People in these categories are likely to transmit their pathological forms of interaction to their children.

If the parents are indeed successful in hiding their fighting from their children, they deprive them of the opportunity to observe effective self-assertion and anger expression and may thereby contribute to their children's development of anger inhibition problems similar to those exhibited by the parents. In the waiting period between the time of provocation and the fight, the children may sense the suppression of anger, and this can foster similar suppressions in them. Many parents naively believe that their children are not aware of their arguments when, in fact, they overhear every word. In the heat of battle we somehow fail to recognize that only a completely deaf person would not hear what is going on, but the child's silence is considered confirmation that he is not hearing. Actually it may stem from his curiosity. He dare not say a word lest he miss something. Or it may stem from fear, withdrawal, or "tuning the parents out." The child who does overhear the fighting is generally getting healthier exposures than the one who doesn't. The former may at least be learning something about the effective use of anger, whereas the latter is deprived of such healthy experiences.

"I know we don't need a new vacuum cleaner, but I didn't know how to say 'no' to the man." The parent who cannot effectively assert himself with others outside the home or who cannot protect himself from being taken advantage of by outsiders also serves as a poor model for the child. The mother who is easy prey to the door-to-door salesman or who does not speak up when overcharged teaches similar inhibition to her children. The father who stands by and lets others push in line ahead of him or who passively permits himself to be taken advantage of should expect his child to exhibit similar passivity. Although there are times when the issue is too trivial to argue over, the inhibited parent may excessively use this argument as a justification for inaction. Declaring

the issue "too small to make a fuss over" can be a way of avoiding the anxiety the parent would feel if he were to assert himself.

"Did you hear what happened to old man Burke? The idiot electrocuted himself with his electric hedge shears." Some parents express inappropriate and exaggerated hostility through insensitivity to the harm and suffering that may befall others. Some go even further and react to such calamities with humor. Although making light of someone else's tragedy is common and can serve to lessen one's anxiety over it, these parents utilize the humor mechanism much more for its value as a hostility releaser than as an anxiety alleviator. The highlight news at the dinner table may be a detailed description of an automobile accident in which the gory details are dwelled upon with an attitude of morbid fascination and mockery of the injured party's ineptitude—without a trace of compassion or sympathy for his plight. Such behavior may contribute to the child's developing similar attitudes, and he may thereby become markedly handicapped in his ability to form meaningful, benevolent involvements with others. The ability to feel compassion and to be able to place oneself in the position of another is central to what we call intimacy in human relationships. Parents who lack these abilities, in part because they are submerged under their overwhelming hostility, cannot engender these vital feelings in their children.

"And then my father called my mother a witch and then she called him a son of a bitch." The general principle I believe we should try to encourage our children to follow is that one should try to resolve differences of opinion in the most rational and civilized manner. Calm deliberation should be the first approach. When this fails, angry feelings may arise; and these, when mild, can serve to enhance one's motivation and effectiveness in settling the issue. It is far more effective to use polite words as vehicles for hostile expression than to use vulgarity. However, it is only human to be carried away at times and to slip into using more primitive and generally less effective language. Physical force should be reserved for rare situations when all else fails and then only either in self-defense or when the threat is truly grave. Generally, the greater the anger, rage, and fury elements, the greater the impotency and the less organized and efficient the attack. Martin Luther King and Mahatma Gandhi were ultimately far more effective with their deliberated passive resistance as a mode of anger expression than haranguers like Fidel Castro and Adolf Hitler.

The younger the child, the less appreciative he can be of these subtle distinctions, and the less capable he is of utilizing the more sophisticated levels of hostile expression. The ideals, however, should be presented to him in a language appropriate to his age and level of comprehension. The parents who occasionally use vulgarity with one another in their altercations (and this applies to most) should communicate to the child that they are not proud of themselves for having resorted to more primitive modes of handling anger, but that no one can be expected to handle every situation in the ideal manner. They should express the hope that the child will most often be able to settle his differences by more civilized methods, but at the same time they should allow him the opportunity to accept the fact that he, like all humans, cannot be expected to handle every situation in the most mature manner and that occasional lapses into the more uncivilized modes of anger expression are expected and not significantly reprehensible.

The parents, however, who use vulgarity with one another as a matter of course—who resort frequently to screaming fits and hysterical outbursts, who spew verbal venom at the slightest provocation—cannot but foster similar maladaptive modes of handling hostility in their children. Like the parent who, while smoking, warns his children about its hazards, such parents cannot effectively discourage their children from inappropriate use of vulgarity.

"My father gave my mother a black eye after she threw a dish at him." In some homes physical violence is the traditional mode of hostile expression. The child grows up with the notion that this is the way all people act. He tends to generalize from his experiences in his home and assumes that what he observes there is the pattern elsewhere. It is no surprise then that he ultimately uses similar methods of expressing hostility in his relationships outside the home. That is the way he was brought up, and that is the way he expects people to act.

Other factors besides simple imitation of parents may contribute to the child's use of these most primitive methods of hostility release. Parents who are so angry that they are frequently violent with one another are less likely to be giving their children enough affection. The latter, as a result of their deprivation, become angry and are therefore more prone to be violent. The feelings of inferiority and inadequacy resulting from such rejection may produce in the child the feeling that he is really not good enough to get anything better than scorn and maltreatment from others. It is as if he reasons, "It is better to be mistreated than to be totally ignored." Such reasoning may contribute to the formation of a sadomasochistic personality disorder in which the individual comes to consider the infliction of pain (either physical or psychological) to be the proof of one's affection.

PARENTAL ANGER TOWARD THE CHILD

"Anyone who hates children and dogs can't be all bad." This comment, generally attributed to W. C. Fields, reflects both the inferior status to which children have been traditionally relegated and their use as targets for adult hostility. The child is a most convenient scapegoat. He is too small to adequately protect himself from adult assault, and he is too dependent on his parents and other grownups to flee their attacks. One's pent-up anger can be safely released on one's children without significant fear of retaliation from either the child or others. (Although in extreme cases of child abuse society may intervene, the legal and other practical complications of such intervention are so formidable that only a small percentage of severely maltreated children are so protected.) All sorts of suppressed resentments can be taken out on one's children. Mother will feel better about the endless irritations that housework inevitably produces in her after a screaming bout with the kids. Father's pervasive anger resulting from his dissatisfaction with his career and life situation can be lessened by periodic outbursts at his children. And one need not wait long for the child to do something to justify such adult release. The principle was well portrayed a number of years ago by a popular magazine cover that featured a series of four pictures. The one in the upper left showed a man being yelled at by his boss. He is silent and fearful. In the picture at the upper right was the same man, now at home, screaming vehemently at his wife. In the lower right the wife was shown, shouting at her son. And in the lower left, the boy was seen screaming at his dog. (I, at the time, thought that it would have made an interesting addition to include a fifth picture depicting the dog tripping the boss—thereby completing the cycle.) The sequence describes a universal phenomenon. We let out our anger when and where it is safe. And our children are the safest targets. They can't fire us from our jobs. They can't fight back too effectively. People without children are deprived of this rarely mentioned advantage of parenthood.

"My daughter is turning into a tramp." The process of denying qualities within ourselves that we consider unacceptable can more effectively be accomplished by criticizing them when they appear in others. The sexually inhibited mother may react to her teen-age daughter's emerging sexuality by vociferously condemning her for every manifestation of sexual expression, no matter how safe and innocent. In addition, the mother may project onto her daughter her own unconscious sexual impulses, which she is too guilty to admit into conscious awareness; and she may thereby see the youngster as more sexually involved than she is.

It is as if the mother were saying, "I don't harbor such loathsome thoughts and feelings. She does." Each denunciation of the *daughter* serves to strengthen the mechanism by which the mother denies *her own* sexuality and thereby assuages the guilt she has over her sexual impulses. By punishing her daughter she is, by substitution, punishing herself and may thereby further diminish her guilt. Another element that may contribute to the mother's censure is her jealousy (either conscious or unconscious) of her daughter's sexual freedom without attendant responsibility. Intrinsic to jealousy is resentment, and strict adherence to religious or moral principles may serve to justify the mother's hostile release. All these mechanisms may be operative in producing the feeling in the mother that her daughter is "turning into a tramp," and they may result in the youngster being exposed to false accusations, humiliations, and diatribes.

"Just because you go to college, you think you're smarter than your parents." Parental jealousy of children is common and was described in detail in Chapter 1. It can be a significant source of parental hostility toward the child. The further the child exceeds a parent in those pursuits that both value, the greater the parent's jealous resentment may be—gratifications over the child's accomplishments notwithstanding. Parents who have been frustrated in their desires for higher education will, at some level, resent their child for attaining one, even though they may have been instrumental in his having gone to college and even though his accomplishment may be a great source of pride and vicarious gratification for them. Their resentment of him may be released through berating comments such as "Just because you go to college, you think you're smarter than your parents." Or the parent may express his jealousy by failing to appropriately compliment the child on his attainments. Other parents may actively demean the accomplishment: "When I was a kid, football *really* was a sport. Those big Polish guys from the Pennsylvania coal mining country were really players to contend with. They don't have guys like that these days."

"He takes after his father—the same stubborn streak, the same laziness." A number of years ago I was asked to see an eight-year-old girl who was admitted to the hospital because of slow physical growth, which was considered by the pediatrician to have a psychological basis. At the time of the girl's delivery the mother, who had been expecting to give birth to only one child, was openly upset when told that she was soon to deliver a second. The patient, the second child, was identical to her sister. When the mother saw her, her first thought was, "This one looks like my husband, the other one seems to be more like my side of

the family." From that time on, the two were treated differently. The sister was mother's favorite and was doted upon, whereas my patient would be left to cry for hours without her mother's responding. When older, my patient was punished for the most minor infraction while her sister could do no wrong. Over the years both girls were seen at the hospital for periodic checkups, routine inoculations, and minor illnesses. The hospital records revealed an ever increasing disparity in their height, weight, and general physical condition. By the time I saw them, at age eight, my patient was five inches shorter and fifteen pounds lighter than her sister. She appeared wan and lifeless; her sister was happy and blossoming. Socially, my patient was described as having no friends and spending most of her free time watching television. The sister was gregarious and sought after by peers. In school, my patient had always done very poorly although she never had to repeat a grade. The sister, on the other hand, had always done well. Intelligence tests done at the time of my consultation revealed my patient to have an IQ a full twenty points lower than her sister. My interviews with the parents revealed the mother to have deep-seated feelings of resentment toward her husband that were rarely expressed to him but were clearly being displaced onto her second-born girl. Although this example is dramatic, it clearly demonstrates the way hostility can be displaced onto a child and how devastating its effects can be.

"*A zadeh you call a 'shithead'*? Fuck you!" The story is told about a pious old Jewish grandfather (a zadeh, pronounced *zay-dah*) who repeatedly implored his grandson Hymie to come into the house, and each time his requests were ignored. Eventually, the grandfather threatened, "Hymie, if you don't come into the house this minute, I'll punish you." Finally, Hymie responded, "Shut up, shithead!" To which the indignant grandfather replied, "A zadeh you call a 'shithead'? *Fuck you*!" The humor here lies in the unexpected rudeness of the boy and the unanticipated response of the religious old man. Children are not supposed to be disrespectful of their grandparents, and zadehs are just not expected to use profanity, especially not to their grandchildren.

I will confine myself here to the question of adults using profanity to children. Once again, the ideal should be that the adult handle difficulties with a child so early and so effectively that he does not build up the kind of anger that results in using vulgarity. However, it is unrealistic to expect ourselves to be invariably successful in this regard. Occasional expressions of inappropriate language to a child can help him appreciate that the adult has his flaws and, in addition, enables him to observe someone getting his anger out of his system. One could even argue that the child is not very much influenced by cool and logical demands and warnings. He is more impressed by the dramatic. Raising one's voice often gets results when calmer methods fail. Shouting lets the child know that the adult is serious and means business. If the use of vulgarity is rare, then it can serve to impress the child with the seriousness of the adult's intentions. If used indiscriminately, however, the child will not take the profanity seriously, and it will lose its effectiveness.

"The first thing you have to do is attract his attention." This principle is well described in the anecdote about the farmer who owned an unusually stubborn mule. In seeking advice from friends about how he could overcome his animal's recalcitrance, he was finally referred to a man named Jed who had established the reputation of being particularly effective with such critters. On his arrival Jed was brought to the mule who was standing stiffly in the field, adamantly refusing to budge. Jed walked around his "patient" a few times, silently deliberating how he was going to handle this "case." After a few minutes he went to his truck and returned with a club. Taking a secure position in front of the animal, he looked him straight in the eyes, raised the club, and then bore down on the mule's skull with all his might. The farmer was distraught, angrily accused Jed of cruelty to dumb animals, and asked him why he had done such an inhumane thing. Calmly Jed replied, "The first thing you have to do is to attract his attention." With children as well, there are times when we may have to resort to some dramatic act, such as a loud and angry shout (not a blow, however), to "attract their attention."

THE CHILD'S ANGER TOWARD THE PARENT

"He has the worst temper tantrums. They can drive you crazy." The temper tantrum is the toddler's natural mode of response to frustration. Not having yet developed more sophisticated and precise methods of communication, the child resorts to this generalized and dramatic act that is bound to attract attention to his frustrations and irritations. An occasional reaction of this kind is normal and expected, especially in response to a provocation that justifies, in the child's mind, an angry response on his part. For example, the three-year-old whose parents leave him at home while taking his older siblings to a theatrical performance may need a wild outburst to release his resentment over what he sees to be cruel rejection and abandonment. The best response to such a flare-up is to calmly proceed to leave, squelching all the while the guilt that may be engendered by the child's crying and at the same time desensitizing oneself to the blood curdling shrieks. Calmly reassuring the child that when he is older he too will be allowed to attend the theatre may par-

tially assuage parental guilt but has little effect on the child. Living as he does in the present, he has minimal appreciation of future events and can derive little if any gratification or solace from anticipating them. In addition, while in the midst of a temper tantrum, he cannot be particularly receptive to any verbal communication—reassuring or otherwise. If, during the tantrum, there is some danger of damage to limb or property, the child should be carried or forcibly removed to a place where he can rant and thrash in safety. With this approach, tantrums should be infrequent.

Tantrums become a problem when the child learns that they have manipulative value. This occurs when (1) the tantrum occurs in response to the denial of inappropriate requests and (2) the parent submits to the child's demands in order to avoid the temper outburst. For example, the three-year-old may come to appreciate that a temper tantrum thrown in a crowded store will predictably result in his mother's buying him a toy. Allowing such a pattern to become established can be expensive, deprives the child of the opportunity to learn about frustration tolerance, and enhances the likelihood that the temper tantrums will be used as a manipulative device elsewhere. Such a pattern can only be broken by the mother's gritting her teeth and bodily carrying the shrieking child out of the store—all the while desensitizing herself to the critical thoughts she knows are going through the minds of her observers.

"I can't stand to see him so angry at me." This attitude toward the child's anger was discussed in greater detail in Chapter 1. It will suffice here to say that some parents live by the dictum "If he is angry at me, I must be abominable." The principle is adhered to even when the anger is totally unreasonable and even when it is the irrational anger of a child. In some families a somewhat masochistic mother, for example, may allow herself to be manipulated by her husband into being the sole disciplinarian. With this maneuver he can delude himself into believing that he has his children's full devotion—reasoning that they will never be angry at him if he never punishes them. This "good guy" is doing no one any favors—neither his wife, his children, nor even himself. His fear of anyone's anger does not help his children learn to tolerate it in others. He creates for them an unrealistic image of what human beings are really like, thereby making it more difficult for them to have reasonable expectations about others regarding angry reactions to what they do. And, his maltreatment of his wife cannot but produce hostilities in her that are being repressed or displaced; otherwise she would not be letting herself be so utilized. Lastly, parents who cannot tolerate anger in the

child, or in anyone else, may not recognize the fact that, no matter how hard they try, there will always be someone who will not only be unappreciative of them but even dislike them intensely. They maintain the notion, derived from childhood, that they can be loved by everybody in the world. Because their feelings of self-worth are so dependent upon the perpetual good will of others, they will resort to practically any maneuver to reduce their experience of others' anger.

Children will recognize early such parental hypersensitivity to anger and will learn to use it as a valuable manipulative device. Their most unreasonable demands may be complied with if they threaten the parent with any angry display. They become indulged, overprotected, and "spoiled." They grow up poorly prepared to relate to others in the world, who are not so fearful of their anger and not so quick to indulge their every whim.

"I'll never get used to his long hair. From the back he looks just like a girl." One of the unknown heroes of our times is the person who invented long hair for boys. Of all the ways in which an adolescent can rebel against authority and establish for himself a sense of difference from the older generation, growing long hair is certainly one of the most innocuous. Of course, there are youngsters who cannot settle for this harmless form of defiance and may resort to more dramatic forms such as drug abuse, illegal acts, and pregnancy. When one considers these alternatives he can appreciate how indebted we are to the initiator of the long hair craze, the value of which is dependent upon parental disapproval or, even better, disgust.

When the long hair trend began in the mid 1960's, adolescents could predictably rely on parental revulsion and derive thereby the full benefits of their nonconformity. During the late 1960's, when the fad had its greatest value as a parental irritant, I advised parents that they do best for their youngster by vociferously expressing their disgust and embarrassment (if that is what they honestly felt) but to be sure that under no circumstances should they prohibit their sons from growing their hair long. I recall one father who did not heed this advice and the results were most unfortunate. His long-haired boy was in therapy for frequent lateness to school and little interest in his classwork. After the boy had continuously refused to cut his hair, the father brought him to a barber and held him down while his hair was cut to traditional length. Following this, the boy completely refused to go to school, became much more recalcitrant at home, and stopped treatment as well. I am not claiming that the forceful cutting of the boy's hair was the sole cause of his deteriorated psychological state—only that it was a contributing factor. Psychologically he felt emasculated and dehumanized and reacted with irrational and self-destructive rage.

It was also during the late '60's that I described how, if the principal or headmaster of a high school was genuinely revolted by the style, he would do best for his students by taking frequent opportunity to decry the new hair style, complain about his difficulty in distinguishing the boys from the girls, but at the same time have no rules prohibiting the boys from wearing their hair long. By the early 1970's the custom enjoys widespread acceptance and has even been taken on by adults—so it is rapidly losing its value as a mode of adolescent rebellion. Because the need for such devices is deep, there is little question that something new will soon be devised. Whatever it turns out to be, parents would be well-advised to react in accordance with the principles I have presented here.

"Who do you think you're talking to? Your mother?" When I attended New York City's Bronx High School of Science in the mid 1940's, there was a gym teacher who, in addition to his usual duties as physical education instructor and teacher of health classes, was the school disciplinarian. In this capacity he was required to keep order each morning when the students congregated in the auditorium awaiting classes to begin. Generally, he stood on the stage with a thick pole in his hand. When things would get particularly disorderly (which happened about once every three minutes or so), he would thump the stick and gruffly demand a return to order and quiet. And when someone was particularly discourteous or sassy to him, his traditional reply was, "Who do you think you're speaking to? Your mother?"

There is great wisdom in these words. A child will say things to his mother that he wouldn't dare utter to a teacher, principal, or others in a position of authority. He recognizes that the repercussions for indiscreet language to such adults are graver than for identical comments made to his mother. Up to a point, such an attitude is healthy. The child should have the basic feeling that his mother will react less punitively than outsiders to his misbehavior. When, however, a mother is ineffective in commanding some degree of restraint on the child's part, he may be impaired in learning to make the proper distinctions regarding what he can say to people in the various categories he will encounter. He may then find himself in trouble with people like my old gym teacher.

"To a zadeh you say, 'Fuck you'?" Although the punch line may sound the same, this is an entirely different zadeh joke. While driving his busload of tourists through the Lower East Side of Manhattan, the guide expounded: "We are now passing through the Lower

East Side of Manhattan. Since the middle of the nineteenth century this section of the city has been a settling place for newly arrived immigrants from European countries such as Poland, Russia, Ireland, Italy, Austria, Hungary, and others. People of many religious persuasions have lived here. Generally, the newcomers have tended to keep their old-world customs, but their children have usually taken on American ways and gone on to other parts of the city and the country. In recent years Puerto Rican immigrants have settled here as well as many blacks who have come up from the South. Although this region has often endured poverty and great human suffering, the descendants of these immigrants stand among the great builders and leaders of our nation.

It is here that we can see many who still adhere to their old-world customs. Look over there, for example; we see an old long-bearded Jewish man wearing the traditional long black frock coat and wide-brimmed hat. The book in his hand is no doubt a religious one, and it is likely that he is well versed in the Talmud and other great works of Jewish wisdom. We see him leaning over and talking to a young boy, possibly his grandson. Notice also that the boy, although only seven or so, is also wearing similar clothing, and his hair is curled down at the sides in the traditional fashion of the orthodox Jews. The old man may very well be imparting to the youngster some sage advice, something he has garnered from the written accumulations of human wisdom. Let us stop here and listen. Perhaps we too can learn from this wise old man." At this point the eagerly listening tourists hear, "To a zadeh you say, '*Fuck you*'?"

The old man's surprise and indignation reflect the notion, strongly subscribed to in every culture I have heard of, that it is grossly inappropriate and disrespectful for a child to swear at an adult. Adults on the other hand, although they may admit that it is somewhat improper to use profanity to children, do so with impunity. I doubt if there was ever a child who didn't say to himself at some time or other, "He can curse at me all he wants to, but I can't curse at him. It's not fair." The child's resentment over this inegalitarian situation is justified.

I believe that the parental indignation stems, in part, from traditional attitudes toward anger. Since vulgarity is often (but not always) an expression of intense anger, it is squelched because of the parent's misguided ideas about the dangers of anger expression. The child's hateful words are particularly unbearable to the insecure parent or the one in whom there is some deficiency of affection for the child. Such parents do not feel that they have, or do not in fact have, the strong reservoir of loving feelings that would enable them to better tolerate unloving feelings directed toward them. The healthy parent recognizes that the child's feelings toward him are ambivalent, just as his are toward the child. He communicates to the child that it is normal and expected that he will on occasion harbor even the most vile thoughts toward his parents. He allows the child angry expression when appropriate and, although interdicting the use of profanity toward a parent, recognizes that the child, like the adult, will at times use it toward him. An appropriate response to such profanity might be, "I can see how that makes you angry. But you still can't talk that way to me. That's the kind of language for you and your friends out in the street." He adheres to no double standard, and admits that his occasional use of profanity to the child, although expected, is as reprehensible as the child's toward him.

There is another argument, which I have not yet mentioned, for instilling a certain amount of inhibition in the utilization of vulgarity. If profanity were to be freely accepted, it would lose much of its psychological charge and thereby its effectiveness as a discharger of hostility. If all the presently unacceptable words were to become acceptable and openly used in any and all situations, new ones, I am sure, would have to be devised to continue to provide us with this safe mode of hostility release. We therefore do our children a disservice if we allow them full expression of socially unacceptable words. Fortunately, those parents who do allow their children such free expression find that the child's exposures to others outside the family provide him with the necessary degree of emotional charge for these words to still enable him to use them as effective releasers of anger.

ANGER WITHIN THE CHILD AND ANGER BETWEEN CHILDREN

"You must have been very angry when the coach had you sit out the whole game on the bench." This form of parental consolation and pain assuagement has become quite common in recent years—primarily as the result of the popularization of some widely-held, but nevertheless misguided, psychological principles. Many child therapists believe that the mere expression of feelings is in itself the primary, if not the exclusive, goal of therapy and either ignore or give very little attention to appropriate utilization of these feelings. They believe that the mere labelling of the child's unexpressed feelings, in order to alleviate his guilt over them and facilitate their expression, is all that is necessary. They do not seem to appreciate that this is a good first step, but that little is accomplished if the child is not, *in addition,* encouraged to direct his

feelings toward specific goals in order to accomplish something more than mere catharsis.

For example, the mother of the boy who comes home from his Little League game upset that the coach kept him on the bench throughout most of the game is advised to say, "That must have made you very angry." If he responds, "Yeah, I felt like kicking his head in," the parent can then feel that she has been very helpful. The child has expressed his resentment, and all will then be right with the world. "The hateful feelings having been let out," we are told, "loving feelings are now free to express themselves." The child's appropriate response to such a parental comment is, in my opinion: "Of course I was angry. Wouldn't you be?" In addition, there is a patronizing quality to the mother's comment that lessens any of its possible commiserative value. For these reasons, the mother's comments can add further irritation to that which the child already harbors.

If the child is significantly inhibited in expressing his anger, the comment is not going to facilitate more guiltless release. If the child is already very much in touch with his anger, he can only be insulted by the statement; and so it is not only unnecessary but ill-advised. In both cases, the parent's comments should direct themselves to the problem that brought about the child's irritation in the first place: "Now what can you *do* so that won't happen again; so that you won't be so angry again?" Encouraging the child to talk to the coach should help. The boy might then be advised to practice more, or the confrontation may make the coach aware of his oversight. Either course should bring about an alleviation of the situation that generated the anger. If these courses of action should still prove ineffective, then the child should be helped to find other alternatives: transfer to another team, parental intervention, and so on.

"How did you feel when Gail broke your doll?" The "How did you feel when . . . ?" question, borrowed by sophisticated laymen from the psychiatric inquiry, is supposed to help a person express his feelings and thereby feel better. In recent years radio and television reporters have been using the question with the implication that learning about the interviewee's *feelings* about a particular event enriches our understanding of what has gone on. Questions of these gentlemen of the public media usually go like this: "How did you feel when you learned that your husband was still alive after being trapped three days in the caved-in coal mine?" "How did you feel when you learned that you lost the election?" "How did you feel when you first saw your son after his release from three years in a prisoner-of-war camp?" The correct answer

to these and all such similar questions is identical: "How do you think I feel you idiot? Get out of here before I hit you." Unfortunately, most people are not free enough to express this on nationwide television and so provide either the obvious answer or formulate the response that they consider will be the most acceptable to the audience.

I cannot be too critical of the layman for using this form of inquiry. He has been taught by experts in the field of psychiatry and psychology that it is a most valuable question. There is hardly a trainee in psychotherapy who is not repeatedly advised by his supervisors to "get out the patient's feelings" and that a good way to do this is to ask him, "How did that make you feel?" With rare exceptions, the question is absurd. If a person knows how he feels, he can only consider the question naive, simplistic, extraneous, or an affront. If he is so repressed that he indeed has no conscious awareness of his emotions, that question is not going to get them out. He will only respond with puzzlement, denial of feelings, a rationalization, or he may possibly say what he thinks the therapist wants to hear.

I can best describe the kinds of questions that can be helpful in eliciting feelings from a repressed person by using a clinical example. A thirty-year-old woman who was once in therapy with me, was involved with a man who treated her with indifference and often cruelty. She rarely complained about the indignities and humiliations she suffered in the relationship. In session one day she related the following episode: "Tom told me that he might be driving past the Rialto theatre sometime Sunday afternoon; and if I wanted to get together with him, I should wait there. So I got there at about eleven-thirty in the morning, just to be sure, and waited until seven. I guess he forgot." There was not a trace of resentment in this patient as she described the experience. To have asked her how she felt would have been a waste of time. She had already told me the rationalization she had given herself to justify the repression of the anger she must have inevitably felt: "I guess he forgot." Accordingly, I responded, "That must have made you furious!" I was not surprised when she denied any irritation, and she reiterated her statement that everybody is entitled to forget. To which I incredulously replied, "I cannot believe that in all the time you were standing there, there wasn't one little thought of resentment, one little flicker of angry feeling." "Well," she answered, "now that you mention it, I did think a few times, 'Where the hell is he?' but I put those thoughts out of my mind because he's really a very nice person." By focusing on the "Where the hell is he?" comment I was able to help bring this patient in touch with some of the repressed anger she felt toward her boyfriend.

The comment would not have been elicited by the question, "How did that make you feel?" What I did was to say what I thought she must inevitably be feeling and to imply that it was the expected feeling. I reduced the guilt she felt over expression of anger and made it safe for her to admit hers.

Eight-year-old Sarah, then, who is afraid to express the anger she feels over Gail's having broken her doll, is asked by her mother, "How did you feel when Gail broke your doll?" Mother would do far better for Sarah's inhibitions to say, "Even though you're not showing it, I know that deep-down you're very angry at Gail. And I don't blame you. I'd be angry as well. Now what do you think you can do about this? If you don't do anything it might happen again." This comment not only communicates to the child that anger is the expected and socially acceptable response, but structures the situation in such a way that it is clear to the child that she must effectively express her anger if she is to avoid a repetition of the situation that provoked it. Such structuring can be far more effective than merely encouraging a child (or anyone else) to *act* in a desired fashion.

"Hardly a week goes by when he doesn't have a terrible fight on the way home from school." The parents who panic at the gory descriptions of the bloody battles their sons describe provide him with an important ego-enhancing experience. The greater the parental discomfort, the more powerful and masculine the youngster will feel. The astute parent recognizes that, while the youngster may be complaining bitterly about the pains he may have suffered during the melee, there is an accompanying sense of pride also being displayed. He is not enumerating his wounds to elicit the response, "You poor child. Come, let mommy hug you so you'll feel better." Rather he is looking for the reaction (implied, if not stated). "How I admire you for your courage in standing up to such overwhelming forces. How brave you are, how manly."

These after-school battles serve other purposes as well. They provide an outlet for the hostilities that may have been built up during the school day, hostilities for which there is no acceptable release within the school building. Boring classes, restrictive classroom situations, scapegoating teachers, and classroom bullies build up frustrations and resentments that can be discharged by "beating up" someone. Hostilities toward parents as well as hostilities stemming from internal neurotic sources can also be released in these battles. Although neurotic elements may be present in bringing about these afternoon battles, the parent should appreciate that healthy growth experiences are also occurring, even though it may be difficult at times to know where one ends and the other begins. The phenomenon is similar, I believe, to the playful fighting that puppies often engage in. There are times when one isn't sure whether they are fighting or playing, and at times there is a shift from one activity to the other.

"Nice boys don't fight." Such comments, when repeated often, can contribute to the child's inappropriate inhibition of anger expression. Parents who inculcate in their children the notion that the youngster who occasionally fights is "bad," and "not nice" contribute to his becoming inhibited in expressing resentment when he should appropriately be asserting himself and standing up for his rights. Although he may be considered a "model child" by parents and teachers, his peers may consider him a "goody-goody" or may use him as a scapegoat.

"My father can beat up your father." Life invariably contains inequalities—a situation most conducive to the development of comparison between those who have less and those who have more. The step from comparison to competition is probably culturally determined and is more likely to occur when self-worth becomes equated with possession. (I am not referring only to material possessions but to any entity, physical or characterological, that the particular society considers estimable.) Ours is certainly a fiercely competitive society, and we are taught very early in life to compare ourselves with others as a measure of our self-worth. Mothers sit for hours comparing their children's development. Fathers talk about how they bettered the next one in business, sports, etc. Both parents may speak endlessly about how superior they are to others regarding material possessions, success, benevolence, virtue, and so on. The child models himself after his parents and other significant figures in his milieu, and it is not surprising that quite early he measures his worth, in part, by how much he exceeds others: "I can throw a ball farther than you"; "I'm taller (smarter, older, heavier, prettier, etc.) than you"; "My father can beat up your father." This kind of competition is just one example of the competition that is ubiquitous in our society.

As mentioned, the hostile and competitive elements do not exist in isolation but are inextricably interconnected and reinforce one another. And losing out in the competition for mastery and success, either in reality or fantasy, naturally evokes resentment.

ANGER BETWEEN SIBLINGS

"They never seem to stop fighting, doctor." This is one of the most common complaints made by parents to the child therapist (regard-

less of the reason for referral). "We've tried everything and nothing works. What can we do?" they ask. Why is it that nothing works? I believe the reason is that sibling rivalry, with all its *Sturm und Drang,* with all the frustration and exasperation it causes parents is, in part, a manifestation of irrepressible healthy forces within the child. In most children these elements press so strongly for expression that they are exceedingly difficult to suppress. There are probably constitutional components operative in determining the extent to which the child will assert himself in the expression of his rivalrous feelings, for even at birth children differ in the degree of their assertiveness. And these congenital differences may play a role in determining how much the child is going to express himself in the rivalrous situation. However, the youngster who does not exhibit a significant degree of sibling rivalry is an inhibited child, a child who has been defeated by those around him in his struggle for self-expression.

"Don't touch that," "Stay away from that," etc. Two central elements in the sibling rivalry phenomenon are hostility and competition. I do not know whether we have an innate pool of angry impulses that would demand expression regardless of how gratifying our lives may be, but I do know that frustration ultimately results in anger. The child is exposed to continual frustration. Everywhere he goes he is told, "Don't do that," "Don't touch this," "Stay away from there," "You can't have that," etc. Even the most permissive parents frequently prohibit their children from ingesting certain substances and walking and climbing in dangerous places. Such frustrations inevitably produce hostility in the child. Quite early in life, however, he learns that anger is not the kind of emotion one can express with impunity. Society has well-defined rules governing its release, and he who breaks them may suffer dire consequences. The child learns that expressing his resentment to his parents (the source of his earliest frustrations) may result in scolding, punishment, and withdrawal of affection. And since the child is so dependent on their good will for his feelings of well-being, as well as for the necessities of life, he develops mechanisms that enable him to handle anger without fear of retribution. For example, the normal child may express his anger symbolically in fantasies and stories (those read to him as well as those he creates himself). Physical activities and temper tantrums allow for some degree of discharge. Normally, a certain amount of repression is possible, and generally some expression of anger will be displaced onto others. Adults, such as teachers, relatives, and neighbors, are poor targets because they, like his parents, have powerful methods

of retaliation. Peers are safer. However, the child is dependent on neighborhood friends for companionship, so too much release in that direction may result in painful social isolation.

"A fight a day keeps the psychiatrist away." Siblings, then, by a process of exclusion, are by far the safest targets on which the child can vent his hostilities. They are a captive audience; they cannot totally reject a child. The repercussions for venting anger on them are far less than for any of the other outlets.

There are other sources of anger as well that may be directed at a sibling. Life outside the home inevitably produces additional frustrations and resentments. Friends are never as consistently loving as we would like them to be, and "beating up" a sibling can provide the child with renewed faith in mankind. The school situation invariably has its disappointments, and the resentments it produces are often reduced through some act of cruelty toward a sibling. More complicated mechanisms may also be operative. By rigidly imposing parental rules on the sibling and mercilessly punishing him for their infraction, the child strengthens his own conscience. He may project his own unacceptable impulses onto the sibling, and by castigating him he may deny the existence of these qualities within himself. (This is a central mechanism in prejudice.)

"You always give him the biggest piece of cake." During the first few years of life, the child's dependence on his mother is so strong that he resents having to share her affection with anyone. For the firstborn child, the only rival during this phase of life is the father. When a second child appears, there is yet another person whose role seems extraneous and who vies with the child for the mother's time and attention. Regression to more infantile patterns of behavior is a common manifestation of rivalry with the new sibling. Observing that the newborn gets mother's attention by wetting, soiling, demanding the bottle, etc., the older child hopes to regain her involvement by utilizing similar maneuvers himself. As the child grows older and the father assumes increasing importance for him, siblings are looked upon as unnecessary rivals for his affection, as well as for the mother's. The healthier the home, the more love there is to go around and the less the child need complete with his siblings for parental affection. But even the most loving parents cannot satisfy the child's needs completely. Children are quite greedy when it comes to demanding love, and they never seem to have enough. (I don't think they differ very much from adults in this regard.) Accordingly, the competition is intense, although not consistently overt. No matter how giving the parents may be, the child tends to see his siblings as receiving preferential treatment, thereby inciting further com-

petition for the parents' affection. In the home where there is indeed a deprivation of parental affection, sibling rivalry becomes even more intensified.

"The oldest was always a hellion." The firstborn has only adults to identify with, whereas subsequent children identify with other children as well as parents. This is one of the reasons why firstborn children tend to be more serious and striving than their younger siblings. (The fact that the parents are less anxious about the younger children than they were about the first may also play a role in this phenomenon.) Such assertiveness may make the firstborn more prone to express his rivalrous feelings. Being the oldest also makes it safest for him to act them out. Lastly, he may have more reason to be rivalrous than subsequent children: he was "king of the world" until his siblings came along; he knew what it was like to live in paradise. The subsequent children never know what they have missed and so have less to be angry about.

"We restrain our praise of Bob because it makes Jane feel so bad." Properly moderated, competition between siblings can be useful and can serve as a stimulus for a child to emulate the attainments of a sibling—if not in the same area of endeavor, then in another for which he may be suited. In fact, healthy competition in socially constructive areas of endeavor should be encouraged in such a manner that winning doesn't become the primary aim, but rather a fringe benefit. For example, when two siblings are collecting bottles for glass recycling, the parent should try to engender the feeling of gratification that comes from performing a socially beneficial act. In addition, he can praise the child who collected the most (the children will invariably know who that was and often the exact number each has collected) to add incentive for future constructive ventures.

There are some children, however, who do not rise to such challenges. Whether or not this is due to psychological problems or intrinsic inferiorities, it should not be used as a reason for depriving those who do compete of its benefits—as long as they have been fair and ethical in the competition. The successful should not be retarded in their growth out of sympathy for or guilt over those whom they leave behind. I am not suggesting that the less accomplished be neglected; every attempt must be made to provide them with the wherewithal to compete successfully, in a healthy and just manner. I am suggesting that unrealistic theories about egalitarianism should not be used to retard the progress of the successful to protect the unsuccessful from the pains of their inferiority or failure to achieve.

"In our home, everything is shared. No one owns anything."

Designation of whose property belongs to whom contributes to the child's sense of his own personal self as distinct from others. The child, in the first few months of life, does not have an awareness of himself as discrete from the rest of the world. He must learn this—and distinguishing his property from the next person's is part of this process. The sharing experience also helps the child learn respect for the rights of others, which is accomplished not so much from any adherence to higher ethical principles, but rather from a sense of expediency. If he inhibits himself from taking advantage of others, they are more likely to show similar restraint with him.

"Billy says I'm a sneak (baby, tattletale, etc.)." The younger the child, the more he evaluates himself on the basis of his parents' views of him. As he grows older, if he is healthy, he will incorporate as well the information he has gained from others regarding his assets, liabilities, character traits, etc. Parents tend to overvalue their children and deny their defects. Siblings harbor fewer such delusions and are not famous for benevolent restraint in expressing criticism. They can, therefore, provide the child with important information about himself. The data the child collects from siblings can complement that obtained from parents—providing him with a more balanced and accurate image of himself. However, the sibling may go too far in the fault-finding direction and, if excessively critical, can undermine the child's self-esteem.

"Their fighting is a constant drain on us." The best attitude is for parents to look upon sibling rivalry as similar to the infant's 2 A.M. and 6 A.M. feedings—painful but to be tolerated out of necessity and love of the child. As a method of handling the problems of life, sibling rivalry is primitive and maladaptive, to say the least. It rests on impulsive acting out rather than appropriate action based on contemplation. It relies on violence and scapegoating as a means of coping with frustration and its resultant anger, and it too easily saps the child's energies in destructive forms of interaction with others.

In accordance with this concept of sibling rivalry I generally recommend to parents that, if the children are relatively evenly matched, they should try to let them work out their problems themselves. This involves some practice on the part of the parents in desensitizing themselves to noise and the potential destruction of property. Of course, if one of the children is continually taken advantage of, then parental intervention may be necessary. At other times the parent may want to bring about a cessation of hostilities in order to preserve his own sanity.

"Who started it?" Most often it is impossible to determine "who started," and I do not suggest that parents try to find out. Even when it

is quite clear that one child has "started" the bout under consideration, his initiation of the altercation may have been in response to the other's provocation three minutes earlier, when the parent was not present. Each child characteristically awaits the opportunity to tease and taunt the other in a never-ending cycle, making it almost unjust to select one as the culprit.

The "divide and conquer" approach is most effective in such situations. A short spell (ten to fifteen minutes) of solitary confinement is often all that is necessary for both children to "cool off." Although at times the "innocent" one will be suffering along with the "guilty" one, this tends to even out. To lessen the "innocent" one's indignation that the punishment "isn't fair," he can be told that because it is impossible to decide who was at fault both are being punished and that the time will no doubt come when the other sibling will also be unjustly punished. I do not believe that punishing an innocent child in this situation is significantly traumatic to the child or causes loss of trust in the parent. Deep down the child *knows* that, although he may truly be innocent in this particular episode, he has engaged in his share of *de novo* provocations (covert and overt) for which he has either not been punished or his sibling has been blamed. Since one is not *really* punishing a completely innocent party, one need not fear repercussions for such. The legal tradition that all men are innocent until proven guilty has little place in the child rearing process. The child who refuses to voluntarily serve out his term of social isolation may have to be warned about further disciplinary measures, but generally the above approach will work well. By working well, I mean getting the house quiet, not preventing the next bout.

"I can see how that makes you angry, but you still can't flush her fish down the toilet." I generally also suggest that the parents communicate to the child that the anger he feels toward his sibling is reasonable and expected, but he cannot be permitted to express it through physical violence, destruction of property, and other socially unacceptable maneuvers. Rather, he should be encouraged to express it in its early phase—before the frustration builds up too strongly—in a civilized fashion, with the intent of changing the irritating situation.

"Thank God we only have one child." Although parents with only one child are spared much harrowing commotion and their child may enjoy the gratifications of unrivaled parental affection and approval, he is deprived of the advantages of the sibling rivalry situation, which, I believe, far outweigh the disadvantages. The parents of the only child can overcome these drawbacks, in part, by providing the child with peer

opportunities; *e.g.,* nursery school or a day-care center and sleep-over dates with cousins and friends. Such efforts, however, are poor substitutes for the real thing. School situations are structured and repressive regarding children's fighting. And having guests is often quite artificial, for it emphasises fun and games and doesn't require the child to experience all the discomforts and inconveniences of really living together with another person.

The philosophy of anger expression that I believe parents should impart to their children and the one I have repeatedly espoused in this chapter is well stated by the poet William Blake:

> I was angry with my friend:
> I told my wrath, my wrath did end.
> I was angry with my foe:
> I told it not, my wrath did grow.[9]

---

[9] Blake, William, A Poison Tree. *The Portable Blake,* New York: The Viking Press, 1953.

7

Reward, Discipline, and Punishment

If a society is to survive it must engender in children the desire to engage in those activities that are generally in the social interest and discourage behavior that is not. The more pleasure is associated with socially acceptable behavior, the more motivated the child will be to engage in it and to repeat it. The more fear determines socially desirable behavior, the lower the motivation. For example, the child whose parents are members of a quartet that practices in his home twice weekly and who enjoy classical records as a routine rather than an event will, at an early age, want to join the fun. He craves to experience the same gratifications he observes the significant figures around him enjoying. By three he'll be trying to pluck out tunes on the piano and can be relied upon to practice assiduously if given lessons. By contrast, the child whose parents have no particular interest in music, but who think that it's "good for him" to take piano lessons, has to be reminded to practice, considers the lessons a chore, and will certainly not do well or enjoy his musical experiences.

The reward system can function much as the first family situation above in encouraging desirable behavior patterns. One child comes home from school and proudly demonstrates to his parents the fact that he has learned to write his name. The parents rejoice at the accomplishment, and the child feels proud of himself for what he has done. Another parent responds perfunctorily, or not at all; and the child, getting little or no reward, becomes ill motivated to attempt to get pleasure through scholastic pursuits. Such a child's parents may be quite interested in sports, however; and their enthusiasm may foster his involvement in that area of endeavor.

Inculcating fear into the child, although it may seem the quicker and more predictably effective way of getting the child to perform in a certain way, is far less desirable. The child who is practicing the piano with the fear that if he does not do well he will suffer the displeasure of, and even punishment from significant figures may be so tense while practicing that he may not be able to learn very much. Learning under similar circumstances in school can be equally inefficient. Such fear, when extreme, can be paralyzing, and then nothing can be accomplished. The fearful child anticipates punishment. Sometimes the punishment is subtle—in the form of parental displeasure. But it can also be more direct and overt—no TV, no allowance, spankings, etc.

Although it may be simplistic, the reward-punishment system applies to most forms of human behavior. We go to work because we enjoy the earnings; and, if we are fortunate, the work itself may be a source of personal gratification as well. Although there may be mornings when we don't feel like going, we do go for fear of losing our jobs. We may play hard at tennis for the pleasure afforded us by the physical activity, for the sense of mastery we feel in playing well, and for the ego-gratification of winning. But we play hard also from the fear of the lowered self-confidence that comes from continually losing. Whatever gratifications we may derive from a loving relationship, there are times when we inhibit ourselves from saying or doing something to our loved ones from the fear of invoking displeasure. And so it goes. Whatever other factors may be present in human behavior (and they are multiple and complex), the pain-pleasure element can usually be found. The greater the degree of pleasure, the more the individual can be relied upon to perform the act; and the greater the fear element, the more predictably he will eschew it. But even under the best of circumstances, there is always some of the fear element. Even the most dedicated student studies, at times, from the fear of failure; even the most enthusiastic pianist practices, at times, because of the fear of public embarrassment. In addition, we consider the mature person to be one who will be willing to suffer certain displeasures in the present in the service of attaining future rewards.

Fear of pain, then, is intrinsic to the human condition. The parent who says he does not believe in threatening his children with pain is out of touch with what he is doing. Even the most permissive parent inhibits his child at times. He doesn't let the child climb out the window, walk off the roof, run into traffic, ingest poisons, etc. Each time the child is inhibited from engaging in these acts, he senses the parent's displeasure with what he is doing and will deter himself, in part, not so much out of recognition of inherent danger but more out of an appreciation that repeating the behavior will result in parental disapproval. And parental censure is probably the child's most painful punishment because it produces feelings of lowered self-esteem. We do best for our children when the pleasure element is predominant and the fear of pain an insignificant factor in the acquisition of desirable behavior. But to consider the total absence of the pain element to be the ideal is unrealistic.

Although the word *discipline* can be used synonymously with *punishment*, generally *punishment* emphasizes penalty and retribution; that is, the vengeful gratification for the person *who has been wronged*. *Discipline*, on the other hand, emphasizes the educative value of the disciplinary measure to the wrong*doer*. When made aware of these distinctions, the parent may think that he should make every attempt to discipline and that if he punishes he is being primitive and possibly even injurious to his child. However, I believe that there are times to discipline a child and times to punish him. And I also believe that it is the child more than the parent who determines which shall happen. The important determinants as to which take place are (1) the speed with which the child perpetrates the unacceptable behavior and (2) the degree of anger the wrongdoing invokes in the parent. The innocent two-year-old who, while sitting on Daddy's lap, suddenly bites his father, gets punished. His father generally recoils in pain and shouts at the child. Although he may recognize that the child does not appreciate the pain he has inflicted, the father's spontaneous response is one of anger and, I believe, the desire to release it with concomitant vengeful gratification. The mother who screams at the one-year-old who spills ink or paint on her rug is certainly trying to deter the child from future repetition of the same, but is without question "letting off steam" for her own sake as well. The very young child does not deter himself from socially unacceptable behavior out of the appreciation of its effects on others, but rather because he comes to associate the act with parental censure. Children do not take subtle hints very well. To be shouted at is generally far more effective than to be told the same thing quietly. Children are much impressed by the theatrical. In addition, were a parent to suppress the anger I believe he would inevitably feel in these situations, he would be providing the child with a poor model for angry expression. If the parent is to help the child learn how to properly and healthily express his feelings he has to practice what he preaches. As George Bernard Shaw once said, "If you strike a child, take care that you strike it in anger."[10]

Discipline can be administered when the child's wrongdoing hasn't caught us from behind; when it hasn't hit us like lightning; when it hasn't produced instant rage in us. If we see Johnny walking into the living room with an open bottle of paint, we proceed "with all deliberate speed" and quickly, but delicately, take the bottle out of the child's hands. Strong verbal censure and appropriate precautionary action (putting the bottle on a high shelf) will generally prevent a repetition. If Daddy has been fortunate enough to stop the baby in the lunge phase of his biting attack, he too will be calm enough to discipline and need not punish. Both discipline and punishment have a place in child rearing, and the child who does not experience both becomes handicapped in adequately adjusting to adult society.

Although children traditionally grumble upon being disciplined and react with tears on being punished, they basically want and need these restrictions. The child whose parents do not limit him feels anxious and unprotected. If he has control over them, how much reliance can he have on their abilities to guide him and prevent him from getting into trouble? The undisciplined child is not taught to differentiate between socially acceptable and socially unacceptable behavior. Without such knowledge he becomes anxious when entering social situations because he lacks the wherewithal to prevent his rejection. Furthermore, parents who are so weak that they do not apply appropriate disciplinary restraints are poor models for the child's identification, and he may thereby grow up to be similarly impotent.

Children continually test their parents to see how far they can go in order to *learn* what the limits are. The adolescent, in particular, cannot allow himself passive compliance with parental rules because of the implied childish dependency in such submission. Still he wishes to learn and comply but may need to be forced or threatened in order to "save face." It is as if he were saying to himself (and peer observers, both real and fantasized), "Deep down I really want them to tell me what to do. But I can't ask them because then I'll look like a baby. If they force me

---

[10] Shaw, George B., *Man and Superman, Maxims for Revolutionists.*

into it, then no one can say I'm a child." One cannot have anything but respect for someone who is courageous enough to put up a good fight and then be overwhelmed by superior forces.

A fifteen-year-old girl who was once in treatment with me demonstrated this mechanism quite beautifully. She had run away from home to the East Village section of New York City. About two hours after her departure, she called her mother from the home of an older friend who had already taken up a hippie-type existence. She told her mother, "I'm never coming home again. I'm going to do just what I want. Sex, drugs, or anything else. I'm going to be a hippie and do my own thing. The only thing that'll get me back is if Dr. Gardner sends out the police to take me to Bergen Pines [the local county psychiatric receiving hospital]." The mother then called me for advice. I told her to call the girl back (the telephone number was known to the mother) and tell her that Dr. Gardner said that if she wasn't home in three hours he would call the police and have her brought to Bergen Pines. I had no such authority and the threat was a bald lie. But it was made in response to the girl's request that I give her this face-saving way of returning home. She was obviously frightened over the prospect of being away from home in a filthy neighborhood teeming with addicts, pushers, derelicts, and assorted criminals but would have been humiliated if she had had to admit her fear and her mistake. Two hours later she was home, cursing me with all the four-letter words in her vocabulary. She returned to school the next day and grumbled bitterly to her friends about the indignities she suffered at my hands.

PRINCIPLES OF DISCIPLINE AND PUNISHMENT, ADVISABLE AND INADVISABLE

In presenting the various principles I have found useful I do not claim to have exhausted them all or that each will be predictably effective for all children. Each of them has merit for many children, but none of them is going to be universally effective. Children vary, and an approach that may work for one child may not work for another. The more disturbed the child, the less the likelihood that his unacceptable behavior will change by merely instituting better modes of discipline. Such behavior is related to deeper unconscious problems that have little relationship to the kind of discipline being utilized. In addition, unless specifically stated otherwise, the suggestions made here refer to the prepubertal child. Although most of the principles discussed here are applicable to the adolescent, some are not; however, it is beyond the scope of this book to discuss in detail the often perplexing and complex problem of disciplining the teenager.

In the ensuing discussion, I will use the words *discipline* and *punishment* interchangeably. However, the reader should appreciate that when either is used, the other may apply depending upon the degree of anger the child's act has evoked in the parent. The earlier the parent has been able to intervene and the more rational the measure, the more appropriately it can be called disciplinary. On the other hand, the longer the parental irritation has been built up or the greater the parental rage the more suitable the term *punishment*.

"Let the punishment fit the crime." The child who is making too much noise at the dinner table can be told, "If you don't stop making so much noise, you'll have to leave the table and finish your meal in your room." Here, the child's noise is the irritant. By sending the child out of the room, the parent removes himself from the source of provocation and thereby lessens the likelihood that his anger will build up. The child has the living experience that when he irritates others they will reject him. The child who cheats when playing a game should be told, "Look, I'm not going to continue playing this game if you cheat. It's no fun for me when you cheat." Again, the disciplinary measure suits the transgression, and the discipliner does something to bring about a removal of his source of irritation.

Many situations, however, do not so readily lend themselves to the application of a punishment that so neatly "fits the crime." The child who is making a racket in a moving car on a family trip cannot be asked to leave the automobile. He can be told that if he doesn't stop he cannot buy any souvenirs at the next point of interest. The child who pokes someone in the eye cannot be responded to in kind. He can, however, be sent to his room for a period of social isolation and rejection.

"It's up to you." Adults are continually exposed to situations in which they are threatened with painful consequences for transgressing or not performing in ways expected of them. If you do not show up for work, sooner or later you won't be paid. If you don't pay your telephone bill, your telephone is turned off. The whole legal structure outlines specifically the punishments for the innumerable antisocial acts that mankind has devised. Most of us do not walk around with someone who continually reminds us that a given act may be followed by unpleasant consequences. As children, however, we need someone to tell us what is acceptable and what is not, to teach us what is punishable and what isn't. If the child is healthy, he will gradually incorporate the "rules" into his own psyche, and external reminders will no longer be necessary. It is the parent's job to help the child reach this state of self-reliance. The child who does not attain it is ill-equipped to function in society as an independent adult, for he will not be readily permitted to "get away with things" when he becomes an adult. It behooves the parent then to structure disciplinary situations in such a way that the child will become increasingly reliant on his own inner controls and warnings as deterrents to inappropriate behavior. The parent accomplishes this most effectively if he communicates to the child the basic principle : "If you do x, then y will happen. It's all up to you." The formula is essentially that of the *threat*. There are those who have an aversion to the use of the word, but I have no such hesitation. The aforementioned examples from adult life all have an intrinsic threat, and to substitute euphemisms for the term in no way removes it as a central factor in the disciplinary process, as well as in many other life situations.

There are numerous ways in which the child can be made responsible for his own actions and their consequences. For example, the child who knows he is to make his own bed but who continually neglects to do so can be told, "Each day that you go to school without making your bed, there'll be five cents taken off your allowance. I won't keep reminding you about it ; I'll just make the bed after you leave. Just as your father isn't paid if he doesn't do the work that's expected of him, part of your allowance isn't paid if you don't do your jobs around the house." The adolescent who persists in leaving his clothing on the floor can be told, "Look, I'm sick and tired of picking up after you so that your room doesn't look like a pigpen. From now on, I'm taking all clothes I find on chairs or on the floor and throwing them onto the floor of your closet. I'll only wash what's in the hamper ; and if you find yourself with nothing clean to wear, you'll have only yourself to blame." The nine-year-old who dawdles each morning as he dresses for school can be given an alarm clock and told, "Getting to school on time is between you and your teacher. I'm not going to keep knocking myself out to get you out of here on time. You're going to have to set this alarm clock yourself each night, get up when it rings every morning, and make sure that you're on time. If you're late for school, you'll just have to face the music there." The same principle will work for most children with their homework : "Homework is between you and your teacher. If you want me to help you a little, I'll be happy to but I'm not going to check it over to catch all your mistakes. If you're careless or sloppy you'll get a poor grade." (These last two examples will be effective for most children and presuppose the child's basic commitment to the educational system and his responding with displeasure if he is unsuccessful in it. The child who has no such commitment or who has significant problems that are interfering with successful school functioning may not respond to these measures.)

Experience seems to be a more effective teacher than didactics and verbal warnings. Since the dawn of civilization men have tried to communicate to future generations what they have learned that can make life easier for them. First verbally (through legend and myth) and then through the written word, the wise men of the ages have tried to help those who follow them avoid the mistakes that they themselves have made. The great religious and philosophical treatises of the world are all, in part, attempts to do this. Lifetimes have been devoted to this task by the greatest minds of mankind. Yet, each of us seems to be able to profit little from the accumulated wisdom of man that is at our disposal. We seem to learn best through our own experiences. We seem to have to make many mistakes ourselves in order to *really* learn many of the important lessons of life. The parent who deprives his child of opportunities to learn from his own experiences deprives him of this vital element in healthy growth.

"How can you punish me if you don't know I did it?" Generally, the child under the age of four cannot be said to steal. He may appropriate the property of others; but since he doesn't appreciate the concept of private property, one cannot readily say he steals. Most older children steal occasionally (as do most adults: paper clips from the office, billing errors in one's favor, etc.). But the child who steals compulsively and repeatedly usually has psychiatric problems, and his stealing is not going to be stopped by the kinds of measures proposed here—although my approaches may be helpful, *in part*, in the handling of such children. I discuss here the handling of the child who steals occasionally.

First, it is *not* vital to extract a confession from the child before instituting a disciplinary regimen. One can assume that if Robert's allowance has been found in his brother Jimmy's piggy bank, the money did not travel there by itself and that its presence there is not a manifestation of Robert's benevolence. Jimmy's profession of ignorance and incredulity regarding the miraculous transfer of the funds should not be taken at face value. His facial expression upon confrontation and his emotional reactions to the accusation are more revealing of his culpability. If Jimmy cannot come up with a more reasonable explanation or if the parent is ninety-plus percent sure that he is guilty, disciplinary measures should be instituted. Failure to implement these, because a confession has not been obtained, is a disservice to Robert because it deprives him of parental protection and a disservice to Jimmy because it allows the offense to go unpunished—thereby encouraging its repetition. The parent who will not punish until a confession has been extracted may be using his strict adherence to the highest principles of justice as a rationalization for less noble operations in his relationship with his child. He may wish for the confession as a way of gaining the child's permission to be punished. As long as the child denies culpability, he can justifiably be angry at the parent if he is punished; and his admission lessens the likelihood of anger. The parent who cannot tolerate his child, (or anyone else, for that matter) being angry at him may let the child's offense go undisciplined rather than suffer his resentment. Or the parent may not wish to accept the fact that his child is stealing because he may consider it proof of his deficiency as a parent. He would rather let the "crime" go unsolved than to find that the "criminal" is his *own* child.

Circumstantial evidence should have a respectability in the home that it rarely enjoys in the courthouse. There is no trial by a jury of one's peers; rather there is a "kangaroo court" where the parents serve as judge, jury, and executioner—all at the same time. I am not recommending an atmosphere of the Spanish Inquisition. It behooves the parent to take into consideration the child's needs, to respect his beliefs and wishes, but ultimately to impose his own will on the child when he sees the latter to be acting against his own interests.

Once it has been established "beyond reasonable doubt" that the child has stolen, I usually recommend that the child himself return the stolen item to its owner. The humiliation the child faces is often enough of a punishment to deter him from repeating the theft. The child's embarrassment may be so great, however, that he may refuse to face the owner. In such cases I suggest that the parent return the item, but that a punishment be administered at home to "help the child remember" not to steal again. If the stolen article has been destroyed, eaten, given away, or is otherwise no longer returnable, then its owner should be paid for it from the child's allowance or savings. If the child's available funds will not cover the cost, then he should be advanced the money—but it should definitely be paid back (if not in full, at least in part). In all of these transactions it is most important that the parents communicate to the child their feelings of amazement, indignation, and repugnance over what he has done. (Although in this example a certain amount of humiliation is an intrinsic part of the suggested punishment, it is generally wise to make every attempt to avoid punishing the child in front of his peers. Doing so often makes the punishment unnecessarily cruel.)

It is surprising how many parents, when learning that their child has stolen, reason (without any supporting evidence) that it was done because of material deprivation. They then give the child money or a present so he "won't have to steal." It is hard to imagine a more misguided approach to the stealing problem. It literally rewards the child for his violation and thereby increases the possibility that he will steal again. In addition, ascribing stealing to material deprivation (which it rarely is) avoids inquiry into its real causes—thereby lessening the likelihood that the problem will be worked out.

Besides dealing with the problem of the immediate stealing, the parent should make some attempt to learn about its causes. On occasion, a child will steal money in order to buy candy and other objects to bribe peers to play with him. Such children should be helped to correct the basic difficulties in their relationships with friends and should also be helped to appreciate that their method of obtaining playmates results in their being further alienated and disrespected—outward appearances of companionship notwithstanding. Some may steal because of the desire to "go along with the crowd" and may fear that if they don't they will have no friends. Such children can sometimes be helped to appreciate that it is an act of courage to do that which you know to be "right" even though unpopular. Some children steal as a way of acting out hostility, and anything that can reduce their anger may be helpful. Others do it because of feelings of deprivation of affection, the stolen object symbolizing love or a prized possession or present. Establishing a more meaningful and loving relationship with such a child can sometimes alleviate the problem.

"I never have to punish my children. When they do something wrong, we just discuss it." Some parents consider punishment of children a primitive and cruel practice and think that appeal to the child's rational mind is the civilized way to get him to do what is expected of him. By the time the child is able to talk, they reason, he has enough understanding to appreciate their explanations. One only needs enough sympathy and patience, and the child can be brought to see his parents' reasonableness and then can be relied upon to behave prudently. Parents who subscribe to this theory are often introspective and highly educated people who tend to rely heavily on logic and intellect to cope with the problems of life. They often have little respect for the natural, the spontaneous, and the emotional.

When the child of such parents misbehaves he is subjected to an inquiry that is itself more punitive than most punishments the parents could have devised. His parents seem not to be aware that his mind is wandering, that he is answering perfunctorily, and that he doesn't really understand the errors of his ways. His agreeing with them is a mere expedient to shorten the tortuous inquiry. Short discussions are certainly appropriate, for they can help the child understand what he has done wrong. After such discussions, however, disciplinary measures should be instituted (whether or not the child has been brought to understand why) with a simple but clear explanation of the cause and effect relationship between the misbehavior and the punishment. Simply being punished and getting it over with (lack of understanding notwithstanding) would be a blessing to the child subjected to the so-called non-punitive discussion approach.

"What will the neighbors think?" This comment has a number of unfortunate implications. It communicates to the child the parents' notion (often completely without basis) that the neighbors will hear of the misconduct and actually give it some thought. The remark then creates a fantasy in the child's mind that he may well be condemned by everyone in the neighborhood; that his misbehavior has aroused the ire of just about everyone on the block. The fantasy is at best egocentric and in its worst form has a paranoid quality. In either case it is usually a gross distortion. Most people are so involved in their own children's behavior that they give little more than transient thought to the misconduct of other children.

In addition, the comment orients the child toward external rather than internal deterrents of misbehavior. One hopes to help the growing child reach the point where he will engage in acceptable behavior because it makes him feel good inside himself to do so and where he will refrain from misbehavior because he feels bad about himself when he engages in it. Too much emphasis on the external deterrents may result in the child, restraining himself only when others will learn of his transgression, but not when he knows that there is little, if any, chance of being discovered.

The remark does not engender in the child very much respect for the parent. Although few of us are completely unaffected by public opinion, when the child is told this, he gets the idea that his parent is enslaved by it. He sees his parent also as someone who is less concerned with the implications of the act itself, of its meaning in the child's life, of the repercussions he may suffer than with the feelings of others. It is, therefore, seen as a manifestation of deficient affection on the parent's part, and this is the factor that often makes children so angry at the parent who says it. The child will commonly reply, "All you keep saying is what will *they* think. What about me? You seem to care more about them than you do about me."

Parents can do far better for both themselves and their children if they avoid using this shame-inducing, reality-distorting, disillusioning admonition.

"We keep a united front." Some parents think that if their child sees them disagree on a question of discipline there will be some terrible undermining of the child's respect or trust in them or that there will be other deleterious consequences that cannot be clearly defined. What often happens then is that one parent freely indulges himself in whatever punishments he wishes to administer, no matter how cruel and inhumane, while the other stands by and does nothing in order to keep the "united front." Generally, the parents adhere to this principle as a rationalization for the passive parent's fear of confronting the more domineering. Mother wishes that father wouldn't be so quick to use physical punishments, and it makes her squirm when she hears the children crying so pitifully, but she says nothing because of her fear of her husband. Rather than admit her weakness she justifies her failure to interfere on their behalf by becoming an adherent of the "united front" theory. The children, however, recognize the "front" as the ruse that it is. They are not only quite aware of their mother's basic agreement with them that they are being maltreated but, even worse, consider themselves "abandoned to the wolves" by their mother. Clearly, such an attitude seriously undermines the children's relationship with her. Because of her weakness, she loses her position as protector, and she may become distrusted in general because of her deceit. In addition, she does not provide her children with a healthy model for anger expression, and so they may grow up to be similarly inhibited in self-assertion and hostility release.

If the children are naive enough to believe that there is parental unanimity, they are being provided with an unrealistic view of human relationships. No two people can possibly agree on everything. The belief that there can be such unform agreement can produce disappointment and disillusionment in the child's future relationships (at work and in marriage, for example) where people will inevitably disagree with him. He may then suffer unnecessary dissatisfaction with these relationships because they are not as good as the one he considered his parents to have enjoyed.

"Just wait until your father comes home." Remote punishments are far less effective than those administered at the time of the transgression. To prohibit a child from watching television in the evening for something he did in the morning is far less meaningful a punishment and far less a deterrent to the repetition of the unacceptable behavior than a punishment given at the time of the wrongdoing. It is important to impress upon the child the cause and effect relationship between the

punishment and the "crime," and this is less effectively accomplished if a significant time lag separates the two. It is best to verbalize this at the time of the disciplining to ensure that the child appreciates the relationship: "Now look what you did. You spilled your milk. Now you get a rag and clean it all up yourself."

The mother who says, "Just wait until your father comes home. Is he going to give it to you," is being needlessly cruel. In addition to the punishment he will receive when his father returns, the child suffers the additional painful anxiety of waiting for its administration and wondering how severe it will be. Also, the father cannot discipline with the same conviction the mother could have at the time of the misconduct, and so the punishment loses some of its efficacy. At times, the father may not administer the punishment at all because he is so far removed from the event that he considers disciplinary measures inappropriate. With such a father, the child lives under a sword of Damocles—never knowing if it will fall. The mother who structures the child's discipline in this way is often trying to win the child's love by being the "good guy." She is so concerned about maintaining this image that she seems to care little about the effects on the child and father—the latter always being considered the "bad guy." Other mothers do this from the feeling of impotence they feel in controlling the child. Whatever the mother's motivation, a father who agrees to be the family hatchet man is performing a disservice to himself, to his wife, and to his child.

"Why can't you be like Howard?" Every neighborhood needs a Howard, a boy who is exemplary in every way. That Howard may end up emotionally disturbed has no relevance to his usefulness during his childhood. That he has no friends and is generally despised by his peers is also irrelevant to the parents who extol his virtues to their children. The efficacy of their maneuver in getting Johnny to behave a little better is questionable; but its efficacy in getting Johnny to loathe both himself and Howard is far more predictable.

In the typical case, Howard is willing to suffer the scorn of his peers because of the gratifications he derives from the world of adults. His reputation as the model boy on the block is his most treasured possession, his greatest source of ego-enhancement. Johnny, on the other hand, is constantly being torn down; he can never be as "good," "smart," or "obedient" as Howard, and ultimately he may give up trying. The maneuver, then, which has been designed to make Johnny behave better, usually results in his behaving worse and, in addition, can have a devastating effect on his self-esteem. Of the two boys, however, Johnny is usually still better off. He can at least find meaningful gratifications with his friends. This option is not available to Howard as a means of assuaging the intense psychic pain he suffers as the pariah of his peers (ego-gratifications with adults notwithstanding).

"My Joey would never do such a thing." Children who exhibit the normal amount of unacceptable behavior do not generally have parents who are encouraging (either consciously or unconsciously) their infractions. Those who have behavior problems may have parents who are getting secret gratification from their misconduct.

For example, the juvenile delinquent may have parents who harbor great resentment toward society because of real or fantasied deprivations. The parents, as adults, may be wise enough not to act out their bitterness directly. Their adolescent, however, with the body of a man but the brain of a child, may be less appreciative of the consequences of his behavior and may be used by the parents to act out for them their anti-social impulses. The youngster is not usually directly told to engage in the socially offensive behavior but surmises his parents' secret delight in it from their failure to appropriately punish it and, sometimes, from their deep interest and the gleam in their eyes when it comes to their attention. When a storekeeper complains to a father about his son's having broken the store window, the sanctioning father replies, "My Joey would never do such a thing," or "Ah, leave the kid alone. Boys will be boys. I used to do the same thing when I was a kid." Or he might say, "Joey, tell the man you're sorry." It is not only the father's words that suggest encouragement. His failure to punish Joey and make amends to the storekeeper provides the youngster with additional sanction to repeat the act because he has the reassurance that there will be no untoward consequences, but rather secret delight on his father's part over what he has done.

The mother, who obsessively fears that her teenage daughter will be promiscuous and who interrogates her after each date about every detail of whatever intimacies may have occurred is unwittingly encouraging the girl to have sexual experiences. When the daughter has nothing to report, she senses her mother's disappointment. When the girl provides some experiences, she senses her mother's delight—which is only thinly disguised by her lectures of condemnation.

A boy once tried to set fire to the curtains in my office. When I called his father about the matter he replied, "Can you prove it?" Again, parental encouragement. One father, who when told that his son was setting fires in a friend's home replied, "He's just expressing himself." A father responds to his daughter's disruptive antics with "Isn't she cute?" Another parent rationalizes his child's duplicity with "It was only a white lie." The examples are legion; the phenomenon widespread.

The communication of such double messages is common. Generally, the parent verbalizes the prohibition and criticism, but his gestures and intonations communicate the opposite message. I am reminded here of the song, popular when I was a teenager, "Your lips tell me, 'no no' but there's 'yes yes' in your eyes." Only more fearful and passive young men respond only to the verbal message and refrain from further advances. The assertive ones appreciate, at some level, the concomitant facial-expressive communications and proceeds. It is the "yes yes" in the eyes of the sanctioning parent that tells the child to go ahead in spite of the "no no."

"If you admit you did it, I won't punish you." Some parents consider it vital to extract a confession. Getting the child to be honest, to admit his culpability, become more important than handling the situation in a way that will dissuade the child from repeating the unacceptable act. In their craving for a confession, such parents may resort to saying, "If you admit you did it, I won't punish you." This approach is not only misguided but encourages further unacceptable behavior. The world of reality, to which we are trying to help our child make a reasonable adjustment, will not be so kind. When an adult commits a crime, he receives a punishment. If he pleads guilty and saves the court time and expense, he may get a lighter punishment. If he lies and causes the court unnecessary cost and effort to prove his guilt, he may get maximum and possibly additional punishments. The same principles should be applied to misbehavior at home. The ideal family atmosphere is one in which it is expected that people will be truthful with one another. This is not something achieved through reiteration. (In fact, if it is often spoken about it is likely that there is much deceit.) When honesty is truly the atmosphere, it is rarely if ever discussed. Therefore, it is expected that the child will be truthful about his transgressions. If he isn't, then he should be given an *additional* punishment for the *additional* infraction of lying : "One half-hour in your room for what you did and another half-hour for lying about it." If the child knows that confession will result in his not being punished at all there is little to deter him from engaging in unacceptable behavior. In addition, the approach may be a way for the parent to gratify his own unconscious desire that the child perform the ostensibly unacceptable acts. The child may sense this and then engage in the behavior in compliance with the parent's subtle wish that he do so, while both play the game of confession and absolution in the service of the parent's denying his basic wish that the child transgress.

In some families, the punishments may be so severe that the child may have to resort to lying as his only way of possibly avoiding parental cruelty. The approach to this problem should not, of course, be double punishment but rather more humane punishment to lessen the likelihood that the child will lie.

"If you don't say you're sorry, I'll punish you." Billy hits his sister Helen. Helen goes crying to mother: "Billy hit me."

Mother (to Billy): "Tell your sister you're sorry."

Billy: "I won't."

Mother: "If you don't say you're sorry, I'll punish you."

Billy (pouting and grumbling): "O.K., I'm sorry."

Billy's contrition is nil. His apology is pure expediency. He has been taught to lie by his mother. He has been taught to use the term "I'm sorry" to avoid the consequences of his misbehavior. If he learns his mother's lessons well, he will attempt to use this maneuver with others—much to the detriment of his interpersonal relationships. For others may act as if they accept his apology (and he may wish to believe them), but they will inevitably reject him for his dishonesty and insensitivity.

Helen is forced into playing the game as well. She certainly appreciates that her brother is in no way sorry and can only leave the situation with the feeling that she has been duped, that Billy has gotten away with something, and that both Billy and her mother have put something over on her. And indeed they have. The situation leaves Helen with the feeling that she cannot rely on her mother to protect her from those who would injure her. Billy has essentially been given free rein to strike her again. He need fear no retribution from his mother if he mistreats Helen. All he need do is say, "I'm sorry," and all is forgiven.

The term *I'm sorry* is much overused, and all too frequently in the way that Billy has been taught. Ideally, it should be reserved for those situations in which one has inadvertently hurt someone, when there has been no malice, and when the apology is genuine. The apologizer's feelings of guilt (even though small) should be genuine and his desire to rectify and avoid repetition of the wrongdoing sincere.

"If you don't say 'Thank you' you can't have the present." There are parents who believe that teaching one's child good manners is training him to be a phony. They point out that many so-called polite expressions, such as "How are you?" "Thank you," "You're looking well," etc., are gross misrepresentations and that the speaker doesn't for one second mean what he is saying but utters these platitudes in compliance with social hypocrisy. Generally, parents who believe this try to teach their children to use such expressions only when they genuinely mean what they are saying. If their child is given a present and does not say "Thank you," they do not encourage him to do so. And if the giver feels a little put off because the child has not expressed appreciation, nor have the parents encouraged him to, that is considered *his* problem, not the child's.

I believe that such parents are taking too literal a view of these expressions, possibly in the service of expressing hostility. These terms often do not really mean what they ostensibly say. They really mean "I recognize your existence" and "My feeling toward you is, for the most part, benevolent." If one walks down the street and says "Hi" to an acquaintance who does not respond, one generally feels offended or mystified or hurt. We live in a society in which such verbal interchanges, although at times artificial, play a significant role in our relationships. Whether justifiably or not, they are important communications in our involvements with others. The child who is not taught their correct usage may become a social misfit. He will be considered antisocial and a snob. He will offend most of those with whom he comes in contact (both adults and children) and will find himself a social reject—even though he may have strong cravings and capacities for deep involvements.

The healthiest attitude the parent can impart to the child is that he should try to use these expressions in as honest a manner as possible. He should make every attempt to reserve them for situations when he can use them without duplicity. However, he should come to appreciate that there will be times when the most appropriate thing for him to do is to lie; and that if he does not lie in certain situations he will be performing a disservice to both himself and others. For example, Sally should be taught that when her cousin Nancy excitedly dances into the room and says, "Sally, how do you like my new dress?" it is inhumane to be anything but complimentary. On the other hand, Sally must be helped to discriminate this situation from the one where Nancy is asking for honest and serious advice and where failing to be honest might cause Nancy disappointment and embarrassment. These distinctions, although subtle, are important for the child to learn if he is to get along adequately with others. When Martin refuses to say "Thank you" because he does not like the birthday present his friend Jim has brought for him, telling him that he cannot have the present until he says so will not necessarily make him into a hypocrite. He can be told that it makes Jim feel bad if he is not thanked for the present and that he would feel bad if Jim didn't thank him under similar circumstances.

Perhaps the time will come when we will not be playing such games, but that time appears to be quite a long way off. Until it comes, we do best for our children to make a sober compromise with the tradition, to encourage them to be as honest as possible, but to recognize that at times judicious dishonesty is the wisest and even the most humane course of action—both for oneself and for others.

"When I was your age . . . " This expression, when used to introduce a remark designed to rectify a child's misbehavior (or otherwise set him straight), is guaranteed to produce feelings of instant antagonism. To say to a child, "When I was your age, I never did such a thing," is either false or true. If false, the parent is lying to the child and lies in this category will undermine the child's respect for and trust in the parent. If the statement is true, it serves to demean the child. It essentially communicates to him, "I am a far better person than you because I never engaged in such loathsome behavior when I was your age." There is an inevitable lowering of the child's self-esteem when he is criticized for his misconduct, and this plays a role in deterring its repetition. However, one need not look for ways to increase the loss of self-respect that the situation may result in. As mentioned, disciplining a child in front of his peers can do this. And telling him that he is far less worthy a person than his parent (or whoever the reprimander is) is another way of doing this.

"How can you do this to me?" One of the goals in the upbringing of our children is to get them to react with an appropriate degree of guilt to real transgressions. Such self-regulation, through the guilt mechanism, is vital to the survival of civilization. The parent, however, who says, "How can you do this to me?" goes too far with the guilt-inducing mechanism. He instills in the child inappropriate guilt, guilt over fantasied calamities, guilt over events for which he had no responsibility. The method is, at the same time, one of the most effective and cruel stratagems for controlling a child's behavior and, when used frequently, will predictably produce neurotic disturbance.

The mother, for example, who says, "What a terrible report card. How can you do this to me?" communicates to the child that the damage he may be inflicting on himself by his poor school performance is of little if any consequence. What is important is what the low grades are doing to his mother—the disappointment, humiliation, etc., *she* suffers. Such a mother has an exaggerated involvement in her child's educational experiences. She is probably using the child to gain vicarious gratification through his educational attainments to compensate for her own inadequacies in this area. It is no surprise when such a child responds by becoming a school dropout. It is as if he reasoned (consciously or unconsciously), "She doesn't really care about me, only how she can use me to make herself look good. Well, I'll show her. I'll fail."

Or take the case of a boy whose father responds to normal rambunctiousness with, "You're going to make my ulcers bleed again. You know the doctor said I should have peace and quiet." The son can only be enraged (even if he cannot consciously express it). His normal self-expression can bring about his father's death. The latter's life hangs in his hands. The slightest recurrence of his father's symptoms makes him loathe himself. It's his fault, as he's been told a hundred times. The guilt the child feels is not only related to his belief that the bleeding was his fault but also to his anger at having been placed in such a position. In short, the father's making the bleeding the son's responsibility produces anger in the boy—anger that may be expressed by fantasies of the father's bleeding. There may be guilt over this anger; and if the father does indeed bleed, the son may consider it his fault—in accordance with the belief that wishing something can make it happen. This, of course, further increases the boy's guilt.

A related phenomenon is the "Do it for *us*" maneuver. Here again, the implication is that if the child doesn't do what he's asked, the parents will suffer. "Squelch your own desires," he is told, "for our benefit" or "just so you won't hurt us." This is a one-sided arrangement that does not give proper respect to the child's wishes, that evokes inappropriate guilt, and that produces an unrealistic sense of responsibility for the welfare of others.

Comments like, "You're driving me crazy," and "You'll be the death of me," if used infrequently, probably have little effect on the child. But if they become a primary mode of controlling a child's behavior, the groundwork is laid for neurotic problems involving inappropriate guilt. The child bears a heavy burden: innocents suffer and may even die because of his misdeeds. It is in this way that the seeds of neurosis are planted.

"God punished you." There is no child who does not misbehave. There is no child who does not "get away with things" behind his parents' back. Such occasional misbehavior is healthy; it implies a desire for independence and is the stuff from which innovation and social progress are created. The child who is told that God is watching him all the time, that no transgression of his goes unobserved, and that there is no escape from the watchful eye of The Lord leads a miserable life (to say the least). God the omnipotent, God the omniscient, God, who makes all men account for their sins, is omnipresent. No sin, no matter how small, goes unobserved. What a way to live! The method is predictably effective in inculcating self-regulation into the child, but the price he must pay for his high degree of social adaptation is immense. The child who takes all this seriously is certainly "good." In fact, he will probably be a "model child." But he will also be a frightened child, withdrawn, prone to magical thinking, and strongly predisposed to utilize a variety of mechanisms (both neurotic and psychotic) to lessen his anxieties.

There is another, somewhat less malignant, version of this maneuver. A little girl is told to stay in the house. Against her mother's instructions, she goes into the street. A few minutes later she returns home crying: "Mommy, I fell and scraped my knee." Mother replies, "If you had listened to me and not gone out, you wouldn't have hurt yourself. God punished you for being bad and not listening to Mommy." Although it is true that if the child had not gone out the fall would not have occurred, the injury was in no way related to the child's disobedience. To relate the two as cause and effect is to give the child a lesson in magical thinking as well as to create in her anxieties about an all-seeing God who punishes her instantaneously for the most minor transgression. There are far more humane ways to discipline.

"If you don't go, none of us will go." This is another method of discipline that basically attempts to get the child to cooperate by inducing guilt. The parent's hope is that the inconvenience Sally's obstructionism causes her family will so overwhelm her with guilt that she will join them after all. Usually when this game is played, the parent has no intention of actually keeping the family home if Sally remains recalcitrant. In that situation, Sally is dragged screaming to the car and the family drives off. The threat is made in the hope that Sally will come quietly. One drawback of this conflict of wills is that even if Sally succumbs to the guilt that has been evoked in her, she does so with the delusion that she has the power to obstruct the whole family if she so desires. Placing such power in the hands of a child cannot but undermine her faith in her parents as her protectors and sources of strength. If Sally remains obdurate and is then bodily carried to the car, she loses trust in her parents because they have not kept their word to stay home if she refused to join them. In the rare situation, in which the family actually does stay home, the child's feeling of power is no longer delusional or potential, but an accomplished fact. Parents who are so controlled and manipulated deprive their children of the respect of their parents that is vital to their children's well-being.

Playing one parent against the other. The most common form of this game is for the child, when refused by parent A, to make the same request of parent B. B grants the request, unaware that A had very good reasons for refusing it. In a variation on the game the child tells B that A said it was all right to do such and such, after A had specifically said that it wasn't. It is often hard to avoid being drawn into this game from time to time. One can't check every request a child makes with one's spouse. The thing that most perpetuates this game is its success, and the thing that most effectively squelches it is its failure. Most children try this game at one time or another, and frustrating the child the first few times he attempts it is the best prophylactic against its repetition. It can also be helpful to check with the spouse first before granting requests that sound like they belong in the *New Yorker* magazine's "Things we doubt mother (father) ever said" department. A reasonable disciplinary measure for lying can also serve to discourage this game.

"Shut up this minute and go to sleep." Some parents complain that the worst time of day is the evening, when hours may be spent trying to get the children to bed. No sooner is the child tucked in and the parent ready to relax than a cry from the bedroom resounds through the house: "Mommy, I want a glass of water" or "Daddy, I have to make." When these requests have been granted, they may be followed by "I'm hungry"; "I'm scared"; "Put on the foyer light"; "I can't fall asleep"; etc. The game can go on for hours if the parent continues to comply with every request; his exasperation and anger may mount until he ends up screeching at the child and may have to restrain himself from beating him. This is a common state of affairs, yet there are things that can be done to alleviate the problem. (Please note that I have said *alleviate*, not *cure*.)

The first issue to consider when a child balks at bedtime is whether he is really tired, whether he is really ready to go to sleep. Some parents ask me, "How many hours of sleep does a child of seven need?" They seem to have the idea that I have some sort of chart (like those for heights and weights) that indicates the amount of sleep children of different ages should get. I usually answer that there is no rule and that, just as children vary with regard to the amount of food and air they require, there is no set rule governing the amount of sleep a child of any specific age needs. Children are no different from adults with regard to the amount of sleep they require—some need more and some less. The main determinant of whether a child is getting enough sleep is how alert he is during the following day. If he yawns in school and seems to get droopy in the late afternoon, then he is probably not getting enough sleep. Sometimes irritability can result from insufficient sleep. (However, since psychological factors can also cause the child to be irritable this is a poor criterion.) Difficulty in getting the child out of bed in the morning is also a poor criterion of whether the child has had enough sleep, because there are people who have difficulty getting out of bed in the morning regardless of how many hours sleep they have had and how well rested they may be. A few days' trial can often enable the parent to determine fairly well just how much sleep a child needs.

Parents should also appreciate that sleep, like many other physiological functions, is readily affected by psychological influences. The child whose parents do not come home until mid- to late-evening may get into the habit of staying up later in order to spend time with them. Such a child may then come to actually require less sleep than others his age and less than he would have needed had his parents routinely come home earlier. Such children, in my experience, do not seem to suffer any ill-effects from their longer-than-average hours in the waking state—such seems to be the adaptability of the human body. Psychological tensions may prevent the child from entering into a relaxed enough state to fall asleep. Investigation into the sources of the child's tensions and alleviation of them, when possible, should make it easier for the child to go to sleep. The child with more than the average frequency of nightmares (a few a month is normal), may fear going to sleep because of his frightening dreams. Such a child may require significant changes in his milieu or life pattern (and therapy is only one possible way in which this can be brought about) if he is to go to sleep more comfortably.

Some parents try to get their children to sleep prematurely so they may have some peace, quiet, and relaxed time together. This is a very beautiful goal, and it is often enjoyed by families on television programs; but even the children who watch these programs do not seem to emulate the children on them when it comes to their own bedtime. There are parents who expect the child to go from a state of intense agitation and excitement to one of deep slumber in a matter of a few minutes. Brothers who spend the fifteen or twenty minutes before their bedtime bouncing on the beds, leaping, shouting, and wrestling cannot be expected to slide into a state of pleasant slumber when bedtime arrives. The transition is far more easily made when the child is eased into a relaxed state with warm milk and cookies, a story, or a quiet activity with the parent. In fact, the presence of a parent can make the transition smoothest. Bedtime can be anxiety-provoking in that it involves a separation from the parents with all their implied security. The child is often placed in a separate room, behind a closed door, and often with the lights out. Having a parent with him to help him bear the separation can be most helpful. Reading a story together is an activity that most children enjoy, or just talking about things that are of mutual interest may serve the same purpose. Lying down with the child, cuddling, humming, singing softly, and saying sweet things is probably the most efficacious way of lulling a child to sleep. I do not believe that deleterious consequences need result from a parent's lying in bed with a prepubertal opposite-sexed child. Such cuddling and tender warmth need not be seductive and is not the kind of experience that produces oedipal problems. In fact, such displays of affection are among the most potent prophylactics against the development of oedipal difficulties. Leaving a small light on after the parent leaves the room can further lessen the child's separation anxiety. In fact, I consider parents who do not comply with a child's request for such a light (on the grounds that it is infantilizing) to be somewhat cruel.

Parents who use the bedroom as the place for "solitary confinement" when disciplining the child generally need not worry that the child will then have trouble going to sleep in the same room that has earlier served as his "jail." However, if they use "going to bed early" as a punishment, they may find that he may come to view going to sleep for normal physiological reasons as a punishment as well, and then there will be difficulties getting him to sleep.

Lastly, there are parents who believe that they must maintain a rigid schedule regarding the times at which the different children go to sleep. They believe that they will be depriving the elder children of certain privileges that are their birthright if they allow the younger children to go to sleep at the same time. Somehow, the elder children's self-esteem will be lowered if they have to suffer the indignity of going to sleep at the same time as a younger sibling. Often schedules are arranged at fifteen-minute intervals in strict compliance with these principles. I believe that such parents are unnecessarily involving themselves in childish and petty sibling rivalries: "I'm older than she is so why shouldn't I be allowed to stay up later?" The answer to that question should be, "Yes, you are older and you are entitled to certain privileges that she isn't. However, the amount of sleep that one needs has nothing to do with privileges. Every person is different regarding how much sleep he needs. The time I make her go to bed is determined by how much sleep she needs, not by when the people around her are going to sleep."

Parents who follow these suggestions should find that getting their children to sleep will be less of a struggle. However, because of the anxiety inevitably associated with the transition from the waking to the sleeping state in the child, the parent must expect some balking at times, some game playing, and at times power struggles and threats of disciplinary measures if the child doesn't "shut up this minute and go to sleep."

"All is forgiven" and "saving face." The utilization of disciplinary, and especially punitive, measures can only be ego-debasing to the child. Whatever benefits he may derive from either, in the present and

in the future, they do take something away from his self-esteem. He has been overpowered and outwitted by superior forces; he has been out-maneuvered, "caught in the act," and subjected to various indignities. These are the inevitable drawbacks of punishment. But if one believes, as I do, that discipline and punishment are in the child's best interest (their drawbacks notwithstanding), then he must accept the existence of these untoward side effects.

One way to help lessen the ego-damaging effects of punishment is to take the attitude that "all is forgiven" after the punishment is over. Fortunately children are much more capable of this sort of thing than adults, who often harbor lingering resentments. The child, on the other hand, is capable of bouncing back and resuming his carefree and optimistic attitudes. The adult who "doesn't forget" after the punishment has been completed is being cruel. It is most important to allow the slate to be wiped clean.

Another way to help the child compensate for the blow to his self-esteem that punishment entails is to allow him to "save face"—to permit him to utilize some retaliatory device that helps him feel that the score has been evened. When sent to his room, the child should be allowed to slam the door. The "God damn you" communication thus imparted lessens his humiliation. A girl, when punished for maltreating her brother, should be permitted to say, "I'll never let him play with any of my toys, ever again." The wise parent does not pick up on these further trans-gressions and pin the child to the wall at the moment of his mortification. There are times to let the child be bad, and this is one of them.

KINDS OF DISCIPLINARY MEASURES, ADVISABLE AND INADVISABLE

No one method of discipline will be equally useful for all children. What may be considered a deprivation for one child may be a boon to another. A punishment that may be salutary for one child may be psychologically detrimental to another. What may work for one child, may not for another. The disciplinary measures, then, must be tailored to the needs of the child and judged by their efficacy for that particular child.

The basic disciplinary measure: threatened loss of parental affection. The basic, and ultimately most effective, disciplinary measure is parental disapprobation. Expressing one's disapproval of a child's act can be an effective deterrent to its continuation or repetition. The facial expressions, intonations, and gestures that accompany the censure enhance the efficacy of the parents' communications. The younger the child, the more sensitive he generally is to the threat of parental alienation and the more likely he is to respond to it. Often a raised index finger or a firm "uh uh" is enough to stop a child in his tracks. All other disciplinary measures to be described are effective less because of the pains or inconveniences the child suffers than because of the threatened loss of parental affection intrinsic to them.

"Solitary confinement." "Go to your room" is a punishment that subjects the child to a period of parental deprivation. He not only suffers temporary loss of parental affection but his separation deprives him of witnessing their signs of reacceptance. Its implementation frustrates the gregarious instinct that, I believe, exists within all of us. Solitary confinement is generally reserved for the most recalcitrant prisoners and is a most feared and painful punishment. Fifteen minutes to a half-hour of such social isolation usually suffices to produce the proper amount of contrition for most infractions. Longer periods, such as two to three hours, are generally excessive and cruel. The measure will not generally be effective if the child can entertain himself with television, building models, etc., so these activities must simultaneously be interdicted. Also, for the younger child with temper tantrums, "confinement to quarters" for the duration of the siege is an excellent measure. It deprives the child of the attention and the manipulative gratifications of the tantrum and can help preserve the parent's sanity.

For many children being relegated to their room is an excellent disciplinary procedure. However, its implementation requires a certain amount of parental vigilance; and this can be a definite disadvantage if the child refuses to cooperate, "take his punishment," and stay in his room. At times, the child has to be threatened with extensions or not-so-gentle replacement in his room if he comes out prematurely. Also, the child who asks every minute, "Is the time up yet?" can make the measure more of a punishment for the parent than the child. For the younger child, standing in the corner, being made to sit in a special seat, or being required to leave the room can be as effective as being sent to his room, in that it shares with the latter the element of separation from the parent.

Going to sleep early (with or without supper). This is similar to the punishment of being sent to one's room in that it exposes the child to deprivation of parental affection. However, it is an ill-conceived and inappropriate measure. One can get a child into bed early; but getting him to sleep early is another matter entirely. Worse, to associate sleep with punishment cannot but affect the child's attitude toward going to sleep in general. Under the best of circumstances going to sleep at night is a difficult thing for most children because of the separation anxiety it evokes. Using early-to-bed as a punishment reinforces in the child the notion that there is indeed something bad about going to sleep. Parents, then, who use this as a disciplinary measure are asking for trouble. They should not be surprised when they have even more difficulty getting their child to sleep than they did before utilizing this method of punishment.

Depriving the child of supper as added punishment invites even further problems. Although the parent who utilizes this punishment (with extremely rare exceptions) plans only to punish the child with a few hunger pangs (rather than to withhold food to the point of nutritional deficiency), there are psychological implications to its withholding that can cause the child difficulty. In most parts of the world, being provided with basic sustenance is considered the birthright of all humans. Starving someone as punishment for a crime is generally considered extremely inhumane. Even the prisoner in solitary confinement is given subsistence rations of food and water. Even the man who cannot or will not work is provided with basic subsistence by society. The child should expect his food as a matter of course, just as he expects water, clothing, and shelter. (I am, of course, concerning myself with the home in which these necessities are available.) If one is deprived of food when one is "bad" and gets it when one is "good," it is not hard to see how this interpretation can contribute to distorted attitudes that are at the root of psychological problems concentrated on eating. The person with compulsive self-starvation may be depriving himself, in part, to punish himself and thereby assuage his guilt over "transgressions," both real and fantasized. The compulsive eater may attempt to gain the feeling of euphoria that comes with being "good" and loved by mother. Of course, these, and other psychological disorders related to the ingestion of food, are complex and have many other contributing factors; but central is attributing to food a significance that is not intrinsic to it. Using food deprivation as punishment fosters the development of such distortions.

It is important to differentiate basic food withdrawal from occasional withholding of desserts, ice cream, and candy as disciplinary measures. These foods are not basic staples necessary for survival, but dispensable additions. Using them for the purpose of occasional reward and punishment does not present psychological dangers.

"You can't watch any more television tonight." In Western society, where television is so ubiquitously enjoyed by children, reducing viewing time can be a valuable disciplinary measure. However, the child must be one who has previously proved himself to be an enthusiast; otherwise it loses its value as a punishment. Since most children probably watch too much television, this measure has a fringe benefit. With the increasingly widespread use of color television, there are homes in which

an effective punishment can be that of requiring the child to use the black-and-white set while everyone else is viewing the show in color. (I am sure that the inventors of color television did not appreciate this added boon of their discovery.)

"Ten cents off your allowance for that." Withholding part of the child's allowance is another effective way of getting children to do what is expected of them. Of course, the child has to have an allowance in the first place, if this method is to be utilized. I have, on occasion, suggested that parents institute the practice in order to be able to subsequently withhold funds as a disciplinary measure. Generally, I suggest that a part of the allowance be automatically given for basic necessities (a kind of subsistence allowance), for such things as candy and saving for birthday presents. The remainder is given as payment for doing certain chores and for "being good." It is the latter part that is subject to deductions if the child does not fulfill his obligations or is "bad." (Some people object to the use of the word *bad* in describing a child's misbehavior because they believe that the child may assume that he is being considered totally worthless and loathsome. I do not share their objection to its use. One can communicate to the child that one considers him bad at the moment, not an inveterate criminal, and that one still appreciates his potential for "good" behavior.)

Some parents regard allowance deductions as a poor disciplinary measure because it implies that the child is being paid to be good and thereby discourages his being good for its own sake. I believe that there are times in life when we genuinely enjoy doing the "good" thing (for inner gratifications) without any external rewards, but there are other times (much more common) when we do it out of expediency. However much we may enjoy our work, there are times when we don't wish to do it but do so anyway because our earnings would be reduced if we were not to perform our tasks. I believe that part of the child's allowance is analogous. If he does not perform his chores part of his allowance is deducted. The same principle holds for his father, who will sooner or later not be paid if he does not perform the work that is expected of him. Using the allowance in this way helps prepare the child for this important aspect of his future life.

"You can't go out and play." This punishment must be used cautiously. For some children it can be very effective; for others it may bring about more misbehavior than the child exhibited originally. The child who has many friends and who daily involves himself with them in a gratifying way may be deterred from misbehaving with the threat of being kept inside. The thought of remaining indoors while everyone is

outside having a grand time can be a very effective sobering device to the child who is getting out of hand. However, outside play is both physically and psychologically healthy and to deprive the child of this activity too frequently may interfere with his emotional, and possibly even his physical, development. The child who has problems in his relationships with friends, who may only rarely be asked to join in, or who shuns involvements with peers should not be further impeded in this regard by being kept in the house as punishment. Every sign of interest in joining his peers should be supported and encouraged. To keep such a child indoors when he evidences interest in peer play is cruel and psychologically detrimental.

The demerit system. This can be a very effective disciplinary method. The child is told that if he accumulates a certain number of demerits for misbehaving he will not be permitted a particular forthcoming present, event, etc. For example, Laura is told, "Between now and next Saturday, every time you're bad you're going to get one demerit. If you get ten demerits you can't sleep over at Helen's house." When Laura persists in horseplay at the dinner table, she is told, "O.K., that's one demerit for not stopping when I told you to cut out the racket. Nine more, and no visit to Helen's house." If Laura is like most children, she will "shape up" instantaneously. The method satisfies many of the desiderata of a good disciplinary measure. The punishment is administered at the time of the transgression; it usually deters the child from repeating the undesirable activity; it is humane; it is precise (the child knows exactly what the punishment is); and the measure requires practically no effort by the parent. Setting up the system saves the parent the trouble of figuring out an appropriate disciplinary measure for each new form of misconduct. In addition, it serves as a general antidote to various types of misbehavior. This is one of the beauties of the method.

For the plan to be effective the goal must be one that the child is desirous of attaining. If not, one must find another objective, the threatened loss of which will make the accumulation of demerits meaningful. The system is best utilized with short-term goals of reasonable importance. To prolong the duration of its application or to use a psychologically vital experience as the goal can be cruel. For example, to prolong the period more than a week or so or to threaten deprivation of a birthday party is excessive. A birthday party is almost a child's birthright. To deprive him of it can be inhumane. It should be a day of forgiving, forgetting, and general amnesty. Christmas presents should be in the same category. It is hard for me to imagine a parent not being able to find other ways to discipline a child than depriving him of Christmas presents or his birthday party.

"*We never spank our children.*" Some people claim that there is no place for spanking in child rearing, that it is cruel, and that it is ego-debasing to both the adult and the child. They argue that the physical pain and humiliation the child suffers does him much more harm than any benefits he might derive from the experience. I believe that spanking, used judiciously, has a place in the upbringing of children. It should, however, be the punishment of last resort—used only when all other forms of discipline have failed.

The pain inflicted should not be excessive. Therefore, straps, paddles, and other devices designed to increase the pain should not be used. The backside is the traditional area of choice—and with justification, because the child suffers the least pain when he is hit there. Occasionally, one may have to slap the child on the arms or legs because he may not "get the message"—so protected is he by his gluteal fat. Frequent use of the buttocks can result in their becoming eroticized in some children and this may contribute to sexual problems. Striking the child's hand is an excellent alternative form of "non-verbal communication" when the buttocks will not do. I have a personal aversion to slapping a child on the face, but it is certainly an ancient tradition (especially when the child says things that are particularly offensive) and probably has a place (rare and only upon extreme provocation) in the parents' disciplinary repertoire. Punches and blows to the head, abdomen, and other sensitive areas are definitely cruel and excessive. The child's pain should be more psychological than physical, and this occurs more readily when he has been taught over a period of time that spanking is the worst punishment. The duration should be short. If the child is being "beaten," his spankings are probably both too prolonged and too intense. Lastly, a strong shaking will often serve the same purposes as a spanking.

Spanking has the advantage of enabling the parent to vent the anger the child's behavior has provoked in him. However, as already mentioned, it is preferable for the parent to handle the situation effectively before significant frustration and resentment have built up in him. But we cannot always be successful in preventing a quick buildup of anger, and the "wallop" may then be the most expeditious way of releasing it.

All parents are aware of those times when the child "seems to be asking to get spanked." This is a real phenomenon; and it is not, in most cases, particularly related to the desire for masochistic or sexual gratification. Rather, the child has built up tensions and resentments to a pitch where he needs an excuse for having an outburst of rage. The spanking can provide him with just the kind of justification he requires. He *needs* the outburst, and the wise parent gives the child the opportunity to vent his feelings. After the *Sturm und Drang*, one observes an amazing transformation of his personality. He is calm, friendly, and relaxed—"a pleasure to have around the house." Giving the child justification to let off steam, to have a temper tantrum (one or two smacks on the backside may suffice) may be all he needs to return to a state where his benevolent feelings toward those around him can reveal themselves.

Concluding Comments

In closing, it is worth repeating that reward (both internal and external) is far preferable to discipline and punishment as a method of eliciting desirable behavior from the child. Although discipline and punishment are predictably necessary, they represent a failure of the reward approach. The more the child's desirable behavior is motivated by the pleasure it affords him, the more he can be relied upon for self-regulation, and the healthier and happier he will be.

The number of punishments parents can devise, like the number of transgressions children can contrive, is legion. I have described the most common, but there are certainly others that may be useful. Depriving the child of certain expected conveniences and services can be effective. For example, the child who is driven to school can be made to walk (if the distance is not excessive), or the parent can delay repairs on a treasured item (bicycle, record player, etc.). Communicating one's residual resentment over a child's misbehavior can be a potent measure because it employs the most fundamental punishment of all : withdrawal of affection. For example, the parent who says, "I'm in no mood to watch you jump off the diving board. I'm still too angry at you for what you did to your brother," deprives the child of the praise for mastery, which is one of his basic cravings. The parent who says, "No, I won't play checkers with you now. I just don't feel friendly enough after all the trouble you made before," deprives the child of vital parental companionship. Obviously, such measures must be used sparingly because to utilize them frequently can be psychologically harmful.

Professionals warn parents of the importance of consistency. If the child is punished one day for a particular form of misconduct and not punished the next, the development of self-regulatory processes will be impaired, and he may become anxious as well because he will not be certain what the parental response will be to his misconduct. Although such advice is basically true, only the most rigid and compulsive parents can possibly follow it. Most of us vary in our degree of tolerance for our children's antics, and we may let them get away with things one day that we punish them for the next. Most of us make threats to our children that are never followed through with, for we have more things to do in life than devote ourselves to the upbringing of our children. We must let much of their misbehavior pass if we are to get any satisfactions of our own. We must think of ourselves as well. If we are miserable in our enslavement to our children, they will get little benefit from our dedication to the task of rearing them. We must be relatively happy too if we are to be any good to them. The parent who is martinet enough to be highly consistent is probably such a wretch as a human being that he is a poor parent, regardless of the benefits his child may derive from his consistency. The ideal then is to achieve a *relative* degree of consistency so that the child basically learns which forms of behavior are acceptable and which will *often,* but not always, result in discipline or punishment.

Dr. Fitzhugh Dodson, in his book *How to Parent* states

> What will be the result if we learn to use the successful teaching methods and avoid the unsuccessful ones? Will we then raise a "model child"? I hope not. As a psychologist I am not too impressed with "model children." A "model child" is neither a happy child nor a self-regulating child. He is a child with a façade. He has been intimidated into a certain outward conformity, but there is considerable emotional disturbance hidden inside him. If we end up with a preschool child who is quiet and respectful of adults at all times; who never rebels or gets out of hand; who is pleased to do whatever adults want him to do without complaint; who has no negative feelings about anything or anyone; who has no interest whatever in sex; who never lies; who never hits his brother or sister or friends; who is moral, unselfish, and of high ethical principle; who is conscientious, clean, and respects private property—then we are not really dealing with a child at all. We are dealing with a person who has been intimidated into being a miniature little adult masquerading as a child.[11]

I am in full agreement. The healthy child is *not* the well-disciplined child. The healthy child is the one who learns most of the rules and has the independence, individuality, and guts to break them once in a while.

---

[11] Dodson, Fitzhugh, *How to Parent*, Los Angeles, Calif.: Nash Publishing, 1970.

The healthy child is the one who gets B's in conduct on his report card. These are the children who grow into the creative, self-sufficient, reasonably rebellious, constructively doubting, questioning adults who are responsible for the progress of mankind. If all children were of the well-disciplined type, we would still be living in caves.

8

Children's Play

Play is the child's natural form of expression, for it brings him into a communicative relationship with others in his world. Adults visit a good friend to talk with him about things of mutual interest. The child visits his friend to play with him. Most parents are concerned when their children do not play well with others, because they seem to appreciate that this social deficit is a psychological liability. And, for the psychiatrist, an impairment in the child's ability to play successfully with peers is a very sensitive criterion for the presence of psychiatric disturbance.

Above all, play is pleasurable. The pleasure may be intellectual, as found in problem-solving games; emotional, as manifested by laughing, singing, and other kinds of exhilaration; or physical, as in running, dancing, and jumping. The pleasure of the infant's play, especially, is in this last category. He loves to be cuddled, bounced, caressed, and to laugh with exhilaration. The toddler who plays in the mud does so for similar gratification. Pleasure, in moderation, is probably the most potent preventative of and antidote to psychological disturbance. Pleasure enhances self-esteem, and lowered self-esteem lies at the very foundation of most forms of psychiatric disturbance. While we are enjoying ourselves we are distracted from stress and morbid deliberations.

"She loves playing peekaboo." At about the age of eight months most children manifest what is called "separation anxiety," which is related to the phenomenon of "stranger anxiety." The child has reached the developmental level where he can differentiate his parents from strangers; he becomes frightened when his parents leave him and may become fearful of strangers. He may also, at this age, not fully appreciate that when an object is not visible it may still exist. When his parents are out of sight, he may fear that they no longer exist—that they will never return.

In playing peekaboo the child experiences transient periods of separation from a parent—during which he suffers separation anxiety. When the parent reappears, there is a sudden alleviation of the anxiety with a concomitant feeling of relief and even exhilaration. It appears that he is willing to suffer the anxiety because of the pleasurable sensations he experiences on the parent's reappearance. The game appears to follow the Aristotelian principle that "pleasure is the absence of pain"— or, better, the cessation of pain.

"He never goes anywhere without his blanket." Some children develop a deep relationship with a small blanket, a doll, a stuffed toy, or other portable object. Going to sleep without it is unthinkable; and if the family forgets to bring it along when they leave the home, the child may become distraught. Many families have returned home, at no small inconvenience, in order to retrieve the forgotten object. The object may have been so caressed and dragged on the floor that it is no longer recognizable. It may have become so filthy that others consider it a health hazard, and yet the child will refuse to part with it long enough for the mother to wash and dry it.

This valuable possession is often called a "transitional object" by psychologists and psychiatrists because it serves as a transition between the child's early egocentricism (in which his primary love-object is himself) and later object relations (in which he can relate to and love others). Generally, it symbolizes the mother and serves to provide the child with mother's comfort and love when she is not available. At night, when the child suffers the prospect of being alone for a long period of time in a dark or dimly lighted room, this substitute for mother's love and protection is especially welcome.

I do not know why some children go through this phase and others do not. Generally, most children lose interest in their transitional object by the age of five. There are some, however, who maintain the dependence into their teens (this is more common in girls than boys), and a few (again, especially girls) will even take their favorite doll along with them when they go to college or get married. The desire to have a transitional object in the pre-school period is probably normal and certainly not, in itself, a sign of psychological disturbance. Beyond that period, the longer the child persists in maintaining the magical relationship, the more suggestive it is of a psychological problem (probably of the dependency type).

"Who wants to be Snow White in the play?" Play allows the gratification of desires that may not be realized in reality. In play the child can be whoever he wishes, be wherever he wants, and gain, in fantasy, all the satisfactions attendant to the transformation. Reality considerations are ignored to varying degrees in the desire to gain the benefits of play. And it behooves the adult to allow the child to let his fancy run free when it is to the child's benefit to do so and to bring him back to the world of reality when there might be some danger in allowing the total ignoring of reality factors.

A good example of the former process occurred at a day camp I know of. The three- to five-year-olds were doing a play of *Snow White and the Seven Dwarfs*. When the counselors asked who wanted to be Snow White, five children volunteered. Similarly six boys wanted to be the handsome prince. Three boys wanted to be Grumpy; two wanted to be Happy; three girls wanted to be the mean old witch; four girls wanted to be the queen; etc., etc. Rather than disappoint anyone, all children got the part they wanted. The theatrical spectacle that day was a sight to behold. At any time one could see on the stage three or four Snow Whites, a few handsome princes, no less than ten or twelve dwarfs, etc. Everyone was having a wonderful time. "Where is it written (other than in the book)," I said to myself, "that there should only be *one* Snow White, *one* handsome prince, and exactly *seven* dwarfs?" This is the kind of unreality encouragement that can help the child gain the gratifications of his world of play.

On the other hand, when children divorce themselves too much from reality, they may do some things in their play that may be dangerous. Most children know that when they don a Superman cape, it will not really enable them to fly. However, there are occasionally children who have to be cautioned or restricted in this regard, lest they harm themselves. The more common problem is the child whose appreciation of his limitations are blurred by companions who encourage dangerous exploits. It is very hard for many children not to rise to the challenge

"I dare you." It is as if their whole self-worth is being tested by the exploit, as well as their acceptability to their peers. The parent does well to impress upon the child that it is usually a sign of greater bravery to refuse to accept the dare, that the more courageous and manly thing is to defy the majority in accordance with one's own opinion regarding the wisest course to take. If one can be successful in developing such attitudes in the prepubertal child (and it is not something that is easily accomplished), it is less likely that he will be swept up in the various kinds of destructive adolescent behavior often engaged in primarily, if not exclusively, because of an inordinate fear of defying the wishes of the majority.

"Daddy, look what I drew!" Play provides the child with a sense of mastery that is vital if one's life is to be meaningful. The child who builds a model boat gleams with satisfaction over his accomplishment. He often beckons his parents to share his joy and admire his accomplishment. The wise parent directs his compliment to the product of the child's efforts. "What a beautiful boat!" is the most effective form of praise, because it directs itself to the created object. It communicates to the child that he is worthy of praise because of the concrete act he has performed. To say to the child, "What a wonderful boy," is not as effective in enhancing his self-esteem because it does not directly link up the praise with the attainment. When a compliment is given a child, without direct reference to some specific accomplishment, it has little effect in enhancing feelings of self-worth.

Play can provide the child with the wherewithal and the sense of mastery that are vital to his feelings of self-competence and high self-regard. In sports he acquires physical competence and dexterity. In play at home he builds things, solves puzzles, makes up skits, and plays checkers. All these provide him with a sense of mastery.

Many factors contribute to the formation of psychological symptoms, but one of the most important is compensation for feelings of inadequacy that relate to a failure to have achieved a sense of mastery. The child who fabricates fascinating exploits and experiences to his classmates does so, in part, out of the desire to compensate for his basic feeling that he has nothing genuine to offer that might elicit their esteem. Although he may possess qualities that might engender their respect, more often he has not developed endearing qualities and lies, therefore, in the futile attempt to gain their affection.

This basic need for mastery appears very early in the child's life. In the latter part of the first year he may wish to hold his own bottle rather than have his mother hold it for him. During this same period, he wishes to hold his own spoon, and the mother who insists that she feed the child herself performs a disservice to the infant. To avoid a mess, a few minutes of extra work, or possibly to save a few cents worth of food, she deprives the child of a healthy growth experience that is vital to his psychological well-being. The toddler who walks away from the parent (but who looks back after every five or six steps for reassurance that the parent is still there) wants to prove that he can do things on his own. The three-year-old who stands on tiptoes in order to press the elevator button enjoys a similar sense of mastery and accomplishment.

Children are constantly going to their parents with "Look, Mommy, what I drew in school"; "Look Daddy, I wrote my name." And when children play house they are practicing the techniques of domesticity that will ultimately enhance their capabilities as parents, homemakers, and providers. The examples are legion because the phenomenon is ubiquitous. The number of times a day the average child performs an act which is designed, in part, to enhance his sense of mastery are probably countless, and the parent who deprives the child of such opportunities or fails to encourage them is crippling him indeed.

"Bang, bang. You're dead." Play provides a gratification of wishes and impulses that may not or cannot be fulfilled in reality. If the wish is socially unacceptable, play allows symbolic gratification and release so that the child need not suffer the guilt he would have if he fully appreciated the underlying meaning of his play. He cannot hit his father, but he can hit a father doll. Play, therefore, has cathartic value. Sports allow the release of hostilities that would not otherwise be permitted expression. Games of war and cowboys and Indians provide similar releases. In order to derive the gratifications of such play, there must be a make-believe element, a "willing suspension of disbelief," as the Romantic poets used to call it. Sigmund Freud once said, "The opposite of play is not serious occupation, but reality."[12]

Our lives are inevitably filled with frustration. The child is constantly being told, "No." He cannot touch everything he wants; he cannot open every drawer, every closet, every window. He cannot pick up, hold, throw, etc., everything he wishes to. He is surrounded by restrictions. The frustrations he feels inevitably engender hostile feelings within him, and he cannot express these directly toward his parents because he is too beholden to them for his survival. Besides, they often actively restrict him in expressing his hostility toward them. He is told, "That's not the way you talk to a mother." Even the enlightened mother suppresses him

---

[12]Freud, Sigmund, The Relation of the Poet to Day-Dreaming, translated by Joan Riviere, *Collected Papers*, Vol. 4, New York : Basic Books, Inc., 1959.

in this regard. She may say, "I can understand that you're angry and you can be as angry as you want, but I'm still not going to let you throw rocks through the window." The pent-up hostilities can be released in many ways. Displaced discharge onto a sibling is common. Hostile fantasies are another outlet. Dreams, especially nightmares, provide the child with further opportunity for release. Monster movies and sadistic cartoons on television allow for vicarious expression. And play is a further way for the child to discharge his hostilities. The games of "Superman" and "Batman" provide the child with a specious feeling of power he does not otherwise possess and allow hostile release as well in a socially beneficial context. (Killing and jailing public criminals is a most noble endeavor.) In addition, by identifying with such omnipotent figures, he also provides himself with a feeling of power over and protection from the dangers of the world (both real and fantasized).

"I never let my children play with guns." This is a common boast of certain parents who consider their position proof of their psychological sophistication. It is often stated with a definite attitude of condescension toward those who allow their children this traditional form of play. "There is enough bloodshed in the world as it is," they smugly claim, "and letting children play with guns just encourages even more." "Violence has to be taught," they profess, "and I'm certainly not going to teach it to *my* child." The parent who is taken in by all of this may begin to feel that he, and others like himself, are breeding children who will end up as thugs, homicidal maniacs, or fanatic militarists. He may guiltily think that crime in the streets, senseless brutality, wanton murder, and military holocausts are, in part, the fault of parents like himself who allow their children to play with guns.

The proponents of this theory fail to appreciate the simple fact that it is the man who controls the weapon and not vice versa. It is the hostility of man that breeds violence and warfare, not the accessibility of weapons. Weapons are merely instruments that allow man to vent his rage more effectively, that enhance the destructive power of his fury. Were every gun in the world destroyed—all other things being equal—man would quickly utilize other weapons to vent his anger. He might even resort to throwing rocks—if that were all that was left to him—and, in his present state, he would do it. And if rocks were inaccessible, he would use his fists, feet, and teeth—so strong appear to be his hostile impulses.

The basic problem to be dealt with is anger, discussed in detail in Chapter 6. It will suffice here to state briefly that I do not believe that there is an innate pool of anger demanding expression or an instinct for anger continually pressing for release. Rather there is an hereditarily determined physiological system that provides the vehicle for expression of anger. The child, like everyone else, is continually exposed to frustration, which inevitably produces anger. I believe that a group of children reared on a desert island (or in a similar environment where they had no access to modern weaponry) would handle some of the inevitable frustrations of life by using rocks and sticks or, if these were not available, parts of their own bodies.

The child today can select the toy gun. If that cannot be obtained, he will strike with his baseball bat, throw his truck, or use whatever else is at hand that has the potential for inflicting pain (either in reality or in fantasy). To proscribe toy guns accomplishes nothing. Both the normal child and the disturbed child (who may have an inordinate need for hostility expression) will not be affected by the absence of toy guns. Both will readily resort to the thousands of other objects that can be used to express hostility. In fact, making an issue over the toy gun (for example, when the child, against mother's wishes, plays with guns in the home of other children) creates a new, totally unnecessary power struggle that adds to the child's frustrations, increases his anger, and thereby requires him to utilize even more instruments like toy guns, which allow the release of hostility. (Easy access of adults to real guns, of course, is another issue entirely.)

"Let's play house." Although more common among girls, younger boys are readily brought into this game when girls are playing. The game satisfies many important psychological needs, and it assists the child in the process of identifying with the parent of the same sex. Most parents appreciate that the child who frequently or primarily chooses to be the opposite-sexed parent in the game may be having some psychological difficulty. (In Chapters 1 and 4 I have discussed my opinions on sexual identity—specifically regarding what I consider to be each sex's primary and secondary roles.) The kinds of toys parents provide and the roles they encourage when their children are playing house can affect the development of their sexual identification. Girls, I believe, should be given dolls to foster the role of child-rearer; and boys such toys as trucks and tools to encourage the role of breadwinner and family protector. In addition, I would provide each sex with toys typical of the opposite's primary area. I would occasionally give a boy a doll and encourage him to take care of the baby while the mother is out working. I would want to counteract some of the traditional social stigma associated with the male's involvement with child-rearing. Similarly, I would occasionally give a girl a car or set of tools to foster interest and pleasure in tradition-

ally masculine pursuits. Competence in these areas has too long been considered unfeminine, and I would want to contribute toward a change in this attitude on the part of society.

In playing house the child gains a sense of ego-enhancement as he fantasies himself an adult with all the accompanying prerogatives. He practices adult behavior and thereby begins to learn the role he will ultimately have to assume in society. Development of conscience is also enhanced in the game. The girl who, while playing the mother, says to her younger brother (who may have been relegated to the ignominious role of the "child"), "Don't cross against the red light," or, "If you do that again, I'm going to spank you," is clearly repeating her mother's words (possibly with a little exaggeration). In this way, she strengthens the incorporation of these dictates into her *own* psyche. Under the guise of admonishing her younger brother, she is really warning herself.

"Let's play doctor." Playing doctor and nurse provides the child with an opportunity to satisfy his curiosities about the anatomy of the opposite sex. For most children, such games are played not so much to gratify sexual urges as to see what they have been so strictly prevented from observing. The child without opposite-sexed siblings may become a strong devotee of the game, but even the child with siblings generally considers the genitalia of opposite-sexed neighbors far more interesting than his own siblings' sexual organs. The child does not differ very much from his parents in this regard, and it was probably they who communicated to him in the first place the notion that one's neighbors' sexual organs have certain indefinable, but nevertheless very real, differences that make them extremely fascinating organs to look at. No matter how healthy the home attitude may be regarding undressing in front of one another, the parents must still instruct the child about the social rules regarding hiding certain parts of one's body if he is to adequately adjust to the world outside his home. Therefore, even under ideal circumstances strong curiosities are engendered, and these can be satisfied by playing doctor and nurse.

Most children do not use the game as a prelude to sexual play and stimulation. To do so occasionally, however, is probably within the normal range of children's behavior. But to become obsessed with the game, to frequently play it to the neglect of other activities, and to stimulate to the point of orgasm probably reflects the presence of psychological disorder.

When parents discover their children playing doctor and nurse, I suggest they make a comment that recognizes the child's interest as normal, that lessens the guilt and embarrassment he may feel on being discovered, and that communicates that there may be certain social repercussions. Therefore the game must be restricted to the more superficial forms of physical examination. (Evaluation for the presence of diseases of the penis, testicles, vagina, and rectum will be left to the family physician.)

"Let's play dentist." Play also allows for an assimilation and desensitization to painful experiences. The phenomenon known as "shell shock" in World War I and "war neurosis" in World War II and subsequently is an example of this psychological mechanism. In these disorders the individual has been overwhelmed by the horrors of warfare. He characteristically relives the traumatic experience, not only through conscious reiteration but also through hallucinatory experiences and dreams. Characteristically, he may suddenly go into a panic state and try to hide from or flee bombs, shells, and bullets that he may really believe are endangering him. These hallucinatory experiences serve a purpose. They allow a piecemeal desensitization to the traumatic episode. Each time the individual reexperiences the event it becomes less painful to him. Ultimately there is a gradual assimilation and acceptance of the trauma and he can think about it more dispassionately.

A similar process is operative in grief and mourning. The deep pain that one experiences at the death of a loved one is lessened by repeatedly thinking about the deceased, talking about him, handling cherished memorabilia, and dreaming about him. Each mental contact is associated with a somewhat less painful emotion than the previous one, and there is gradual desensitization to the grief.

Playing doctor and dentist and thereby focusing on a specific operative procedure may serve this same purpose, both before and after the traumatic experience. Similarly, playing monster, war and cops and robbers may also enable the child to work through the fear he may feel at viewing such experiences on television and in the movies.

"Daddy, you just sat on my friend Judy!" The imaginary friend is one of childhood's most intriguing and engaging phenomena. Generally, he suddenly appears on the scene when the child is about two to three years old and resides in the home for a year or so. Both his birth and death are precipitous and unannounced. His arrival is as mysterious as his departure and involves no particular fanfare. That he is visible only to the child himself seems to be of no particular concern to the child. For reasons that I do not understand, he does not move into every home; and when he does become a guest, he may not befriend each child in the family. The criteria he uses to determine who will be his friend are never disclosed to adults (not even to psychiatrists). Although some claim

that he prefers children without siblings, I am not impressed with the evidence for this, and it has not been my own observation. Although children usually have imaginary friends of their own sex, choosing one of the opposite sex is common and not, in itself, pathological. Lastly, he is a great source of amusement to parents, who can usually be relied upon to treat him with the respect a special guest deserves.

The child will never again have a friend as loyal, dependable, and compliant. He never fails to appear when needed, and never overstays his welcome. He has no objection to being bullied, and thereby provides the child with a scapegoat for hostilities that could not be directed toward others. He readily takes the blame for the child's misbehavior and has never been known to object to false accusations. He is an excellent conversationalist (mainly as a listener, but many comments are attributed to him), and he exhibits a rare patience for the child's often endless verbal ruminations. There is no game he will not agree to play, and he never loses interest before the child does.

The imaginary friend is a willing learner of all the rules of the household and never seems to tire of their reiteration by the child. He listens with interest to the child's innumerable admonitions: "Bad boy. You made in your pants"; "If you run into the street, I'll spank you"; "Don't you ever speak that way to me again." His purpose in this regard, of course, is to help the child himself learn by repetition the rules of society. He is also an excellent attention-getting device. When the child feels neglected by adults who are not concerning themselves with him, talking about the imaginary playmate can be the conversation piece that redirects adult attention to him.

With all these assets, however, he has one liability. (No one is perfect!) He is very sensitive to slights by the child's parents. Both he and the child become easily offended when parents forget to include him in family activities. When Sally indignantly says, "Daddy, you just sat on my friend Judy," she wants her parents' agreement that this valuable friend does indeed exist. When Bobby plaintively asks, "Where is Larry going to sit?" he wants parental reassurance that his invisible friend has a place in the family scheme of things. Many other communications to the imaginary companion (especially those that require parental cooperation and compliance) serve to confirm his somewhat precarious existence. For example, he may be angrily told that he cannot come along on the family picnic because he has been bad.

Sometimes the imaginary companion takes a protective or retaliative role. This is especially true when the friend takes the form of an animal. The pet lion or tiger is available at a moment's notice to scare away or trounce those who would cause the child any harm or inconvenience—no matter how slight. The beast may also serve as the externalization of the child's own unacceptable angry impulses and guiltlessly acts them out. He is thereby a most convenient and useful pet. The animal companion can also help the child desensitize himself to inner angry feelings that he may fear or feel guilty over. The animal becomes the incarnation of such hostility. By externalizing, the child denies the anger as his own and can decide at any given time his degree of contact with his symbolized hostility. His frequent contact with his ferocious friend allows a piecemeal accommodation to his own dangerous impulses. This process is part of normal development.

There comes a time when we recognize within ourselves impulses that have been considered unacceptable by our parents. This is a necessary first step in becoming acculturated. Those who never achieve such recognition are in a poor position to get along, even minimally, with others. They do not know what will be acceptable behavior and what will not—a crippling situation indeed. The child's externalizing his unacceptable impulses, by attributing them to his imaginary friend or pet, indicates that he is aware, at some level, of their existence within himself. The slow desensitization process ultimately results in the child's acceptance of the hostile impulses as his own. And he has then taken another step forward toward psychological health. This process of fusion can be assisted by the parent who refuses to accept the child's allegation that it was his imaginary friend who caused the trouble: "No, Stevie did not break the vase—it was you—and you're going to have to stand in the corner for doing it."

In the final few weeks of the friend's sojourn in the home, the child exhibits a peculiar relationship with him. At times the companion is very much there, and the child reacts with his usual indignation when the family does not show him proper respect. At other times, the child says absolutely nothing about him; and when his name is broached, the child becomes embarrassed and suggests changing the subject (a request with which the wise parent will readily comply, because the topic appears to be a very sensitive one). And then, as suddenly as he appeared, he leaves—never to be heard from again. Referring to him now only brings about the child's puzzlement. There is no mourning over his loss. He is no longer needed. He has been a useful friend during a specific phase of the child's life. He has now moved on into a younger child's home.

"Mommy, buy me a toy." Because of their appreciation of many of the aforementioned psychological benefits to be derived from play, parents, teachers, psychologists, and psychiatrists provide children with

toys to facilitate the salutary benefits of play. The more sophisticated these adults are concerning its psychological benefits, the more elaborate the toys they buy. This, in my opinion, is an unfortunate trend and benefits the toy manufacturers more than the children. Since the make-believe element is so important, the reality element may serve to restrict the child's fantasy and thereby deprive him of some of the psychological benefits of play. An excellent example of this phenomenon is to be found in a psychological test known as the Thematic Apperception Test,[13] commonly referred to as the TAT. This test consists of a series of cards depicting common life situations about which the person being tested is asked to tell a story. There is one card, however, that is completely blank. This card is at the same time the most anxiety-provoking and the most revealing. There are no stimuli to catalyze fantasy; there are no "contaminants" to free fantasy formation. The story elicited by this card is similar to the dream in that it is a complete creation of the imagination and is in no way determined by specific reality stimuli. In a similar manner, we learn far more about a child by asking him to make up a story and relate it to us verbally than we would if he were to depict it in a drawing. In order to draw it, he must restrict himself to a small fraction of all the elements in his mind; and he is confined not only by his technique, but by the size of the paper, the colors available to him, and the allotted time for drawing. The story a child tells about a very expensive doll that simulates a real child as accurately as possible is far less revealing than one that might be told about a human figure made by putting a ball of clay on top of a pencil. The empty dollhouse elicits far richer stories than the well-appointed one with numerous articles of furniture. Elaborate and expensive toys tend to have more parts that may break down and may therefore be ultimately less useful to the child. A set of electric trains, no matter how realistic and beautiful, has far less flexibility of travel than a string of blocks. In addition, the latter is the preferable toy for the pre-schooler, who generally cannot set up and operate the electric trains himself. He gets far more fun from pushing his trains wherever he wants (rather than confining them to the tracks) and can fantasize bridges, tunnels, etc., more elaborate than those provided by the manufacturer. The economically deprived child, then, has this advantage over his more affluent counterpart—his other disadvantages notwithstanding.

"That must have made you very angry. I think you'll feel better

---

[13] Murray, Henry A., *Thematic Apperception Test*, Cambridge, Mass.: Harvard University Press, 1943.

if you pound some clay." It is important to appreciate that the mere *release* of hostility is only *part* of the healthy adaptation to angry impulses. Ideally the child should be helped to express his anger to remove the irritant that engendered it in the first place. Those who hold that the mere expression of angry feelings suffices suggest that the child first be approached with comments designed to catalyze the expression of angry feelings: "You must be very angry that you weren't invited to Anne's birthday party"; "It must make you very angry that Daddy wants to watch television rather than play with you." They then suggest the child be provided with media for angry expression: clay for pounding, blocks for throwing, etc. I agree that the initial comments can be helpful as a starting point. They serve to lessen the guilt the child might have over his angry feelings and foster their expression. It is the second step—of providing clay and blocks—that I take issue with. Such maneuvers only guide the child toward *displacement of his feelings away from the direction toward which they should be turned.* Although pounding clay may have a little cathartic value, it does not result in any basic change in the situation that produced the anger in the first place. Therefore, there is a greater likelihood that the uncomfortable angry feelings will be regenerated than there would be if the anger were directed toward rectifying the situation that originally brought it about.

The girl who was not invited to the birthday party may feel a little better after throwing sand or kicking a ball around. However, she does far better for herself if she can learn something about how or why she may have alienated the friend. If she indeed brought about her own rejection and is able to rectify this, she will suffer fewer future rejections, have less to be angry about, and thereby have less pent-up anger to express. The father who prefers the television set to playing with his child might be pried away from it if the child were to openly express his resentment. If the child is successful, then he will no longer be angry over that situation. If not, his anger will only abate when he accepts his rejection and can be helped to find substitutive satisfactions.

"I believe competitive games are harmful to children." Some time ago, while I was playing checkers with a five-year-old boy, he exhibited what I thought was an exaggerated investment in whether or not he was winning. In order to help alter what I considered to be an inappropriate attitude, I said to him, "Alan, the important thing is how much fun you have while playing, not whether you win the game." To this he replied, "No, you're wrong; the *important* thing is whether you win the game." The boy was, for the most part, right. We pay lip service to comments such as mine; but who of us would enjoy tennis, bridge, or chess were there no winner? My revised advice to him would be, "There are two important things: how much you enjoy playing the game and whether you win; both can be fun." There is no question, then, that competitive games can be ego-enhancing and can provide a sense of mastery and competence that are vital to the development of the normal child and that are so lacking in most psychologically disturbed children. When the competitive element becomes all-important, however, the child may be deprived of the important pleasurable aspects of play.

"*Should I let him win?*" This question can be reduced to the following conflict: if the adult plays honestly and wins most games, the child may be humiliated and deprived of the opportunity to gain the feeling of accomplishment associated with winning; if the adult purposely loses, the child may benefit from the gratifications of winning, but the adult's dishonesty may cause the child to lose trust in him. (Siblings, of course, have no such conflict. They provide true rivals with whom the child can experience the lessons of life through game playing.) Although I am a strong proponent of being honest with children (generally it is a *sine qua non* of therapy), this is one of the situations in which I consider falsification of the truth to be justified. I allow the child to win or lose depending upon what is desirable at that time for that particular child. I have not found children to have basically lost trust in me over this duplicity, probably because there is so much openness and honesty in compensation and possibly because winning and losing are usually so balanced that the child does not become suspicious. Such duplicity, used sparingly and with discretion, serves to enhance the child's self-confidence and makes him feel worthwhile and competent. Especially at times when the child's self-esteem may have been lowered, the winning of a hard-fought game or giving the adult a "shellacking" makes the child stand a little taller in his own eyes.

One might, of course, avoid the whole dilemma by openly giving oneself a handicap, as is done in many sports. This obviates the lying problem but diminishes the child's gratification in winning, and so the benefits are lessened.

"*Timmy's such a sore loser.*" A child with great feelings of inadequacy relies heavily on winning to compensate for his low self-esteem. He plays a hard game, puts all his energies into it, and moans at every loss. It is as if his whole worth as a person depended upon the outcome. The adult should not fall into the trap of letting these children always win. The world will not be so kind, and furthermore, the game has little to do with the primary issue—low self-esteem. Such a child might be told, "You think my whole opinion of you is based on the outcome of this game. That's just not so. My opinion of someone is based on many, many things that are more important than whether he wins or loses a game." Other comments like "It's only a game"; "It's not the end of the world if you lose"; and "I'll still like you if you lose" can be tried. In addition, actually playing and having the experience of not being ridiculed and embarrassed for losing can be emotionally corrective. However, these approaches will only be minimally helpful if the trait is deep-seated. Such children need more intensive approaches (such as psychotherapy) to enhance the low self-esteem that is causing them to be sore losers.

"How about a game of checkers?" There is much we can learn about a child by careful observation of his play. To demonstrate this I will describe how the game of checkers can be a valuable source of information about the child's basic wishes, frustrations, etc. The discussion will also serve to provide examples of some of the principles of play I have presented as well as of some others I have not. The game of checkers probably antedates chess. It was played in the days of the pharaohs and is mentioned in the works of Homer and Plato. This enduring and ubiquitous appeal attests to the fact that the game provides many psychological gratifications.

Before one can adequately appraise the child's responses while playing the game, it is necessary to appreciate what is normal play for children of comparable ages. I have not conducted a formal study of the degree of proficiency one can expect at various age levels. The ages presented here are derived from clinical impressions and should be used only as indefinite guidelines. They have their greatest value in the extremes; that is, for those who deviate most from the norm.

The average child of five to six should be able to play the game. When he first learns to play, he is apt to see a magical relationship between the color of his checkers and his chances of winning. He plays a strictly offensive game and is not too concerned with his partner's potential danger to him. He restricts his focus to a small segment of the board, forges doggedly ahead, and tries to jump his opponent regardless of the consequences. He does not devise any traps or grand plans. He sees single, but not double or triple, jumps and has to be told that he can jump farther. Deriving great pleasure from kings, he tries quickly to get to his opponent's side. But once he acquires a king, he tends to leave it and try to get more, rather than to move it out and attack his opponent from the rear. His delight in acquiring kings, along with the inability to use them effectually, is the hallmark of the child's play at this age. Lastly, he frequently interrupts the game to determine whether he is winning, by counting the number of checkers that he and his opponent have taken off the board, and tends to disregard the fact that this sort of reckoning fails to take the kings into account.

By the age of seven to nine, the child should appreciate that the immediate gain of winning a man can be more than counterbalanced by his opponent's subsequent move. He plays more cautiously and his focus broadens, but he still sees only one step ahead; that is, his opponent's single subsequent move. He knows how to use his kings for simple pursuit. He readily sees double and triple (and quadruple!) jumps and enjoys them tremendously. He recognizes that the winning player is determined by the number of men on the board, kings and regular men, and not by what has been captured.

It is not until age ten or eleven that the child can really play a game in which he is able to plan ahead beyond his opponent's next move. He can devise traps, sacrifice to gain more in the end, and engage in various gambits. As in any intellectual pursuit, there will always be the precocious ones and the laggards, but this has been the norm in my clinical experience.

Prior to beginning play the passive or fearful child complies with his opponent in the decisions and ground rules that must be agreed upon. For example, if asked which color he wants, he may respond, "It doesn't matter, you take whichever you want." He fears doing anything that might result in his opponent's displeasure and possible resentment of him. Most children play according to one of three rules pertaining to whether one has to jump; namely, (1) a player must jump if he is in a position to; (2) he has the option; (3) if he does not jump when he could have, his opponent may take the faulty man. The fearful or passive child lets his opponent decide which rule to use; most others have a definite preference.

The insecure child often will hesitate to play for fear he may lose. He may instead suggest a game of pure chance where there is less likelihood of humiliation. He asks, "Are you good?" or partially protects himself from the embarrassment of his anticipated loss by stating beforehand that he is a poor player and that the opponent will probably win. He may insist on going first each time, hoping to increase his chances of winning. Such children interrupt the game frequently to count checkers in order to see who is winning and may become "bored" or "tired" when they are losing.

As the game progresses, a child who is losing may wish to change the rules in the middle of the game in order to improve his chances. I usually tell such a child that the game is "no fun if we do not play by the rules" and that, if he wishes to continue, he will have to abide by the original rules. However, one might add, "If you want to make up special rules for the next game, which apply to both of us, I'll be glad to try that."

The child from a chaotic, disorganized home, who may not have developed the degree of compulsivity necessary to adhere to rules, can also be told that the game will continue only on the condition that the rules are adhered to. This is salutary in that the game serves as a vehicle for engendering in the child a sense of organization and adherence to regulation in a manner that can be pleasurable. The self-absorbed, egotistical child who will not wait his turn learns a lesson in self-restraint and respect for the rights of others, as he is required to wait while the adult is thinking about his next move. The suspicious child plays cautiously and defensively. He hugs his pieces to the sides and rear of the board and may spend long periods of time deliberating in order to avoid being jumped or trapped. The child who cheats during the game might be told, "Look, this game is no fun if you're going to cheat. If you want to play with me, you'll have to play it straight. I'm sure your friends feel the same way."

If the child is clearly not deriving gratification from the game, it can stem from a variety of causes. The obsessive child is too wound up in his doubting, indecisiveness, and procrastination to enjoy himself. Also, his obsessive distractions detract from his pleasure. He may be concerned with whether the checkers touch the marginal lines of the squares, and he has to be sure that the non-crown side of the checker faces upwards on the men and crown side upwards on the kings. The depressed or anxious child also derives little satisfaction from the game. He will often fidget, play too quickly, show poor concentration, and make many errors that he is intellectually capable of avoiding. The hostile child may play an aggressive and serious game with great interest in winning. He will respond with glee at every advantage and then rub salt into his opponent's wounds. If the hostility is severely repressed and the child fears retaliation for its expression, he might be afraid to win in anticipation of his adversary's hostile reaction. This fear may be expressed in such comments as, "Don't be mad at me if I win."

The adult's hostility may also manifest itself during the game. On a few occasions, I have found myself winning too many games or trying hard to beat a child and realized that I harbored anger toward him that I was not aware of previously. The game brought these feelings to my direct attention, and they were then handled more appropriately.

The way in which a therapist's error might have been utilized to the benefit of a boy in treatment is demonstrated by the following experience of a psychology student I once supervised. The child made a poor move, to which the therapist responded, "Are you sure you want to do that?" The boy looked up, slightly irritated, thought a moment, and then replied, "I did it and don't want to change it." The child's manner and facial expression communicated his attitude, "I made the mistake, and I'm man enough to accept the consequences."

This was, indeed, a mature and healthy response on the boy's part, but unfortunately the therapist did not take full advantage of the further therapeutic opportunities this incident provided. Had he said, "You're right. I'm sorry I treated you like a baby. Good for you for stopping me," he would have revealed that he, too, was fallible, and thereby lessened the chances of unrealistic hero worship. Such hero worship can create difficulties in one's relationships because, like other distortions in interpersonal relations, it lessens the likelihood that we will deal effectively with reality. It would have further communicated that the therapist was mature enough to admit his errors and that such an admission enhances one's manliness rather than detracts from it. In addition, he would have reinforced the boy's mature reaction, thereby increasing the likelihood that it would become ingrained in his personality and be utilized in the future. Clearly, parents can follow the same principles when they play games with children.

The egocentric child who is chronologically old enough to play at a level where he attends to his opponent's strategies may focus only on his own pieces in a manner similar to the younger child. Such a child can be helped to become more "socially aware" by such comments as "Watch out for my king"; "You fell right into my trap"; and "If you had moved there, you could have had a double jump." These remarks, also, of course, help him improve his game and thereby enhance his social adaptability. An insecure child may not be able to learn better playing techniques from another. The more secure one will learn receptively and utilize what he has been taught.

During the game, praising the child for good playing (while concentrating on the deed rather than on the child—for reasons previously discussed) can be ego-enhancing. Comments such as "That was a very clever move"; "Gee, I fell right into your trap"; and "Boy, you really had me sweating there for a while" can be helpful.

As previously mentioned, the game has greater psychological value to the child if the adult is also enjoying himself. One way of stimulating this, if his interest is lagging, is to let the child get far ahead of him;

then when he has only two to three checkers left, to the child's eight to nine, he plays as hard as he can.

Competent playing, even if he has lost, gives the child a feeling of mastery that can be especially helpful to one with low self-esteem. If he has learned a few techniques from the adult that have improved his game, his utilization of this knowledge in games with peers can be salutary.

The child who prefers his fantasy world to that of reality may worry obsessively at the end of the game about how it might have been otherwise; for example, "If I had moved there, *then* I would have gotten a double jump" or "*If* the checkers had been like this, then I would have won." To such children, I respond in such a way that the child is directly confronted with reality: "Yes, it's true that *if* your checkers had been that way, you might have won. But, they *weren't*. Maybe in the next game you'll be able to beat me by doing that."

Lastly, the game gives the child a lesson in certain aspects of real living. One is responsible for one's fate and suffers the consequences of one's actions. Whether a person wins or loses is, in part, determined by his own acts. If one plans ahead and is appropriately cautious, then one does better than if he sits back and leaves things to chance. The lesson of being master of one's fate is present in most skill games. However, one is not completely master; one must reckon, too, with others in the world whom one must compromise with, avert, deal with head on, and at times, succumb to. All these lessons can be learned in microcosm in a relatively painless way in games such as checkers. And many other lessons of life can also be enjoyably learned by the child in the context of his play.

9

Education

Difficulty in learning is probably the most common reason for referring a child to a therapist. Many children's psychological problems are either denied or unrecognized by parents until the child enters school and more objective observers detect his problems. Or the more rigid demands of the school situation may cause problems to manifest themselves when the child enters school for the first time. The child's learning problem is best understood as an attempt to resolve or adapt to difficulties present in both the child and his parents. And since the root of the learning disorder is most often in the home, a detailed understanding of the child's family is necessary if one is to adequately appreciate the factors bringing it about. However, it is important for the reader to appreciate that I discuss here only those learning difficulties that are psychogenic in origin; that is, those resulting from family disturbances. I will not be discussing the learning disabilities associated with organic or physiological disease of the brain, of which the most common type is referred to as "minimal brain dysfunction."

Extreme learning disability results in total separation from school. When older, such children will often be referred to as "dropouts." There are children, however, who "drop out" at lower levels, but the law does not permit them to leave the school situation. Such "grade school drop-outs"—and even "kindergarten dropouts"—remain physically in the classroom but learn little. Many of the problems in this chapter can manifest themselves during this early period and, if not rectified, may cause the child to literally waste his whole educational career. For years, he may attend school and learn practically nothing.

Psychotic children may, however, exhibit an uncanny ability to learn such things as species of dinosaurs, railroad schedules, and baseball statistics. They may have such a vast storehouse of knowledge in their areas of interest they may give the impression that they are, at the very least, brilliant. But their knowledge is quite restricted and totally unrelated to the human scene. Although their memory for baseball minutiae may be prodigious, they cannot, and may never have, played the game. Although walking railroad information booths, they have little interest in using a train to visit any person or place of interest. In other psychotic children, the failure to learn may give the impression that they are retarded. In reality, they are pseudoretardates; that is, they are perfectly capable of learning but are prevented from doing so by severe emotional problems.

"Gee, dad, when I grow up I want to be like you." The healthy child wants to learn, in part, out of the desire to identify with, emulate, and grow up to be like an admired adult figure. For the healthy child of five to six, reading and the mastery of simple arithmetic principles can be exhilarating. He can finally read! He can finally figure out for himself the previously undecipherable symbols that have always been all around him and that adults readily understand. He can count money just like "big people." A major step forward has been made into the adult world. It is a true milestone in the life of the child. However, for the child who equates adulthood with weighty obligations and loathsome responsibilities, these advances are not only unwanted but feared; and one should not be surprised to see him sit by silently as the others are swept up in the excitement of learning.

"I don't trust my kids with those 'highbrow' and 'commie' teachers." Parental attitudes toward the child's teachers and other school authorities have an important effect on the child's commitment to the educational process. If the parents are basically in sympathy with the authorities' aims and respectful of them, so will the child be. If the parents are not, the child's respect for them may be undermined and his

ability to learn from them compromised, if not made impossible. The child is not likely to identify with a teacher his parents despise; the risk of losing his parents' affection is too great for him to take that chance.

In some families that have not reached their vocational, economic, or social aspirations, there is a constant condemnation of the successful, which often stems from jealousy. The teachers may then be berated as "intellectuals" and "snobs" and criticized as condescending to the less educated. This is sometimes extended to their being inappropriately labeled "Communists" and considered to be devoting their primary energies toward the violent overthrow of our government. The child can hardly be expected to learn from someone he thinks is secretly plotting the extermination of his parents. Parental jealousy may also manifest itself in the condemnation of those engaged in intellectual pursuits as less manly than others. The boy who becomes very studious may then be considered by his parents to be turning into a "sissy" and possibly even veering toward homosexuality. His classmates may have acquired similar notions from their parents, and this can serve to significantly dampen what might have been deeply gratifying scholarly endeavors.

Observing teachers and other educated people to be such an object of scorn to his parents, the child cannot but fear that if he too were successful in that area they would similarly hate him. Doing poorly (and even failing) may then be the only way for him to keep their affection. The phenomenon is similar to the depression that some people feel on obtaining a long sought-after goal. For example, the president of a large company, whatever esteem he may enjoy, is usually the object of much inappropriate and displaced hostility. Presidents, governors, and mayors have traditionally been considered to be the cause of all the woes of their constituents. When an individual finally finds himself occupying such an office, he may find the hostility directed toward him intolerable. In some cases the person slows his pace as he gets higher; others decline the honor; some quit or acquire a convenient sickness that prevents them from keeping the position; some do so poorly that they get demoted back to a job where they will be less subjected to criticism; and some even kill themselves (although many other factors are operative, the fear of jealous scorn is often contributory to such suicides).

"He has a defiant attitude toward all authority—the teachers, the principal, and especially my husband and me." Some children openly express the anger they feel—anger that generally stems from difficulties they may have in their relationships with their parents. Not only may they exhibit this anger at home, but much may "spill over" onto others—such as teachers and other school personnel. The deprivations they suffer may result in their taking the attitude that "I get little if any love from my parents so it's not very likely I'm going to get more from anyone else. I might as well get my kicks wherever and whenever I can. Hurting others and destroying things are among my greatest joys." Such children live for the moment. Expecting little pleasure in the future, they try to get as much as they can in the present. They are not interested in waiting for the remote gratifications that education promises. In fact, they do not believe that such gratifications really exist or that they can attain them. By disruptive and antagonistic behavior they not only release anger but also gain the morbid gratification of hurting others. In the classroom they may be obstructionistic, arrogant, and disobedient. Rules for them are made to be broken. In fact, the rule is their "cue." Learning what a particular rule is provides them with information as to what form of behavior would be particularly provocative to the teacher.

Such children do not seem to have developed a sense of guilt in the way I have described in Chapter 5. They feel no remorse over the hardship they cause their teachers and the interference in the learning of their classmates that their disruptive behavior causes. The threat of punishment may serve to deter them from acts that may be immediately detected; but when they know they can "get away with it," there are few, if any, internal mechanisms that inhibit them. Because they have not had the experience of emulating admired parental figures (with the exception of the parent who is admired for his own antisocial activities), they are less likely to identify with a teacher—and as I have described, such identification is central to the educational process. Lastly, their intense hostility may be directed against their peers; and their resultant alienation may cause them to be even more angry, thereby perpetuating a vicious cycle.

Children with the degree of hostility I have described learn practically nothing in school. Generally, psychiatric treatment alone may not be adequate to help these children because many of them are as obstructionistic with the therapist as they are with others. Work with the parents as well as the child can sometimes be helpful. In many cases there are significant cultural and social factors that may also be contributing to the child's behavior—and when this is the case, the problem is particularly resistive to change, regardless of the approach.

"Very nice report card, Bobby; now take out the garbage." A parent's complaint that his child isn't learning in school does not necessarily mean that the parent himself is fully involved in the child's learning process. Often the parent's interest is minimal, or he is ambivalent.

(The noncommitted elements may even be unconscious.) Children reflect and comply with their parents' real, even though unexpressed, attitudes; and the parent with a basically healthy investment in education will transmit this to the child, either overtly or covertly. One child comes home from school, proudly displays his work, and is given enthusiastic support and praise; another is ignored or receives only a perfunctory reply. The response, "very nice," to a child's report card can be said in a number of ways. It can convey pride, enthusiasm, and genuine pleasure with the child's accomplishment. Or, it can be said in such an offhanded manner that the child gets no feeling at all that his parent is genuinely pleased. Such a deadened response to the child's efforts only dampens his enthusiasm for learning.

The family atmosphere that is probably most conducive to the child's learning is one in which the parents themselves are genuinely curious and get great pleasure from the acquisition of knowledge. Observing his parents to be deriving so much enjoyment from learning, the child wants to join in the fun and get some of the pleasure himself. In homes where there is very little, if any, intellectual curiosity, the child's desire to learn, to discover, and to master the unknown becomes atrophied.

"It's not what you know, but who you know." Some parents consider the educational process a necessary evil, an experience to be tolerated only until one is old enough to go out into the world and begin earning a living. Education is not looked upon as living, per se, but rather as a painful period of preparation for life. The total purpose of education may then be the diploma, which is looked upon as a ticket to a higher paying job.

Some parents go even farther and do not consider the diploma to be enough but feel that it's really knowing important people that finally determines whether or not one is going to be successful. During his education, the child is encouraged to meet the "right people," people who can be counted upon to "do things for him" after graduation. The parents, too, have their "contacts" who can "pull strings" and thereby ensure that the youngster will be "well placed." It is no wonder, then, that children exposed to such attitudes are bored in school.

"What percentage of graduates from this school get into Ivy League colleges?" Parental overcommitment to the educational system is a common problem. A parent who may have been unsuccessful in obtaining the education he wanted may hope to satisfy vicariously, through the child, his frustrated desire for academic success. To an extent this phenomenon is normal. When, however, the parent's need for

such compensation is so great that he places undue pressure on the child, the foundation for a psychogenic learning problem is laid. The child usually senses that his parents' deep involvement in his school performance has little to do with their genuine interest in him and is more related to their own inappropriate needs. Such a child may respond by doing poorly; and his parents may respond with "How can you do this to us?" Although these children are "cutting off their noses to spite their faces," for many of them the personal loss is worth the vengeful gratification. Or, the child may be made so anxious by the parental pressures that he may "freeze" on examinations or be unable to concentrate on his schoolwork.

Parents of such children may involve themselves in every detail of the child's school experience. They never seem to "get off his back." Every homework assignment is checked to be sure it is completed and correct. The threat of not ultimately getting into Harvard or Yale looms over the child from the earliest years of school. The child may be rewarded with money for good grades ("fifty cents for each B and a dollar for each A"), but such bribing does not teach him to appreciate the value of academic accomplishment in its own right—and thereby deprives him of this important gratification.

If the child reacts to these pressures by balking, the coercion is intensified. "Rules" are then set up: "No television until you finish your homework"; "You can't go out and play until you finish your homework"; "You have to quit Little League"; etc. Such threats rarely work—rather they usually exacerbate the problem. Such parents do not seem to appreciate the wisdom of the adage "You can lead a horse to water, but you can't make him drink." As I have stressed, the child learns best when he wants to, not because he is made to. The creation of an environment that stimulates the child's interest, curiosity, and enthusiasm most predictably encourages him to learn. In such an atmosphere the child wants to do his homework. He may do it, in part, to avoid the anxiety of failure (just as the healthy adult, at times, tolerates the unpleasant because he appreciates the benefits to be derived from doing so), but his primary reason is the gratification that learning affords him. Homework then primarily becomes an issue between the child and his teacher. The parent, in my opinion, should be available to help the child if he requests it—but only in a manner that fosters further inquiry and self-reliance. He should not be doing it for him or screening the errors to ensure that the child hands in a good paper.

There are parents who do not stop with formal school education. A host of other activities are forced upon the child "because they are good for him" : music lessons, dancing lessons, religious training, judo, karate, drama, enrichment tutoring, etc. The child may be on an endless merry-go-round to become "well rounded" and "cultured." I certainly see no objection to a few of these activities in moderation, but many children are engulfed by them. They may become joyless automatons, robbed of their youthful spontaneity and lust for life, while obediently performing for adult approval. Others rebel, channel their energies into thwarting their parents, learn very little, and meanwhile are deprived of many of the gratifications of life, especially the satisfaction that can come from learning.

"Ma, I have a stomachache. I don't feel like going to school today." A common way in which some parents justify overprotecting their children is through excessive concern for health. The most minor ache or complaint is used as an excuse for keeping the child home from school. All the child need say is, "Ma, I have a stomachache," and he is put to bed (usually in front of a television set) and catered to and pampered all day. He is generally too "sick" to do homework, but usually gets better in midafternoon, around the time his friends come home from school.

The degree of incapacitation one suffers in association with a physical illness is strongly determined by psychological factors. The family attitude toward illness is very important in establishing the child's reactions to the inevitable physical disorders he will suffer. In the healthy home, the attitude is one of doing one's best to go about one's business and not letting the illness get the better of oneself. Medication may be taken to ease one's discomfort. Bed is only for those who are significantly incapacitated and really need rest for their recovery. In such homes not only is there less incapacitation resulting from illness, but there is actually, I believe, less illness. The reason for this is that in such an atmosphere there is less likelihood that anyone will develop purely psychosomatic complaints. These flourish in a home where the sick are indulged and rarely occur in less indulgent families.

I try to encourage parents who are playing the "bellyache game" with their children to keep them home only when there is clear-cut, bona fide evidence for physical illness. Mild nausea, slight pain, mild fever (below 100° Fahrenheit), headaches, and other such nebulous signs and symptoms are to be ignored and the child pushed out or carted off to school. If the parents are not certain whether the illness warrants keeping the child home, I advise that they err on the side of mistakenly sending him. I try to reassure them (and this is often very hard to do) that there will be no terrible consequences if the child exhibits his symptoms in school. At worst he will be sent home, but this is not going to cause a serious intensification of his illness.

In short, homes that are sickness-oriented are generally homes in which the illnesses are more likely produced by family attitudes and expectations, rather than the sicknesses causing the family preoccupation in the first place. And poor school attendance and learning impairments are the inevitable consequences of such a family pattern.

"If you don't send me to an out-of-town college, I won't go at all." The child who has been overprotected becomes egocentric, intolerant of frustration, and self-indulgent. He may have omnipotent fantasies about himself that are fostered and perpetuated by his parents. He wants to go to college, not because he may learn something that might be useful and interesting, but because he considers it a place for fun and games. If he lives in a city, the "out-of-town" campus is envisioned as a place that can provide him with a life of pleasure. His parents, who may have limited means, may wish him to live at home and attend a local, community-supported school. They may masochistically submit to his threat: "If you don't send me to an out-of-town college, I won't go to school at all," lest their child be deprived of that all-important college education. They are so beholden to the magic of the diploma that they blind themselves to the obvious fact that after four years he will be no more educated than he is now. They must deny also the cruelty of their son who would expose them to further privations for his own self-indulgence. But this should be no surprise to them, because the years of catering to him cannot but impair his sense of appreciation for the pains and discomforts of others. Generally such parents want the suffering for the masochistic gratification it offers them (their protestations to the contrary notwithstanding), and their son helps them obtain these satisfactions by maltreating them.

I usually try to impress upon such parents that little will be learned if the youngster's desire for an education is so shallow that he will go only if it is an experience incidental to a life of pleasure. Generally I have been unsuccessful in getting them to appreciate this obvious truth. I try to communicate that such a youngster might do better going out into the world at that point. He would then be provided with a few reality experiences, which would place him in a better position to decide whether or not he wants to go to college. In either case he will probably be more motivated to pursue whatever course he chooses. Unfortunately, such advice has rarely been heeded. And, afford it or not, the child is sent off to "the college of his choice" where he selects an "easy" major known for its abundance of "crap" or "gut courses."

"He has the worst luck with teachers." Some parents deny that their children could be anything but perfect and consider the child's school difficulty to be the result of teacher inadequacy or school system deficiency. They further cripple the child by fostering in him delusions of competence and encouraging his tendency to blame others for his own deficits, thus depriving him of the opportunity and incentive to remedy his deficiencies.

Many children (especially between the ages of six and eight, in my experience) have a tendency to blame others for their disappointments and misfortunes. In fights it's always the other kid who starts; they are the innocent bystanders. When disliked, it's the other children who are unfriendly, snobbish, cliquish, etc. They have great difficulty accepting their own participation in bringing about their difficulties. They may be too insecure to tolerate any defect. They may not consider themselves to have counterbalancing assets, and this makes it most difficult for them to allow for deficiencies. Parents who blame the teacher or the school when such children get into difficulty only entrench and perpetuate this problem.

Some parents' first thought, when a child gets into difficulty in school, is to transfer him to a private school. These people believe that private schools, unless proven otherwise, are better than public schools. They point out that there are smaller classes and a greater sense of intimacy at a private school and that there the child will get "more attention." But while there is no question that there are some very fine private schools, there is also no question that there are some terrible ones enjoying good reputations that they are most unworthy of. This has become more the case in recent years when more parents have been sending their children to private schools in order to avoid having their children bussed or associating with youngsters from ethnic groups that they consider undesirable. Accordingly, some of the most inferior private schools have found themselves swamped with applications. The same faculty that, only a few years ago, was considered abysmally inadequate is suddenly transformed into a body of experienced, sensitive, and dedicated teachers.

Some parents are often blind to the obvious fact that many of the private schools that long ago enjoyed good reputations still had their share of poor students and those with behavior disorders. The greater the percentage of such children, the less the likelihood that the rest will learn optimally. (I believe that the laggards and the troublemakers inevitably "drag" the more motivated down with them. They sap the teacher's energies, reduce her efficiency by the unhappiness they cause her, and distract her from giving her utmost to the rest.) Most private schools have their share of children of alumni who would not otherwise have been accepted. However, depending, as they do, on private funds for their existence, private schools are more susceptible to accepting children of wealthy donors, children who also might not otherwise qualify—a factor that many parents overlook. In addition, parents often have the delusion that their child will be the only one transferring there because of difficulties in the public school system. They somehow envision their child as being surrounded by bright, shining, uniformed, well-behaved, strongly motivated youngsters and blind themselves to the obvious fact that many of the others are also there because of significant maladjustment in the public school system.

There is no question that there are some very fine private schools where some children would do better. There is no question, however, that many, if not most, children do not do better if they are transferred there because of the parent's belief that the child's school problem lies with the school and not within the child himself. Since the problem more often lies within the child than the school, changing schools usually does not help. The strongly motivated child will learn in all except the most deplorable educational settings. The child with significant problems will learn little, if anything, in the best of schools.

"She's afraid to go to school. The doctor says she has a 'school phobia.'" Although, strictly speaking, this is not a book on the treatment of psychological disorders of childhood (rather, it is my hope that what is contained herein may help prevent some of them), there is one disorder that I would like to comment on both because it is common and because an understanding of its causes and certain aspects of its therapy may be of help to those dealing with the child with a mild or incipient case.

The term "school phobia," as its name implies, is a disorder in which the child exhibits an exaggerated fear of either going to school or staying in the classroom. His fearful reaction may vary from mild anxiety to gross panic. He may balk on leaving home, become agitated, sweat, vomit, shake, and in extreme cases enter into a state of terror. Generally, the closer the child gets to the school building, the greater the fear. And the panic reaches its peak when the child is in the classroom—separated from his mother. In fact, if the child's mother is allowed to remain with him in the classroom, there may be little, if any, anxiety. Usually, the child justifies his fears of the school with vague descriptions of the maltreatment and discontent he suffers there. He doesn't like his teacher; the kids always pick on him; the school lunches are no good; it's a very long walk; etc. Generally there is only a modicum of truth to these allegations, and they are created as justifications for the school avoidance because the child does not truly know what he is really afraid of. Often he will say as much, but usually the rationalizations are provided as long as adult authorities keep asking him *"why"* he doesn't want to go to school.

Like all psychological disorders, there are many contributing factors. One element is the presence of phobias in the child's parents. Some parents are extremely distrustful of the world or exhibit phobic attitudes toward many aspects of the environment. They are constantly communicating to the child that terrible things can happen outside the home: the neighborhood is too rough; streets are too dangerous for bike-riding; the child will get lost, and so on. When the child does venture forth into the world—which he has come to see as perilous—he knows that he can flee back home at the first sign of danger. But in school he is captive; running home is not possible—so he either refuses to go or is panicked when sent. The school phobia, then, may be only one manifestation of generalized phobic attitudes derived from the parents.

Parental overprotectiveness is another possible contributing element. The child's "fear" of going to school may be his way of complying with his parent's (more often his mother's) desire (usually unconscious) that he not go to school—school representing a step toward the child's independent existence outside the home. Children of such parents become overindulged, pampered, and unwilling to tolerate the usual stresses and strains to which school (and life in general, for that matter) necessarily exposes one. Such mothers are particularly resistive to the therapist's attempts to get them to cooperate in getting the child to school. Every sniffle, every stomachache, every rainy day serves as an excuse for them to keep the child at home.

Another factor that is often present is somewhat more complex. It relates to the child's unconscious hostility toward the parents—again, usually the mother, who is the one generally more involved with the child's upbringing.

The child who harbors significant hostility toward his mother may feel so guilty about and fearful of his anger that he may unconsciously repress it from his awareness. He may have been brought up in a home where he has been made to feel excessively guilty over his angry thoughts and feelings. Or, he may believe, as many children do, that his thoughts have magic power and that angry thoughts can actually harm the person at whom one is angry. In either case the child may repress his anger from conscious awareness in order to avoid anxiety, but he may want to be forever at his mother's side to be sure that nothing will happen to her—such as an accident or sickness—while he is in school; in other words, to be sure that his hostile impulses toward her will not be realized. In the school situation, there is an enforced separation—a separation that prevents him from the reassuring and anxiety-alleviating observation that she is still alive. The fear, in the school phobia then, usually has nothing to do with school, but with separation from the mother. And it is for this reason that the child will often be free from panic if his mother is allowed to remain in the classroom with him.

These are a few, but certainly not all, of the factors that generally contribute to the so-called school phobia, but it is not a question of either one or another working in isolation from the others. Rather, in any given child, each element can contribute, in varying degrees, in combination with the others; and additional elements, peculiar to that child, may also play a role.

In treating school phobias there are two schools of thought regarding the question of whether or not the child should be pressured to return. Some consider it anti-therapeutic to advise the mother to force the child because this only increases his anxiety and resistance to therapy. (The child knows that the therapist has suggested that the mother coerce him.) Those who follow this approach may arrange for home tutors and wait for the child to work through his problems to the point where he himself makes the decision to go, even if he has to push through a little anxiety to do so. The child is treated with dignity, and ego-degrading coercion is avoided. Others feel that every attempt should be made to get the child to school at the earliest possible time, even though he may be suffering considerable anxiety. They hold that the longer he stays out, the harder it will be for him to return. Providing him with tutors only supports his phobic withdrawal and entrenches his pathology. Keeping the child home deprives him of the desensitization experience that is an important part of treatment.

Subscribing to the second view, I advise the parents to do everything possible to get the child to school, starting the next day, or even that same day if feasible. I suggest that they not get into discussions with the child about the various rationalizations and excuses he provides for not going to school. I tell the child that there is a law that he must attend school and that neither he nor his parents can break it. If excuse notes have been given, I advise their discontinuation. Although this is, in a sense, a medical disorder, its treatment, I tell the parents, is not best accomplished by giving the child medical excuses to stay out of school. I recommend that they approach each morning with a matter-of-fact attitude about school—that the child is expected to go—and that they exhibit surprise when he refuses. I advise them to pressure the child to go *up to the point of panic* and only then to allow him to return home. However, there should not be one school morning when they do not at least take the child to the school building. If he cannot make it inside in the morning, then another attempt is made after lunch hour. If he has to leave school midmorning, then he returns again after lunch. Waiting until the next day only prolongs the problem. When he is at home during school hours, no television or play is permitted—only homework. Making things pleasant at home can intensify the problem.

I prescribe tranquillizers up to lethargic doses and then drop the dose slightly, maintaining the child on a sub-lethargic level. I speak personally to the child's teacher and other school authorities and apprise them of my approach. I attempt to enlist their aid and sympathy. I advise them to make no special concessions for the child and request their tolerance of his procrastinations, balking, crying, agitation, and at times blood-curdling shrieks. I reassure them that they will not be psychologically damaging the child by pressuring him into the phobic situation, up to the point of panic. I explain to them that desensitization is an important part of the child's treatment and that the longer he stays away from school, the harder it will be for him to return. When there is a play-acting, hysterical, and manipulative element in the outbursts (as there often is), I inform them of this and advise them not to be taken in. I reassure them that my experience has been that refusal to indulge the child in his screaming outbursts usually results in their progressive diminution (as the child comes to appreciate that they don't work), whereas complying with them only perpetuates them.

Interestingly, my experience has been that most often school personnel agree with this approach. Occasionally, someone who considers himself psychologically sophisticated becomes indignant and is overtly or covertly uncooperative. ("Well, you're the doctor.") I explain to the mother (the one who is most often involved in taking the child to school) that it will be rough-going but that letting the child stay home, although easier, is in the long run the less desirable course because it will only prolong the child's illness. The child is present when I describe my plan to the parents, for to discuss this out of the child's awareness would only foster a distrust of me that would be so anti-therapeutic that a successful outcome of therapy would be unlikely.

All this may sound very cruel, especially to those who have used what they consider the more "humane" approach. I can only respond that I have tried both ways and that the main drawback of the "softer" approach is that some children never get back to school. My success with the "hard line" has been much greater. The children will often curse me terribly. "That big fat meany Dr. Gardner; you listen to every stupid thing he says," or "He's the stupidest doctor I ever saw in my whole life." In spite of their most vociferous vilification of me, however, they typically come willingly to each session. We learn about the underlying psychodynamics *while* the child is going to school, not before. Working-through is not a sterile process that takes place in the therapist's office; it is only meaningfully accomplished in association with living experiences. Desensitization, that is, suffering the separation anxiety and having the experience that the anticipated repercussions (especially the mother's death) are not forthcoming is a part of the therapeutic process. And this is one of the reasons for my advising against the mother's staying in the classroom with the child.

After school we discuss what happened in school and other matters of psychotherapeutic concern. Whatever ego-debasement the child may suffer in being so coerced is more than compensated for, I believe, by the sense of accomplishment he feels when he successfully stays. Also, there is no question that permitting the child to avoid the phobic situation is, in itself, ego-degrading to him. Staying home alone because he is "too scared" to go to school like the other children lowers every child's self-respect. Lastly, I recommend the above approach for all children with school phobias, regardless of how free, open, or child-oriented a school may be. If a school is so compliant with a child's wishes that it will "respect" his wishes not to attend, it is not going to provide him with an education.

In the sessions with the child and his family I work on the fundamental issues that have contributed to the problem. Generally these involve the child's anger and his attitudes toward it, his appreciation of the inappropriateness of his parents' phobias, and the overprotection problem. In my work with the parents I appreciate that it is unreasonable to expect them to cure deep-seated neurotic patterns in a short period of time. What I try to do is to get them to see the inappropriateness of some of their fears and, when possible, inhibit themselves from acting out on them. For example, I try to convince the parents that other children the patient's age are permitted to cross themselves at certain "dangerous" streets, to swim in the deep water, etc. I try to get them to allow the patient such exposures, tolerating and squelching their fears as best they can. If they exhibit such symptoms as claustrophobia, airplane phobias, etc., I am usually successful in getting them to communicate to their child their appreciation that these fears are irrational and that they wish that they didn't have them. If I am successful in helping the mother to involve herself in pursuits that will make her less dependent on the child as he grows older, she may then lessen her compulsion to overprotect him. And most important for the child, my efforts with both him and his parents are geared toward his gaining a greater sense of independence, autonomy, and self-sufficiency so that he will not be so receptive to parental overprotective pressures.

By the time a child has been referred to me, the school phobia problem has become deeply entrenched and intensive therapy may be required (along the lines I have described) in order to alleviate it. My hope in presenting this clinical material is that more parents and teachers will be able to interrupt this common problem in its incipient stages and thereby prevent its progression.

"She just can't get through biology." Some children have a specific "block" in learning certain subjects, and this inhibition exists purely on a psychological basis; that is, there is no known organic disease of the brain that could explain the learning inhibition. In addition, there is good evidence that environmental factors have caused it. For example, there are children who may be ashamed that their parents are foreign-born or speak only a foreign language or "broken English." They may consider the fact that they are different to be proof of inferiority, and they may so eschew all hints of their foreign background and so attempt to hide all traces of their original language that they develop a psychological block to learning any foreign language at all. A child who lacks spontaneity and self-assertiveness may do well in subjects like mathematics and science, where the answers are precise and reveal little of the inner self; but in liberal arts subjects like creative writing, where imagination and self-expression are required, he may fail abysmally out of the fear of exposing himself. Children who have been brought up in homes that are extremely sexually inhibited may have great anxiety learning biology, where one must discuss subjects like anatomy and reproduction. A youngster whose physician father may have placed undue pressure on him—either to go into medicine or not to—may thereby find high school and college subjects that might prepare him for medical school to be particularly difficult. This may have nothing to do with intellectual impairment, but rather with the anxiety associated with his interests in these subjects. These are but a few examples of how a subject's specific symbolic significance can make it anxiety-provoking and therefore difficult, if not impossible, to learn.

"My father never even hits me." A number of years ago, when I was in residency training, a nurse reported overhearing a conversation

among three of the children on the ward. The first complained, "My mother's a bitch. She's always yelling at me." The second chimed in, "That's nothing. My father's always hitting me." To which the third replied, "My father never even hits me." The story is a sad one, but it well demonstrates a basic truth about human relations: if one has a choice between being hit and being ignored, most would choose being hit. There are essentially three kinds of interaction among people: the benevolent, the malevolent, and no interaction at all. When the first is not available (or the individual does not think it is available), then one is left to choose between the second and third. People we call masochistic have chosen the second type; that is, they gravitate toward relationships in which pain is inflicted on them. Some of the people we call schizophrenic have chosen the third type; that is, they withdraw from others entirely and gain whatever gratifications they can from their inner fantasy world.

When parents are involved with other adults and a child is unoccupied, he will usually interrupt the adults and ask to be played with. If he is put off and further ignored, he will ultimately become provocative. A "scene" may then ensue in which, although there is much *Sturm und Drang*, the child is without question very much the center of attention. The child generally knows his parents well enough to have been able to predict the outcome, and yet he does not seem to have learned from his previous experiences. Actually he has. He has learned that there are times when the only way he can get attention from his parents is to provoke them—otherwise he will be totally ignored. And he chooses the less lonely, albeit more painful, course. Similarly, there are homes where there is little if any response to the child's efforts in school (and possibly in many other areas of endeavor as well). He may find, however, that doing poorly in school may be the only way he can "get a rise out of" his parents. A poor report card brings on a wave of involvement that he would not have otherwise enjoyed. There are long lectures, visits to school, repeated questions about whether he has done his homework, etc. If in response to all this he starts to do well and if his parents then lapse back into their previous state of disinterest, it is unlikely that the child will maintain his improvement.

Masochism can be a way of gaining self-aggrandizement. The masochist essentially says: "How noble I am to be able to suffer what others may not be able to bear. People will certainly admire me when they learn of my forbearance in the face of pain." A child of a masochistic parent (or parents) may come to appreciate that when he does well in school his parents have nothing to complain about to their friends and relatives, nothing with which they can elicit sympathy, and so they have little to say about him. When, however, he does poorly in school, then he becomes "news." For hours at a time the parents may bemoan their fate; their misfortune brings them a degree of attention and commiseration they had not previously enjoyed. And the child may continue to do poorly in order to make his parents "happy" with him and "happy" with themselves.

Another pathological form of masochistic behavior is seeking punishment to assuage guilt. The child may be excessively guilty over many thoughts and feelings that he has come to learn are bad. He may attempt to alleviate such guilt by doing things that can predictably bring about his being punished. And doing poorly in school may be just the thing that will gain him the punishment he seeks. However, such guilt alleviation is usually short-lived. Because the punishment doesn't "fit the crime," because it does not relate to the issues that brought about the guilt in the first place, it cannot be too effective in reducing the child's guilty feelings. Only when the basic distortions of thinking and feeling that caused the inappropriate guilt are worked out, can the guilt be truly assuaged.

"She's such a perfectionist." Some children are highly perfectionistic and are too insecure to tolerate doing average or even good work. Either they must be the best or they will do nothing. When they choose the latter course, they justify their withdrawal with the specious argument that "I'd do extremely well if I wanted to try. I've just decided not to." The flaw in their reasoning, of course, is that they probably wouldn't do as well as they would like to think; but they would rather say, "I quit" than suffer the humiliation of having "flunked out." By not trying, they avoid confrontation with their inadequacies and their grandiose expectations of themselves.

A related group are those children who have the idea that only a 100 or an A is an acceptable grade. To them 99 is not much better than zero on an examination. Although such an attitude can be the result of parental pressures, it doesn't necessarily have to be. Some children react to this excessively high standard by not trying at all. They accept defeat before they try and so at least save themselves the trouble and disappointment of working toward a goal they consider themselves incapable of attaining. In the extreme such children may also become dropouts. These children differ from the previously described group in that they *do not believe* that they can reach their high standards, whereas the former group delude themselves into believing that they *can* reach perfection.

There are some perfectionistic children who fear that if they do well, they will be expected to operate continually on an extremely high level of excellence. They believe that one *should* be capable of such performance, but that they themselves are not. They do not seem to appreciate how unrealistic and completely unattainable such a goal is. In response to this false notion about human potential, they attempt to gain for themselves the reputation of being intellectually limited. In this way no one, neither they nor anyone else, will have very high expectations of them. In this way they can avoid the humiliations they anticipate they will suffer by not maintaining a perfect record. In the school situation, where one's capacities are most readily "objectified" (with grades, reports, and evaluations), they can accomplish this most effectively. Sadly, such children may not only convince those around them that they are intellectually inferior, but may come to believe it themselves.

"No one likes the 'class brain.'" In some schools a certain amount of stigma is suffered by the better students. Such children are most criticized, of course, by the poorest students, who do so out of jealousy. The bright child may be referred to as a "sissy" or called the "class brain"—often in a pejorative way. The child who is overly sensitive to criticism, who cannot tolerate being different from the majority (no matter how slightly and regardless of the reason) may squelch his academic aspirations and do poorly in school in order to be "one of the boys (or girls)." Such children must be helped to appreciate how they are prostituting themselves, how they are making a terrible sacrifice for a little more popularity. They must be helped to appreciate that the stigma they suffer is the result of secret envy and admiration. In this way they may be helped to maintain their dedication to their studies by more involvement with other academically-oriented students.

"Men don't like smart girls." Most educators are aware that prior to puberty girls are generally the better students, whereas after puberty the boys excel academically. This is in part related to the fact that at any grade level girls are developmentally ahead of their male classmates of the same age. A more important factor in this phenomenon relates to what happens after puberty. Then, the boys start thinking more about careers and the girls about getting married. The specter of living the life of a spinster descends heavily over the heads of most girls during their teens and plays a significant role in their turning away from their studies toward those endeavors, no matter how frivolous, that will enhance their attractiveness to the boys. Although she may ultimately get her husband, the girl has paid a heavy price. She has deprived herself of the opportunity to develop in other important areas. And the older she gets, the

more bitterly she may come to resent how she has been duped by her parents and by society at large. This tragic situation is one of the leading causes of frustration, disillusionment, and unhappiness in the lives of many women.

It is during the high school period that girls start being advised by their well-meaning mothers that they had better not act too intelligent in front of boys lest they scare them away. Or the mother might be a sort of "female chauvinist" and basically believe that females are smarter than males but that the prudent woman "builds a man's ego" and so conducts herself that he is led to believe that he is the smarter one. In either case the girl is advised to "cool it" with her intellectual growth if she is to successfully "get a man." Unfortunately, many, if not most, men *are* so insecure that they would be threatened by a woman who is their intellectual equal. So they cooperate with the woman in the latter's intellectual suicide. They gravitate toward women who have not developed their intellectual capacities anywhere near their potential—except in the area of flattering men and "building up their egos." However, the remedy for this situation does not lie merely in the development of a new generation of women who refuse to play this self-destructive game. A new breed of men will also have to evolve if these women are to have an ample number of suitable men to relate to on an egalitarian basis (whether in marriage or not). And it is in childhood, in the home and in the school, that the foundation for such new patterns can most effectively be laid down.

"He's totally removed himself from his studies. He says he's having an 'identity crisis.'" At best adolescence is a difficult period. (This is not to say that the rest of life is such a breeze.) The adolescent is half child and half adult. I often think of him as having the brain of a child in the body of an adult. He would like to believe himself fully independent of his parents. However, the realities are that not only is he dependent on them for food, clothing, and shelter but that in Western society he has not developed the competence and the skill to provide himself with these commodities. In addition, he is usually still very much psychologically dependent on his parents (generally more than is justifiable—social and economic factors notwithstanding).

As part of the transitional process from child to adult, the adolescent may experience periods of confusion about his identity. This not only concerns obvious questions such as whether he is a child or an adult but may also include questions about the validity of the values of his family and of society as a whole—values he may never before have doubted. He may question, as he has never questioned before, his religious beliefs. He wonders about his sexuality and his attractiveness to the opposite sex. He wonders about his country, his continent, the world, and the universe—and where he fits in it. He may have grave concerns about the future course of his life and wonder about exactly what role he will play. As a child the future seemed like a million years away. Now it is at his very doorstep. Definite choices in this regard have to be made *by him*; they can no longer be made *for him*. He has to try to envision himself in various careers and social positions and take appropriate steps toward the attainment of these goals. All this can be very anxiety-provoking: the decisions are awesome; they affect his whole life; he may regret forever the decisions he is now making. At its best and healthiest, this identity search can be a rewarding and creative period of self-discovery—its anxieties notwithstanding. And even when the confusion becomes so great that the term "identity crisis" seems appropriate, it need not be a deleterious experience.

There are those who can only handle this crisis by taking "time out" to "find themselves." They have to remove themselves from their main activities, to take stock, to think, to try new things, and to try to see things from another vantage point. Most accomplish this on evenings and weekends and remain in school (at least until graduation from high school). Others, however, may have to leave school (whether it be high school or beyond) in order to do this. When this occurs it may be very difficult to ascertain whether the step is a healthy one. One way of determining this is to observe what the youngster is doing while he is trying to "find himself." If he is actively out in the world—involved, committed, trying to make it on his own—then it may very well be a healthy step. However, if he withdraws into himself and tries to find his solutions through philosophizing about them, if he is not having reality experiences against which to test his ideas, he may be labeling the withdrawal an "identity crisis" in order to cover up its pathological significance to both himself and those around him. If the pursuit of his "true self" requires parasitic dependence on his parents and involves no meaningful efforts toward self-sufficiency, then it is probably sick. If "doing his own thing" means a life of hedonistic self-indulgence at his parents' expense (or at the expense of anyone else who is misguided enough to support this way of life), then there is more of a "crisis" going on than just that of "identity." In addition, the longer it takes for the youngster to accomplish this task, the greater the likelihood it is pathological.

Never before in the history of the world have so many youngsters been so indulged. Never before has Western society been more affluent.

Never before has there been such a long gap between the time one is born and the time one is capable of self-sufficiency. Never before has there been so much psychologizing to parents about what their children are doing, how to "understand" them, and how to bring them up to be psychologically healthier. (And this book, alas, is in this tradition.) There is probably no better example of a sick fusion of all these phenomena than a disturbed adolescent being supported (financially and psychologically) in his neurotic (and even psychotic) flight from reality with the rationalization (borrowed from psychology) that he is only having an "identity crisis."

"We don't believe in grades in this school." School systems across the nation are doing away with grades, in part, to lessen competition among students. The children are told that they are to "compete with themselves" (whatever that means). Yet, even without report cards, they still try to determine how they measure up to those around them and know pretty much where they stand. One could argue that they continue to compare and compete because they are still imbued with the rivalrous spirit of their parents and society. I believe that the weakness of such programs is only, in part, related to the years of social conditioning to which the child has been exposed.

We need some degree of comparison to ascertain the value of our accomplishments; we cannot judge them in a vacuum. And we need some degree of competition to provide us with the esteem enhancement that comes from excelling others. It is when exceeding others becomes our primary, if not exclusive, source of ego-enhancement that we get into difficulty. It is then that we are likely to lose the intrinsic satisfactions of the attainment and become so engrossed in competition we may deprive ourselves of opportunities for other sources of esteem building. A certain amount of excelling others to enhance one's self-worth can be healthy. Used to an excessive degree it becomes dehumanizing, as one's main purpose in life then becomes beating others down. Competition, used in moderation, can spur us on to work more efficiently toward our goals. Used in excess, however, it may become an end in itself and may then lessen the likelihood that we will reach our goals. We then become more interested in the winning than in the process and the goal, and this lessens our effectiveness in achieving our aim.

The school can and should be a place that teaches healthy competition, in preparation for the competitiveness of adult life. The fact our society is fiercely competitive is no reason to do away with competition completely, as some would attempt to do. Rather we should tone it down and use it as constructively as possible. Awareness of his progress as compared to others can be a useful tool in providing the student with healthy competitive impetus.

In addition, human beings seem to need some praise, feedback, and other kinds of symbolic pats on the back from those around them. No matter how mature and old we are, all of us, I believe, never completely outgrow this need. Rather than deplore this childish residuum—this need to get the praise and affection from our parents and their surrogates—we should make use of this craving to our best advantage. A teacher's praise and gratification over a student's progress can do this quite well and need not be used in excess to accomplish this.

The main purpose of a teacher's rating or feedback system should be to provide the student with information about his level of accomplishment. Knowing one's level of achievement—to be provided with exact knowledge of what has been accomplished—is fine up to a point. To say, "Jimmy has now mastered multiplication up to the six table," is useful information as far as it goes. But this achievement has little meaning if it is not compared with the level of other children who are learning the multiplication table. Without such a comparison the child, his parents, and his teachers are ill-equipped to determine whether this level of achievement is something to be pleased about or whether Jimmy should work harder to improve upon it. To say, "Jimmy has now mastered multiplication up to the six-times table. The average student of his age in this school has, by now, mastered the eight-times table," not only enables everyone to better appreciate the level of accomplishment, but may also serve to encourage Jimmy to work harder to bring up his level. Or the teacher might report, "Most of the children in Jimmy's math group are progressing more rapidly than he. He needs special practice in the seven- and eight-times tables, as well as in the addition of three-digit numbers." Additional information would be given by adding, "On the basis of our tests of Jimmy's capacities, we believe that he should have by now easily mastered the eight-times table." This comparison to an ideal standard can also serve to help the child better appreciate the meaning of his accomplishment.

The grading system is being replaced, across the land, by verbal and written reports, and certain unwritten rules are followed by teachers in preparing these reports. It is important for parents to understand these rules if they are to know what is going on with their child.

The first rule is *Words with a pejorative connotation—no matter how slight—are strictly verboten.* I can best describe this principle with a recent discussion I had with the teacher of Gregg, a boy I was seeing in treatment. In response to my question on how he was doing academically she replied somewhat hesitantly, "Well . . . he . . . uh . . . seems . . . to have what I would . . . call . . . a . . . a . . . strong need . . . to be right." Since this did not tell me very much, I asked if she could be a little more specific and, if possible, give me an example. "Well," she haltingly replied, "on spelling exercises he seems to want to get all the words *right*." "I'm not sure what the problem is," I replied. "Isn't that a common attitude?" "Well . . . " she said, "he handles his mistakes . . . what I would call . . . *differently* . . . from the other children." (Note the careful choice of the word *differently*. Under no circumstances should his behavior be criticized.) I again requested that she be a little more specific. "Well . . . " she said, "after I have read off the list of words for the children to write down, then I read the list again, this time spelling each word. The children are supposed to look at the way *they* spelled the word and see if they spelled it the same way *I* did." (Note again the careful avoidance of the words *correct* and *incorrect*.) If the child has spelled the word differently from me," she continued, "he's supposed to put a line through his word and write down my way of spelling it next to his. Now . . . what Gregg does . . . (every single word now was carefully being thought out) . . . is to . . . erase the word . . . that he had put down . . . according to the way he liked to spell it . . . and put down my way of spelling it over his original word . . . so it looks like he had written it my way in the first place . . . but I can see that he had erased his way and put my way over his way." I replied, "Oh, what you're saying is that he's cheating!" "No, doctor," she somewhat indignantly replied, "I don't use such terms with children. I consider his behavior to be caused by his strong need to be right."

Another rule that is rigidly adhered to in such reports is one that I call *The rule of the uncompared comparison*. Stated briefly the rule is this: In describing a child's performance, never make any references— no matter how subtle—to the baseline or standards by which the student's performance is being judged. In this way no accurate information about poor performance will be communicated (since the term *poor* only has meaning in relation to its antithesis *good*), and so the child will be spared the painful confrontation with his inadequacies. The examples of this are legion and are best demonstrated in the first report card of the year. "Jane is doing much better in math." That's the whole sentence. The parent can only wonder, "I guess she must have been doing poorly at first and now she's doing better. Well, that's good to hear. But how poorly was she doing at first? And how much better is she doing now? Was she failing then and passing now? Or was she failing then and still failing now? Did she go from a 10% to a 20% average? from a

30% to a 90%? from a 1% to a 2%?" Or we are told, "Billy is trying much harder in social studies." Again, the same confusion and frustration is produced. We're glad to learn that; but how far have his efforts gotten him? No information at all in that department. The real questions most parents want answered are "Is he passing and failing in comparison to the other kids in the class? Where does he stand? Does he need help? How the hell is he doing?" To spare anyone any hard feelings, no one is told how he is doing. No one's feelings are going to be hurt. All those who do poorly are helped to deny their difficulties. And this is supposed to enhance self-esteem. What is enhanced is delusion, procrastination, and the avoidance of painful reality—qualities that, in my opinion, have never proven themselves to be particularly effective ways to ultimately enhance anyone's feelings of self-worth.

Other devices are commonly used to protect the child from confrontation with his inadequacies. Using vague terminology can accomplish this. Words like *slight* and *somewhat* serve this purpose quite well: "Mary is doing somewhat better in spelling" or "Ronald is showing slight improvement in math." Usually improvement is nonexistent or miniscule, and the teacher believes that it would be devastating to the child's ego were he to be told that he has made no progress. Another way of accomplishing this is to use a verb form ending in *ing*, in such a way that vague passage of time is implied: "Bobby is doing fractions"; "Gail is still learning the three-times table"; or "Malcolm is beginning to learn how to organize his time." No one knows exactly how far these children have gotten in their various pursuits—in fact, one strongly suspects that they have made no progress at all. Another ploy is to avoid focusing at all on academic performance and state, "Virginia is trying very hard" or "Thomas is doing his best." These maneuvers do actually teach the child something. They teach him ingenious ways to blind himself to his deficits. In addition, they cannot but lessen his respect for his teacher if he senses her duplicity—and he often does.

Parents who are genuinely interested in their child's education and are confronted with such non-informational report cards do best to try to convince school authorities of their frustration with a system that provides no data about their child's performance in comparison with others—in his group, his class, and beyond. In addition, the parent does well to arrange for private conferences with the teacher and ask very specific questions about the child's performance and progress and to persist until he has real answers. Such a conference will usually be most beneficial if both parents can be present. (Many teachers, including women, persist in the misconception that fathers are more concerned about their children's education, that they better appreciate pedagogical and intellectual concerns, and that they are less "emotionally involved" in their children's progress.) However, whether mother, father, or both meet with the teacher, the parent should not be put off by such evasions as I have described above. He is entitled to know the particulars of his child's development, in which, after all, he has invested a great deal.

"No baseball till you practice the piano." At the present time, many parents provide their children with certain supplementary educational experiences. In the case of the arts, for example, it is because they want their child to have more intensified training than the school can usually provide. In the case of religious training, it is because it is unconstitutional for the school to provide such instruction. This is consistent with the separation of church and state philosophy—so strongly promulgated by those who framed our constitution.

In the ideal school, intensified training in the arts would be provided for those with deep interest and talent. Accordingly, such extra training would not then be restricted, as it often is now, to the more affluent. Until that time comes, however, parents themselves will have to provide these experiences. Training in these areas is often embarked upon because the parent considers it to be "good" for the child. It will make him more "well-rounded" and "cultured," we are told. Poor Mitchell has to get in his half-hour of piano practice before he can join his friends at baseball. He does not concentrate on the music, but rather the clock. When he complains he is told, "You'll be glad someday that we forced you to take these lessons. I'm sorry to this day that I quit when I was a kid." The child comes to dread the weekly lesson, where his lack of proficiency is clearly demonstrated to his teacher. Many teachers scold their pupils for not practicing and angrily threaten to discontinue the lessons if the child doesn't "shape up." Complaints to the parents are made, and they are urged to intensify their efforts to get the child to practice. Even if the teacher is most diplomatic and does not communicate his disappointment or frustration to the child, his lack of progress is painfully apparent to all concerned. Generally, the parents of such children have little, if any, genuine interest in the arts themselves. Their coercion of the child is in the service of showing him off—thereby enhancing their own egos. In some cases their own artistic aspirations have been frustrated, and they use the child for compensatory vicarious gratification. Whatever the parents' reasons, their coercion of the child is psychologically deleterious. He not only learns little, but the experience can sour him on the particular art form forever—depriving him of what might have been some source of enjoyment (although not necessarily to the degree that the parents might have wished).

The child is most likely to involve himself in artistic pursuits when he directly observes his parents themselves to be genuinely enjoying them. He too wants to join the fun and so will be motivated to suffer the discomforts of gaining proficiency. Parents who have no such deep interest themselves, but still wish their child to develop in this area, do best to allow the child exposures and then provide him with lessons, if he wishes and as long as he wishes—and no longer. There should be no provisos about practicing and no threats that lessons will be discontinued if he doesn't. He should be told that he can practice as little or as much as he wants. A teacher should be found (and they do exist) who also adheres to the philosophy that the child should not be made to practice and that he can proceed at any pace he wishes—no matter how slow.

Some parents find these suggestions totally incomprehensible. To them, music lessons are so inextricably bound to pain and coercion that they can conceive of no other way to gain proficiency. In an attempt to "get through" to such parents I will sometimes ask, "Suppose you wanted to take tennis lessons, and two people with whom you lived screamed at you every day if you didn't practice, and your teacher got angry at you if you didn't proceed at the rate *he* deemed advisable. Suppose also that he threatened to stop teaching you if you didn't practice every day. How would you feel? What would you do?" Most agree that they would not put up with such a situation, but often follow their agreement with "But it's different for children, they must be forced. Would you let him stop school if he wanted to?" To this I usually reply, "You can't put school and music lessons in the safe category. By law, your child must go to school. Although there may be many aspects of the school situation to justify his not wanting to go, most children still go and learn in spite of its deficiencies. The way our society is presently structured, there are no laws requiring music lessons. Whether justifiably or not, society does not consider music lessons vital to its survival; however, it does consider a certain amount of education to be. Life is filled with unpleasant things that we *have* to do. Why are you unnecessarily adding to your child's burdens?" Some hear me and others do not. Those who do, and get off the child's back, often have a happier child and often one who still pursues his artistic interests.

With religious training, one often sees similar hypocrisy. Literally millions of parents with little or no genuine religious conviction send their children for religious training "because it's good for them." Parents who think that such a child is going to become religious are fooling themselves. More often, instead of becoming religious, the child becomes aware of his parents' hypocrisy. In addition, he builds up mounting resentment toward them as he is forced to undergo a program of studies that his parents do not basically believe in but are imposing on him "for his own good." Their coercion may make him so antagonistic toward his religious training that he might be deprived of benefits that he might have otherwise gained in a more permissive setting.

Education, be it inside or outside of the school, be it curricular or extracurricular, be it in the home or outside of it, cannot be forced down anyone's throat. To carry the metaphor a little further, it may be forcibly introduced into the stomach but it will never be digested. And the educator cannot teach if he does not genuinely have the belief that what he is teaching is worthwhile and if the student he is teaching has a real interest in learning. Education, therefore, involves two people : a teacher and a learner—both of whom are committed to the process. If only one, or neither, of the individuals are basically involved in it, many other things may be going on, but not education.

10

Television

After the parents and the school, television probably plays the most important role in molding the child's personality. That's saying a lot for a machine, but that machine has come to be the most widely utilized instrument of human communication ever devised. According to the U.S. Surgeon General's Scientific Advisory Committee on Television and Social Behavior, "96 percent of American homes have one or more television sets. The average home set is on *more than six hours a day* [italics mine]."[14] It is probably the most widely used and, at one to two cents an hour, the cheapest baby-sitter ever devised. I believe that more are addicted to it than to alcohol, tobacco, and hard drugs combined. Its influence on us—from birth to death—has yet to be determined, but there is no doubt that it is profound.

---

[14] *Television and Growing Up: The Impact of Televised Violence*, Report to the Surgeon General, U.S. Public Health Service, Washington, D.C.: U.S. Government Printing Office, 1972.

The advertisers. These ladies and gentlemen (and I use the words loosely), more than anyone else, determine what is shown on television. The simple facts are that their main interest is selling products, in making money for both themselves and their clients. In the service of this goal, their main concerns are, above all, not to offend; to provide what will be least controversial, least provocative, and least disturbing to the greatest number of people; and at all costs (and they are usually formidable), to win friends for their clients. To do this they will resort to every kind of duplicity and chicanery that the law will permit. Although their self-serving deceit is most crass in their advertisements, the fare they provide also serves their aforementioned goals.

In defense the advertising people claim that they are only giving the public what it wants. "The public interest is what the public is interested in," they cooly claim. But they know the public's gullibility and pliability, and they know their own power to mold public opinion and make the public want what it never wanted before. They know their power to create cravings. "As unpopular as you may be young man, buy this car and the pretty girls will be flocking around you," they communicate (not necessarily by word) to the poor guy who can't get a date. And the somewhat plain looking girl is promised a magic transformation into a ravishing beauty if she will only buy the lipstick or shampoo they are pushing. And then there are the pills, the ubiquitous pills. There's a host of them for every ailment. Pop a pill into your mouth and all your troubles, whatever they are, will go away. (I have no doubt that this is a contributing factor to our present-day drug addiction problem.)

So advertisers bombard us—instilling the grossest kind of materialism and the sickest forms of conspicuous consumption. In subtler ways, as well, they mold our minds. The styles the celebrities wear—as outlandish as they may appear to us at first—become ours before we realize what is happening. The model of car that the hero detective drives is not randomly selected. The advertisers know that it can very well influence our next choice of automobile. And ingenious photographic stunts, which distort time and space, turn the cheapest kinds of toys into the most exciting devices, which promise to provide our children with hours of thrill and adventure. The Surgeon General's report on the effects of cigarette smoking[15,16] did not stop these people

---

[15] *Smoking and Health*, Report of the Advisory Committee to the Surgeon General of the U.S. Public Health Service, Washington, D.C.: U.S. Government Printing Office, 1964.

[16] *The Health Consequences of Smoking*, A Public Health Service Review, Washington, D.C.: U.S. Government Printing Office, 1967.

from peddling their cancerous weeds. It took an act of Congress to stop the hoax.

Parents who prevent their children from watching television entirely can protect them from these insidious influences. I personally do not believe that such drastic action is warranted. As I will describe, in spite of its present deplorable state, there is still much of value on television. The fact that it may take generations to rectify some of its unsavory practices is not justification for depriving children of its benefits. What we have to do is to teach them discrimination and to help them protect themselves from some of its nefarious influences. I generally tell children that, with the exception of the advertisements of the American Cancer Society, the Heart Association, and other health and public service ads, all commercials have some lies. I use the word *lie* here to refer not only to gross distortions of the truth but to all forms of subtle deception intended to mislead. (There are occasions when this generalization may not be warranted, but they are so rare that I do not feel uncomfortable making it.) Although I recognize that advertisers can and do perform a public service, they have so bastardized their function and have been so prostituted that they have created for themselves an image of corruption that far overshadows the good they do. And we do our children a terrible disservice if we do not start educating them, when they first start watching television, to the steady diet of duplicity they are being fed.

The world of unreality. A certain amount of indulgence in fantasy is probably necessary to preserve our sanity. If we were to be constantly confronted with harsh reality, if we had no mechanisms to desensitize ourselves to the terrible things happening around us, we would probably all go crazy. Fantasy is one way of assuaging such pain. Reveries of wonderful times and beautiful places, of happy experiences and exciting adventures can serve this purpose. Fantasy, however, like the narcotic it resembles, can be dangerous. Resorting to it in excess can interfere with successful functioning. And the fantasies that are continually being provided us by our television sets have clearly gone beyond the healthy level.

With too few exceptions, they contribute to our children's forming a distorted concept of the world, in part, by the simplistic stereotypes they continually present. "Good guys" are handsome, clever, glib, quick-thinking and are more often than not, WASPs. The "bad guys" are usually ugly, often extremely clever, and speak with lower-class or foreign accents. There are good-guy lawyers who, week after week, never lose a case. And there are good-guy doctors who never lose a patient, never charge fees, and whose patients never have to wait for a hospital bed. Good-guy cops and detectives are fearless and always get their man.

With rare exceptions, crime on television sets doesn't pay, and crimes and other knotty problems of life are usually solved in exactly twenty-nine or fifty-nine minutes (leaving one minute for the final commercial). There are marriages in which Mom and Dad never fight and are always immaculately dressed, well-spoken, sympathetic, and understanding. And there are somewhere-over-the-rainbow places where people live happily ever after.

Prolonged exposure to such programs, the overwhelming majority of television fare, is likely to have deleterious effects. It produces false notions about reality, which then contribute to disillusionment, since the world never turns out to be as gratifying as it is for the people on television. There are the handsome jet-setters who spend their time enjoying the pleasures of beautiful men and women in the world's most exotic places while the rest of us lead a relatively mundane existence. Our marriages are never as perfect as those on television, where couples are always living "happily ever after." (This disillusionment with imperfections in one's mate is, I believe, a contributing factor to the high divorce rate.) Some people must surely feel they are cowards because they become fearful in dangerous situations where their television heroes would never flinch.

I believe that the disillusionment of many of today's young people is, in part, derived from their having grown up in the world of television. When they have finally grown up and left their television sets—their main source of information about the world—they have been profoundly disappointed. It's nothing like they expected. "You have lied to us," they say. And indeed we have.

Television and violence. The amount of violence portrayed on television is truly staggering. Children's cartoons are filled with the most sadistic and ingenious forms of cruelty; and the argument the producers give, that the mutilated invariably end up unscathed, does not impress me. Doing something and then undoing it is not the same as never having done it at all. The violence has still been portrayed—whatever its effects—and the subject's magical and impossible recovery primarily serves the purpose of his being available for another round of sadomasochism. Detective stories and westerns abound, and as proof that crime doesn't pay we are presented in minute detail every sordid crime it does not pay to perpetrate. Then there are Superman, Batman, and other super-heroes, who inevitably thwart the most treacherous plots and lethal inventions devised by their ingenious adversaries. And more subtle, but no less hostile, are the comedians. Under the guise of humor they spew forth some of the most venemous insults and scathing denunciations of their fellow men. And slapstick humor serves the same purpose in a more primitive and overt form.

When the television producers say that they are only providing the public with what it wants, they are completely correct if they are talking about violence. Because society cannot permit free expression of anger if it is to survive, it must allow for various forms of substitutive release. And vicarious gratification is one of the safest and most widespread forms of socially acceptable expression for anger. From ancient times, men have expressed their emotions in socially acceptable forms; and in a sense, television is simply the twentieth-century equivalent of the legends, myths, epics, dramas, and rituals of non-technological ages. By reading about or imagining or observing (either in reality or in a visual representation) someone performing an angry act, one can, through the process of identification, satisfy inner desires to perform the act. We enjoy the release of the hostility without having to suffer any social consequences or feel any guilt. Television, with all its faults, has proven itself to be a most convenient instrument for providing such expression. It is always there in the house, ready to be switched on, ready to provide the most gruesome and satisfying release of our pent-up hostilities.

In recent years, with mounting crime in the United States, the finger of blame has been pointed at television. Its steady diet of violence, its critics claim, contributes to crime and provides ideas for children that would not otherwise have entered their innocent little heads. I do not believe this is so. Violent acts are performed by angry people, people whose anger has causes having nothing to do with television. Even though television glorifies violence, desensitizes us to its horrors, and equates violence with masculinity, it does not, in my opinion, make criminals. Most criminals did not get that way because they watched television but because of a host of social and familial factors (especially the latter). To put the blame on television is to attempt to find a simple solution to a very complex psycho-sociological phenomenon. In fact, because it allows for a vicarious release of hostility in a socially acceptable way, I believe that television may actually play a role in reducing crime for most people. However, I also believe that violence on television can encourage a transient upsurge of angry feelings in a small percentage of people already predisposed to antisocial behavior and that on rare occasions such a person may act out on these.

Some might argue that, since violence on television *can* be a contributing factor to criminal behavior (admittedly, only in the angry predisposed), it would prevent some crime and even save a few lives each year to eliminate it. In response, I would have to agree that it might. However, what has then to be considered is the question of whether we are willing to face the problems associated with the imposition of a massive system of censorship on this medium. Would such censorship jeopardize our basic freedoms? Is it constitutional for us to impose it? If it were, who are the censors going to be? What criteria would they use to decide which programs are to be shown? Often the violence is subtle and symbolic. Often it is portrayed in the great works of literature. What do the censors do with plays such as *Hamlet* and *Macbeth*? With the works of Homer, Dostoyevsky, Sophocles, and other great masters whose works are replete with violence? What about news reporting? These days we enjoy televised "on the spot" reporting of all of our wars. Are these to be deleted as well? What about nature films describing the incessant devouring of one species by another—a process vital to the maintenance of life on this planet? Would we ban boxing, wrestling, football, monster shows, most cartoons, and many forms of humor? Are we willing to deprive ourselves of all these? Are we willing to accept this infringement on our freedoms (whether it proves to be legal or not)? Are we willing to accept all these impositions and restrictions for the questionable benefit of an insignificant reduction in crime? I vote no. I vote to stop scapegoating television and direct our attention more to some of the real causes of violence—as complex and as overwhelming as they may be to face.

Television and sex. Just as violence on television has not, in my opinion, played a significant role (if any) in criminal behavior, sex on television has not played a significant role in antisocial sexual behavior. By antisocial sexual behavior, I refer to those forms of sexual behavior in which an individual imposes himself forcibly on another for the purpose of sexual gratification. I believe that those disturbances of the mind that would make a person resort to this kind of behavior have their roots in childhood and are related to unfortunate circumstances in the person's upbringing, not to the things he has seen on television. I believe that the sexuality portrayed on television provides vicarious release for most people. And for these, if television were not available, other forms of release would be quickly found; for example, books, films, theatre, and fantasy. For children, arousal is uncommon, and what they see on television has little bearing on their sexuality.

There are probably occasional individuals who are predisposed to antisocial sexual behavior who might be aroused even further by their television experiences and then act out on them. Such individuals, I believe, would be equally stimulated by a host of other modalities (pornography and fantasy, for example). It is not the stimulus, but the fundamental personality disorder, that is the primary, if not exclusive, determinant of their behavior. The same arguments that speak against censoring television violence also hold in the case of television sexuality. For the small possible reduction in sexual crimes, we would sacrifice much social benefit. Again, these considerations are not relevant to the child, who even when he suffers with sexual pathology, does not have the strength and the physiological wherewithal to sexually impose himself on another. But more important, watching television in childhood is not the cause of antisocial sexual behavior as an adult. Psychopathological factors within the child's family and society are at the roots of such disturbances.

"Scary programs." These programs are something of a paradox. Commonly a child will be frightened by them, yet still want to watch. While cringing in his chair and covering his face (ostensibly not to look), the child will peek through the slits between his fingers (so as not to miss a thing). There are even children who have nightmares about the very same programs they have seen during the day, but they demand that they be allowed to continue to watch. I do not claim to fully understand this strange phenomenon. I would guess that the antics of the monsters on these programs allow for a certain amount of vicarious release of hostility. The greater the horror and gore, the greater the release of hostility. And the more hostile the release, the more terrifying the creatures must be. If the demons were less fiendish, they would provide less of an outlet for the child's repressed anger. It appears, then, that the child is willing to suffer the fears these programs produce for the psychological benefits he can derive from them. He may even have to dream about them at night to desensitize himself to the fears they engender. By reliving the program in his nightmare, he can lessen the pent-up fears that result from them, as well as provide himself with a little more hostile release.

Generally, I do not suggest that parents prevent their children from watching these programs. They should respect the child's need for them. They should appreciate that many of the so-called "good" fairy tales provide identical forms of gratification. They should allow the child to decide himself how much of them he can take. Only he can judge when the fears outweigh the benefits.

Television addiction. In mild doses, television is a tranquilizer. It lulls the viewer into a relaxed state. With longer periods of viewing it acts as a narcotic, with a dulling and deadening effect on the senses. And like the narcotic, its potential for addiction is strong. As the Surgeon General's report suggests, television addiction is ubiquitous. In fact, when the television addict is prevented from watching, he becomes agitated and preoccupied with the desire to resume his viewing—in a manner quite similar to drug, alcohol, and cigarette addicts when they are prevented from indulging themselves in their habit. Unlike these other forms of addiction, which generally do not begin until the teens, television addiction can begin in the first year of life. And there is a certain amount of temptation for parents to get their children "hooked." As mentioned, at one to two cents an hour, it is probably the world's cheapest baby-sitter. On Sunday morning, when parents want to sleep, the most convenient thing is to prop the kid up in front of the TV set and crawl back into bed. The television producers conveniently provide our children with programs that will predictably keep their eyes glued to the set for at least a few hours. With such parental encouragement, it is no surprise that the child becomes addicted.

Whatever benefits may be derived from television, there is no question that addiction is one of its greatest dangers. Vicarious gratifications are fine, up to a point. However, when these substitutive forms of satisfaction are preferred to experiences in reality, we deprive ourselves of the greater pleasures to be derived from the *real thing*. Children who get hooked on their TV sets lose out on the pleasures of work and play with real human beings, in real situations. Accordingly, I advise parents to limit the time children can watch. Generally, I advise a two-hour maximum per day, during which the child may watch whatever he wants. To permit more is to contribute to the child's becoming the kind of non-participating, sedentary, onlooking type of person who is a credit neither to himself nor society.

Television's benefits: present and future(?). With all its dangers and drawbacks, television is a wonderful invention. It enables us to expand our horizons in a way impossible up to the present. It can provide us with glimpses of the way the world was (to the best of our knowledge) at any time in the history of mankind. There is no place on earth and no event that takes place that cannot be brought into our living rooms. I cannot imagine any person—regardless of how strongly he hated the invention—not being inspired and enriched by the experience of watching the first man step on the moon, *at the very time it was actually happening*. It has brought into our homes the greatest plays, films, and literary works of man's creation. Its educational programs have enriched millions. Even its humor—although often crude and sick —has been salutary. And as an instrument for providing vicarious release (something all of us need), it may be unsurpassed.

In Elizabethan England even the most uneducated enjoyed Shakespeare and Marlowe—which was their popular theater. It is probable that there are television programs today that are viewed at any given time by more people than all those who viewed all the plays of Shakespeare during his whole lifetime. (It is hard to imagine that this number was even close to the 60,000,000 who have at one time viewed certain programs.) With such a mighty instrument at our disposal it is indeed a shame that we have allowed its utilization in fostering and entrenching some of society's sickest values, when we could have used it much more as a powerful tool in bringing about the enrichment of man.

....

Epilogue

This book is a compendium of the issues and problems with which most of the children and parents I see in my practice have to deal. The insights I have so gained and the suggestions I have thereby been enabled to offer are applicable, I believe, to the normal child and not just those who require therapy. It is my hope that the reader's understanding of what I have learned and his application of this knowledge will play some role in alleviating and preventing psychological disturbance in those children with whom he is involved. Furthermore, it is my hope that this book will contribute to the healthy development of the children of those parents who utilize what is contained herein. Such parents can thereby gain what is without doubt the highest gratification a human being can enjoy—the gratification of guiding and nurturing the development of a child into an emotionally stable and mature young man or woman. There is no greater reward for the adult; there is no greater gift to the child.

Index

Adler, A., 100
Aggression, *See* Anger
Ambivalence, 33, 42, 48–49, 58, 99, 105, 150, 215–216
Ames, L. B., 96, 118, 135
Anal phase of psychosexual development, 95–97
Anger
  aggression and, 132
  antisocial behavior and, 106, 129–131, 147, 191, 198–199, 242–244
  the child's stories and themes of, 96–97, 135
  the child's toward,
    parents, 37–38, 41, 55, 57, 58, 60, 122–123, 145–150, 197–198, 222–223, 226–228, *See also* Oedipus complex

    peers, 71, 153–154, *See also* Peer relationships
    siblings, *See* Sibling rivalry
  denial of, 136, 138–139
  displacement of, 136, 137, 142, 143–144, 155, 158, 202, 204, 209, 214
  frustration and, 133–134, 197–198
  healthy expression of, 133–134, 137–138, 140–141, 150–153, 159, 160, 166, 197–198, 204–205
  inhibition of, 135–138, 151–153
    the child's, 55, 60, 71, 72–73, 97, 122–123, 128, 136, 138–139, 154, 155, 191, 209, 222–223, *See also* Oedipus complex
    the parent's, 37–38, 128, 138–140, 164, 172
  murder and, 25, 135, 198–199, 243

251

the parent's in
the child, 33, 65, 74, 77, 143, 216
himself, 51, 66–67
Primal scene, *See* Sexuality, the
parent's, primal scene
Profanity, 55, 71, 140–141, 144–145,
See also Anger
Promises, 39–40
Psychopathy, *See* Anger, antisocial
behavior and, *and* Guilt, antisocial
behavior and
Psychosomatic complaints, 95, 100,
214, 218–219, 222
Psychotherapy, 54, 84, 138, 152–153
of the child, 29, 33, 35, 54–55, 58–
60, 119, 121–124, 127, 147–148,
154–155, 165, 182, 203–211, 212,
215, 221–226
of the parent, 35, 39, 113, 123, 215,
225–226

Rage, 133–134, 164, 190, 198, *See
also* Anger
Rank, O., 100–101
Rebellion, *See* Anger, antisocial behavior and, *and* Education, the
child's rebellion against the parents
and
Regression, 51, 156
Religion, 128, 135, 136, 143, 144, 149,
179–180, 230
Respect
the child's, for the parent, 39, 40,
43, 49, 52–55, 56, 57–58, 66, 98,
139, 144–145, 148, 148–150, 171,
172, 178, 191, 210, 213–214, 226
the parent's, for the child, 33, 34–
36, 144–145
Reward and praise, 50, 65, 73–74, 76,
81, 95, 143, 161–163, 190–192, 196,
210, 216, 217, 232–236, *See also* Discipline and punishment

Sacrifices, the parent's, for the child,
33, 39, 40–41, 158
School, *See* Education, the school
"School phobia," *See* Education, fear
of school

"Self-actualization," 64, 101, 230–232
Self-assertion, 132
the child's, 35, 71, 86, 117, 139, 154,
155, 157, 179, 192, 195–196, 226,
229, 230–232
the parent's, 117, 139–140
Self-blame stage, *See* Guilt, the child's,
development of
Self-esteem
the child's, 36, 51, 57, 58, 63–83,
110, 130–131, 138, 141, 153–154,
155, 158, 161, 162, 173–174, 178,
183–184, 189, 193–194, 195–197,
200, 206–207, 220, 223, 225, 229–
230, 232–236
the parent's, 36–38, 40–41, 42–44,
47, 48, 49, 50–51, 66, 74, 138,
146–147, 154, 189, 198–199, 214,
227–228, 229–230, 236–238
See also Respect
Self-image
the child's, 49, 51, 63–64, 157–158,
229–230, 230–232
the parent's, 53, 229–230
Sexuality
the child's
castration anxiety, 96, 98, 116–
117, 122, 123
curiosity and, 96, 97, 110–113,
119–121, 191, 200–201
development of, Freud's theory,
95–99, 121
exhibitionism, 97, 119–121, 200–
201
identification and, 107–110, 199–
200, 229–231
masturbation, 87, 97, 98, 103,
113, 117–119, 120, 123, 200–
201
penis envy, 116–117, 123
reproduction fantasies, 96
the parent's
encouragement of the child's
sexuality, 52, 142–143, 174–
175, 200–201
inhibition of the child's sexuality,
119–121, 126
primal scene, 113–116

COMMENTARY

"Gardner's book, although his basic experience stems from the consulting room, addresses itself to all of us: to the issue of the upbringing of normal children by normal parents."

Rudolf Ekstein, Ph.D.

"This is a splendid book, a gold mine of information for parents which will help them to understand what is going on in the minds of their children."

Fitzhugh Dodson, Ph.D.

"In sharing his rich repertoire of professional knowledge and experience in a format that is highly informative and readable, Dr. Gardner has accomplished a prodigious task. I believe he has aptly fulfilled his hope that the book would appreciably help all parents contribute more effectively to the healthy development of their children. Accordingly, I highly recommend this book to colleagues in all areas of psychiatric endeavor."

Frank J. Menolascino, M.D.